GRIPES

GRIPES

THE LITTLE QUARRELS OF COUPLES

JEAN-CLAUDE KAUFMANN

Translated by Helen Morrison

polity

First published in French as *Agacements* © Armand Colin, 2007

This English edition © Polity Press, 2009

Polity Press
65 Bridge Street
Cambridge CB2 1UR, UK

Polity Press
350 Main Street
Malden, MA 02148, USA

ISBN-13: 978-0-7456-4361-8
ISBN-13: 978-0-7456-4362-5 (paperback)

A catalogue record for this book is available from the British Library.

Typeset in 10.5 on 12 pt Sabon
by Servis Filmsetting Ltd, Stockport, Cheshire
Printed and bound by MPG Books Group, UK

The publisher has used its best endeavours to ensure that the URLs for external websites referred to in this book are correct and active at the time of going to press. However, the publisher has no responsibility for the websites and can make no guarantee that a site will remain live or that the content is or will remain appropriate.

Every effort has been made to trace all copyright holders, but if any have been inadvertently overlooked the publishers will be pleased to include any necessary credits in any subsequent reprint or edition.

For further information on Polity, visit our website: www.politybooks.com.

Ouvrage publié avec le concours du Ministère français de la Culture - Centre national du livre

Published with the assistance of the French Ministry of Culture - National Book Centre

CONTENTS

CONTENTS

Part Three Small Acts of Revenge and Romantic Tactics

CONTENTS

INTRODUCTION

'Now that irritates me! That really gets on my nerves! It makes me furious! Yes of course, anyone can be a bit untidy – that's fair enough as long as it's confined to their own bit of space. You ask my neighbours how many times they've heard me yelling at my husband because he doesn't put stuff away; they're used to it. Not that it makes much difference really – except to make me feel better.' Generously, however, Agnès acknowledges that there are attenuating circumstances for the presumed guilty party by admitting that she is 'a bit obsessive' about housework. 'It's not as if housework is the be all and end all of my life. But when it doesn't get done, it really gets on my nerves!' And then, yet another attenuating circumstance, there is the issue of the ironing, where the roles of irritator and irritated are reversed. Whereas she immediately springs into action when there is tidying to be done, it is a very different story when it comes to ironing, the prospect of which fills her with weary reluctance. Overwhelmed by the tediousness of the task from the moment the torture table is in position, she finds it hard to summon up the slightest motivation. And worst of all is the sudden irritation which overwhelms her at the mere sight of the dreadful pile of ironing. A pile which inevitably keeps on growing. As a result, she has devised a little trick to get round the problem. 'When the sight of my ironing basket really starts to get on my nerves, I put it somewhere where I can't see it anymore, somewhere out of sight. It can just wait – it's not as if it has to be done that day.' Unfortunately for her though, next time she stumbles upon it, the irritation it provokes is even more intense.

This has given rise to the issue of the shirts, an issue which over the years has poisoned what has been, and still is, in every other respect a loving relationship. Happy couples have their stories too. Stories

1

which emerge simply by following the trail of the small (or not so small) irritations within the relationship.

Jean has never yet had to turn up to work without a freshly ironed shirt on his back. On numerous occasions, however, this minor domestic exploit has been achieved at the very last second, and only after he has had to run the gamut of a whole range of intense emotions: anxiety, anger, hatred! And, worst of all, the sound of Agnès's laughter. A loud and hearty laugh completely at odds with his own internal feelings. Jean decided the solution was to buy a professional ironing machine but this failed to make any significant difference. The problem was eventually resolved by employing someone to come in and do the ironing twice a week, which is currently what happens. No more wondering whether or not a shirt would be ironed in time, no more hurtful outbursts of laughter. Until the day when the sociologist asked them to confront their respective positions in a joint interview (each of them having previously been interviewed individually). The shirts were back in the spotlight once more; Agnès laughed so much she could barely speak while Jean struggled to keep his cool. Each recounted a totally different version of events, in terms of both tone and content.

> AGNÈS: Ah, now that makes me laugh, that really makes me laugh!
> JEAN: I don't find it funny at all – it's a serious matter!

The difference between them is even more acute when it comes to the thorny matter of buttons. 'I don't know how he manages it, but the buttons on his shirts are always coming unstitched. Now that really gets him going! . . . He gets so annoyed about it – it's quite incredible. It's true that when I'm ironing a shirt I might notice that the buttons are a bit loose. But that's as far as it goes – I don't pay that much attention. And then – as soon as he puts the shirt on, off flies a button!' Agnès bursts out laughing and laughs so much that she can hardly continue. 'At which point he loses his temper: "Can't you be a bit more attentive when you put my shirts away!" I think that's the only thing we get annoyed about as a couple – this business of buttons.' Fresh outburst of hilarity, from which she manages to pull herself together enough to conclude: 'It must really get on his nerves! Still – he needn't make such a big thing of it.' Jean does indeed make a big thing of it. He cannot understand this apparently over-aggressive attitude towards him, especially as he has tried on numerous occasions to explain his feelings to Agnès in a diplomatic manner. Worse of all is that intolerable laughter which he finds so hurtful. She suspects him of some kind of 'mysterious' behaviour which results in the loss of so many shirt buttons. 'I don't understand how he manages it. Mine are perfectly OK.' He is convinced that the blame lies with industrial sewing techniques which are not sufficiently thorough and need re-inforcing by hand. Since he never participates in any of the domestic chores, he dare not really be any more overt in blaming Agnès. Jean was brought up by his grandmother and he clearly remembers that the first thing she did whenever a new shirt was purchased was to re-sew all the buttons. Which is why, in the thick of the crisis (in spite of being married and having three children), he decided to take his shirts to his grandmother so she could reinforce the buttons. Which made Agnès laugh even more. In the end, (between the first interview and the joint confrontation), the problem was definitively resolved by having someone come in to do both ironing and mending.

One of my researchers received a phone call from Agnès out of the blue. Apparently she felt she had not told the whole story and wanted the opportunity to confide 'off the record'. It turned out that her laughter concealed a suffering, dating back to the day she first met Jean, the man she loves so much. Life is strange and can some-times change course without us even realizing it is happening. Deeply in love with her handsome suitor, she was oblivious to the change of direction her life was taking. Yet she had given up all her profes-sional ambitions for the sake of love, opting instead for an existence totally devoted to the home and the family. The future she could have had was beginning to haunt her dreams, initially in a rather pleasant guise, but then quickly becoming increasingly painful. We must not for an instant suspect Agnès of deliberately inventing the button saga as a strategy to get back at her husband – it evolved quite of its own accord. But very quickly she intuitively understood that this was her own secret little act of revenge, a way of compensating for her sup-pressed frustration and recovering her psychological stability. That laughter especially – in the face of poor Jean's irritation – was incred-ibly liberating. She thought she had found a relatively harmless way of making him pay. Sometimes the person causing irritation fails to appreciate how much the other person suffers.

The moral of this story, selected from many similar tales, takes us straight to the heart of the subject: irritation is never anodyne. Beneath its agitated surface lies an infinite universe of explanations. What an odd sensation, in truth, irritation turns out to be. Disagreeable, even acutely so at times, it nevertheless plays a fundamental role in the way a couple is structured, and can sometimes even produce positive effects. Irritation must therefore be seen as a necessary evil. Its most remarkable feature is undoubtedly the fact that the mechanisms behind it turn out to be extraordinarily precise and by no means random. Close study of this area gives an original and illuminating perspective on the way conjugal relationships function. The subject also throws new light on the dynamics of the multiple identities of the individual. In other words, this book on minor irritations, could, against all expectations, have been written as a theoretical treatise, so rich and complex is its subject. I have chosen instead (for the moment at least) to concentrate on the human aspects of the subject, on the irresistible humour and edgy electricity which pervade these stories, rather than plunging into the deeper waters of a conceptual approach.

This journey into the realm of conjugal irritation promises – at least, so I hope – to be far from dull, even if, inevitably, there are the various prolegomena and definitions to be dealt with first. There is irritation and irritation. We have only to listen to the way people signal its presence to their entourage (ranging from the purely informative and straightforward 'that gets on my nerves . . .' to the violent shriek of 'THAT GETS ON MY NERVES!!!!!') to appreciate that it encompasses a range extending from simple intellectual annoyance to full-blown emotional outbursts capable of provoking the most extraordinary reactions. And yet, from one extreme to another, the mechanism behind irritation is always the same, invariably provoked by the same cause (dissonance) – a relatively unusual situation in the field of social science, increasingly fragmented and sometimes even overwhelmed by the complexity and the multiplicity of factors. It would have been unthinkable to have deprived ourselves of the power and intellectual comfort inherent in this explanatory simplicity. Yet to benefit from it requires a strict definition of irritation which is indeed close to a whole range of negative feelings (some quite clearly defined, others less so), which are not associated with the same mechanism and which therefore threaten to jeopardize precise analysis by blurring the boundaries. These would include bitterness, exasperation, resentment, vexation, impatience, malaise, frustration, disenchantment, dissatisfaction, disappointment, disgust, anger, etc. Several of these feelings and emotions have strong structural links with irritation. Anger, for example, which is sometimes the means through which irritation is expressed. Or dissatisfaction and disgust, both of which will be examined in due course. It is worth noting too that certain bio-psychological traits or particular social contexts can

4

predispose a tendency to irritability. Some consideration will be given to these chronically irritated individuals who are sometimes capable of turning violent. Yet the real essence of the subject lies elsewhere. Just as what causes conflicts within a couple is very different from what causes violence (Brown, Jaspard, 2004), irritation must not be reduced to dissatisfaction, to conflicts and, still less, to violence, if we are to understand it clearly. The best way to capture the subtle yet clear dynamics of irritation is to focus on the most ordinary of ordinary details of conjugal life, in other words on the happiest and most peaceful couples, the ones who could wrongly be said to have no story to tell.

Part One

1 + 1 = 4

— 1 —

THE CONJUGAL ADVENTURE

In reality it all starts with the individual. Our partners are not the only source of our irritation. We are quite capable of irritating ourselves too, for example when faced with a recalcitrant object like that item of flat-pack furniture we are trying to assemble, where screw no. 7 bears no resemblance whatsoever to the diagram; or, in Agnès's case, the pile of ironing. This contentious confrontation with objects provides a fascinating analytical opportunity to observe the extent to which we are not quite all we think we are. The prevailing view of man is that of a rational, thinking individual leading his life according to his own ideas. We embrace this view all the more eagerly in that it is precisely from this introspective standpoint that we observe the world, and ourselves. In actual fact, this is only a part of the whole picture, a very small part, no more than a single level of truth. Traditional sciences such as biology have acquired enough experience for those working in these fields to recognize that these different levels of truth exist and to adapt their work accordingly, selecting specific methods, categories and concepts, a vision and a language which differ radically from one level to another. Hidden beneath the observable body surface lie the circulatory and nervous systems with their own separate laws and, if we probe still deeper, specially adapted formulae enable us to unlock the secrets of molecular genetics, etc. Perhaps one day the same will be true of social sciences, with the particular challenge that, in this case, the mind is the focus of its own study, a complication which brings with it the attendant risks of egocentricity and cephalocentricity. The subject of irritation provides us with a unique opportunity to shift course and take a completely new look at the cultural depths of the individual.

9

Below the surface consciousness, each individual operates in a state of permanent flux, intimately associated with the familiar objects which surround them. Take the first moments of the day, for example: there is no need to ask ourselves where the breakfast cups are, or whether we should have tea or coffee or hot chocolate to drink. Most of our most basic gestures are triggered automatically. This is, however, no random process. When it comes to the most trivial aspects of daily life, no two individuals are the same. Each of us has built up our own personal stock of micro-references, the result of our own history, and it is these that govern our individual reflexes. A fortunate situation indeed, since without it we would find ourselves living in a state of constant mental exhaustion. Cognitive science has succeeded in identifying the specific location of this memory of ordinary things, referring to it as the 'infraconscious', or the 'cognitive unconscious', or the 'implicit memory' (Buser, 2005). In a more theoretical book (Kaufmann, 2001), I demonstrated how this memory functions in a dual complementary mode. On the one hand is the un-conscious brain studied by cognitive science, where pre-programmed guides to action set in train reflex movements. Such 'schemas' as many specialists call these guides, combine to form a sort of secret programme whereby each individual acts out the ordinary routines of his or her existence. On the other hand, there are the objects themselves, transformed through familiarity into a series of visual or tactile references to our everyday gestures. When I open the cupboard to take out my breakfast cup, I do so either without thinking at all, or thinking only in an extremely intuitive and rapid way. It is only if the cup is not in its usual place that I will experience surprise or need to reflect. The mildly unpleasant sensation such a discovery provokes involves a conflict between the two ways in which memory functions. The one which is external to the individual (the object) fails to correspond to the secret programme which dictates the appropriate sequence of gestures. In the case cited here, the dissonance is not particularly brutal and the only consequence may be the need to invoke a conscious thought process – well, where is my cup then? Irritation will be felt only if the cup cannot be found, or if it has been moved from its usual place for no good reason. In more critical contexts, the initial dissonance immediately provokes a feeling of irritation. The more sudden and intense this feeling is, the more urgent it becomes for the individual to restore coherence between the two conflicting elements of the self. In Agnès's case, that meant getting rid of that dreadful pile of ironing. By hiding it, provided the pile was a reasonably small one, or, once it had become too big to be comfortably ignored, by summoning the energy to get it done. 'Once I've moved my ironing basket two or three times, I know that I can't hold out much longer. That sooner or later I'm going to have to get on with it.' It is not necessarily the object that must always be restored to its 'proper' place in order for the irritation to subside. The effect can also be achieved by an adjustment of the sub-conscious schema. 'That's all very well when it comes to shirts. But tea-towels – that just seems ridiculous. Jean doesn't give a damn what the tea-towels look like and neither do I really. So why, when I hate ironing so much, do I still insist on ironing the tea-towels?' Agnès could have stopped ironing the tea-towels, by making a conscious effort with the part of her (the secret blue-print) that was making her do something she considered 'ridiculous'. Instead she came up with a far more radical way of dealing with her irritation, deciding to give up ironing altogether and instead hand it over to be done by a professional. The irritation experienced on an individual level can indicate that a recurring contradiction between the two memories of the self remains unresolved: every night for the last thirty years Léon has been irritated by the sight of the untidy pile of clothes on the chair beside his bed. Alternatively, it can be simply a way of regulating action, as in the case of the ironing, for example, where the absence of any regular pattern, any fixed day of the week, etc., means that a decision about when it is done has to be made each time. Rational arguments are not always helpful in these circumstances: one argument might clearly indicate that the ironing should indeed be done today, while another suggests it should be put off until tomorrow. Some kind of emotional impetus is needed to clinch the decision (Damasio, 1995). In the case of love, the emotional impetus is an agreeable and pleasurable experience. When it comes to the ironing on the other hand, the emotion involved is not so agreeable. Provided it is not too insistent or too violent, irritation can often be a useful, even indispensable, way of provoking an action and reducing mental fatigue.

Domestic emotions

Our relationship with the everyday objects that surround us is dictated by our own personal history. The domestic universe varies enormously from one family to another. The slightest speck of dust is enough to make Agnès spring to action, yet when it comes

11

to attacking the ironing her body refuses to respond. For Lola, the reverse is true. Far from being a chore, ironing is a genuine pleasure. She puts on her favourite music and even manages to dance, iron in hand – admittedly a poor substitute for her now unattainable dream (of becoming a professional dancer). Housework, unfortunately, is not such a simple matter. She is twenty-two, and, like most people of her age, not particularly interested in housework. There are far more important things in life. Nevertheless, she spends a lot of time at home and the general untidiness and the most glaring signs of dirtiness are begining to seriously affect her. She is gradually formulating a new plan of action, which will eventually lead to the vision of a cleaner-looking flat. The floor in particular has become a real obsession. Much as she would like it to be spotless, her body still obeys the old standards, whereby a certain amount of dust was tolerated. 'Oh the floor, the floor! It's not that I don't think about it! It's a case of: oh shit! I must do it, I must do it! It really gets to me!' She hardly knows what irritates her most: the sight of those nooks and crannies that need cleaning or the nagging obsession with the idea of this new domestic standard which is proving so difficult to achieve. Lola's troubled relationship with her floor is the perfect illustration of a variant of individual irritation. Where an automatic reflex is well established, the mere sight of something out of place is enough to provoke a feeling of irritation and the body immediately springs into action. 'It irritates me, it really does . . . but if I had to spend my life on my hands and knees picking up clothes that have been left lying around, I'd do it. That's just how I am' (Agnès). However, a dialogue can be established between the secret blue-print which prompts a series of gestures and the more conscious level of thought. An individual can reason with themselves, or begin to envisage other ways of doing things. A quick flick of the broom is no longer enough for Lola. Irritation shifts its ground and takes a different form. Instead of being simply provoked by the discrepancy between the secret blue-print and the object not in its proper place, it is now the result of the discrepancy between the acquired automatic response and the new ideal of how things should be done, between implicit memory and conscious thought. It no longer takes the form of a short, sharp shock which instantly provokes the required action; instead it complicates the action, blurring the established reference points and, over time, continuing to exacerbate what has already started to become an onerous mental burden. 'It really gets to me', says Lola. The dissonance, a discrepancy between the two discordant parts of the self, has shifted and the social function of the irritation has changed. No longer simply the emotional trigger setting off a specific action in the context of an already established reflex (deciding to do the ironing when the pile gets too big), it becomes instead the preliminary to a reform of this reflex. Of course, the reform may never happen and, in such cases, irritation lingers in a disagreeable and unproductive manner. It is highly likely that, every evening for a long time to come, Léon will continue to be irritated by the sight of that untidy bedside chair. And yet, if he could simply acquire the new habit of putting his clothes neatly away, this disagreeable sensation, which has been the bane of his life for the last thirty years, would be banished for ever. Long-established routines can, however, sometimes prove too deeply entrenched to be changed. Lola, on the other hand, is in the early stages of her domestic journey. Every day the stage is set for all kinds of small adjustments. It seems likely that very soon the irritation provoked by that floor will be no more than a bad memory. Her 'cleaner' ideal will have become the standard dictating her everyday gestures. The first years in a couple's life together are punctuated by irritations which help shape the gradual elaboration of their domestic system. Lola is in the throes of this process, torn between all kinds of contradictory emotions. The washing-up in particular causes her to fluctuate between unbearable irritation and jubilation, on a daily basis. She washes up each morning after breakfast. By the time lunchtime comes around the growing pile of dirty dishes in the sink keeps catching her eye, and even, in the worst case, her nose, and provokes a growing sense of irritation. By evening her irritation has intensified to the extent that she feels positively ill at ease. The following morning brings tangible relief as her irritation is channelled and transformed into the energy of action. 'I say to myself: that's it! That's it! That's everythings' bloody clean again!' For the rest of the morning, she keeps glancing at the sink, but with pleasure this time. 'I glance over at the sink and it looks wonderful, wonderful!' Then midday comes round and the whole process starts all over again.

Eventually, as with the floor, Lola will no doubt move to a new system. One which might involve doing the washing-up more often, after each meal for example. Then her irritation will be more or less over. But so too will be the intense pleasure of doing something to remove the source of irritation. Well-oiled reflexes banish the most powerful domestic emotions, both good and bad. The adventure of setting up home together inevitably follows this pattern since, once established, automatic gestures are also the guarantee of an easy life.

And, in our increasingly exhausting and complex social world, that counts for a lot.

1 + 1 = 1?

However, since housework is not the only thing that matters in life, we can easily afford to sacrifice a few emotions in that domain. We do not, after all, become a couple for the pleasure of getting the washing-up done. The early stages of a couple's life together open a completely different chapter in the saga of irritation.

Up until that point, without realizing it, the individual is two. This is because their familiar environment (which holds a part of their memory) is constantly out of step with the secret blue-print dictating automatic gestures. This discrepancy gives rise to frequent minor irritations, the prelude to the restoration of equilibrium through the appropriate action. So what happens when the other person comes along? When two completely different universes of everyday life, each carrying within it a memory rooted in the handling of the simplest objects, come into confrontation? I had decided to carry out some research on this issue, notably within the particularly revealing context of the morning after the first night spent together, by focusing on what I knew were the deceptively anodyne gestures associated with the bathroom and the breakfast table. I was expecting all manner of difficult confrontations. I did indeed encounter some of these, but by no means as many as I had thought. Feelings of irritation in particular were almost non-existent. Instead there was a great deal of anxiety, embarrassment and unease. And the desire to run away, to forget about the whole experience as quickly as possible. But very little in the way of irritation.

Vincent is a striking example. His first 'morning after' is nothing short of a disaster movie, and he reels off a string of disturbing or hostile comments on the subject of his lady-love. Even the milk tastes strange that morning. Yet he continues as though nothing had happened, as though all these negative emotions were water off a duck's back. The verdict is yet to be reached. He feels as though his life has entered a kind of parenthesis, which is indeed the case. His normal responses and judgements are still there, in some far-off part of his mind, but they are distant and ready to be modified at any time, should circumstances require it. Few irritations are registered precisely because the individual is in this parenthesis, a transition area between two worlds, one of which may be about to disappear completely while the other is yet to be explored. In those stories of first mornings in which the old world triumphs, all kinds of negative feelings are experienced, but not in the form of irritation. This is because the hapless candidates for conjugal life are not interested in trying to resolve any of the contradictions which set them in opposition to the universe they are presented with. He (or she) is more intent on working out how best to escape, or, if the night in question has been spent on home territory, to get rid of the intruder. Dissonance presupposes a (contradictory) unity, either already established or in the process of becoming so. In the circumstances in question, however, the objective is separation. Any elements which might have proved irritating in a situation of forced integration no longer do so. Where circumstances take a more favourable turn, irritation is also absent, for in such cases the old regime is (momentarily) put on hold. Love works its magic and things we might have found surprising pass unnoticed or, if they fail to endear, are confined to some dormant part of memory. 'I found all his little ways charming at first' (Gally). They can also act as a catalyst, inspiring one of the new partners to modify their behaviour accordingly. Colombine was amazed to discover that all those new creams and lotions in her bathroom belonged to Franck, the muscular sportsman she had thought of as such a tough character. All these pots and tubes represented an unknown universe to someone who had hitherto been content with a simple bar of soap. Panic-stricken, Colombine immediately decided it was time to rethink her own attitude to personal hygiene. It is in situations such as this, where one individual is prepared to change radically, or in circumstances where passion takes over, that the illusion can begin to take shape that $1 + 1$ might indeed equal one. An illusion which is not without a ring of truth: $1 + 1$ can indeed make 1 at first. Subsequently, the couple not only discover their internal divisions, but also realize that these are necessary if they are to function successfully as a couple. Initially this comes about with the re-emergence of the individual, happy to dream of love and life together, but not to the extent of sacrificing themselves body and soul. $1 + 1 = 2$. Later, time spent together becomes more clearly defined, contrasting with time spent on one's own (Singly, 2000). $1 + 1 = 3$. Finally, as we shall see, comes the realization that they have been able to ignore the ordinary dissonances between them only because their day-to-day existence was going through such a major upheaval. Not only do these dissonances gradually re-emerge with time but also it becomes clear that the partner has brought along their own baggage of dissonances, conflicting in all sorts of ways with what we ourselves find irritating. $1 + 1 = 4$.

Sparks start to fly

The first irritations experienced by the couple are the sign that the process of unification is under way. Differences between them only flare up in as much as the two partners are making progress with the construction of a shared culture. Sometimes this occurs very early on in the relationship but it is always associated with a shared routine that is beginning to take shape. The fact that Artemiss was so annoyed by the little dog is partly because dogs are just not her 'thing', but mostly because it interfered with the cosy romantic cocoon she wanted to escape into. 'Dogs are not really my thing! There I was round at my boyfriend's and we hadn't seen each other for ages so we were really looking forward to spending the evening together. . . . Problem no. 1: he was looking after a sweet little dog for the weekend, a kind of sausage dog with crazy dreadlocks. Problem no. 2: the mutt in question seemed as keen on my date as I was . . . in other words, very, very keen! You can imagine the scene: my "true love" and I cosily tucked up in the sack getting up to all sorts of exciting things, then suddenly, the creature starts scratching at the door. . . . Out of the kindness of his heart, my boyfriend lets him in . . . not realizing that the dog would start barking as soon as there was the slightest suspicion of any kind of groaning noise. . . To cut a long story short . . . that was it for the night. Yeah, because if we put the thing out, he yapped even louder! And the worst of it was that the brute managed to worm his way onto the bed as soon as we started to drop off to sleep. . . . So if ever you find yourself getting involved in pet-sitting, make sure it's a fish you're looking after.'

Irritation is not confined to the couple. We can just as easily be extremely irritated by a friend, a work colleague, or, sometimes, by a complete stranger. Whatever the context, however, the cause is always to be sought where the coming together of two people, however briefly, is troubled by a dissonance. As their life together becomes closer, with ever more shared intimacy and a greater sense of fusion, so the risk of irritation increases. At the other extreme, sharing a house or flat with others provides an interesting contrast. Often of limited duration and with no pressure for any formal integration, people sharing a house or flat manage to avoid many of the kinds of irritation sometimes associated with communal life, largely because they uphold a culture of tolerance and openness characteristic of young people, what Céline Bouchat refers to as 'the cult of cool' (2005, p. 26). Even those couples living in a shared house or flat generally see it as a way of prolonging their youth and resisting domesticity and the pressure to settle down too soon. However, certain spaces or activities tend to be associated with a more trying and problematic kind of intimacy, leading to feelings of irritation which sometimes come to a head in sudden and violent outbursts. The confrontation over how domestic tasks should be done and the promiscuity of personal products in the fridge are particularly fraught. Thomas explodes: 'The state of the fridge really gets on my nerves. When you discover a courgette that's completely rotten, you feel real hatred!' (2005, p. 72).

Today's couples also start out by worshipping that 'little god of cool' (idem, p. 27). But unlike a flat or house-share, the two protagonists are involved in the complex task of gradually establishing a united life-style. Every domain must be intuitively tested to avoid upsetting either party and in order to identify even the smallest common denominators. At meal times, for example, the combination of each person's likes and, more importantly, dislikes results in a new eating pattern which represents a departure from each person's past history (Kaufmann, 2005). Eline and Jack have thrown themselves energetically and wholeheartedly into the task of constructing their conjugal unity. The fact that they are a young couple who find it easy to discuss things means they often take stock of their experiences where other couples might settle for a more intuitive kind of adjustment. Take the issue of going out, for example. They realized at an early stage that their rhythms were completely out of sync. As Eline explains: 'When we first met, our life-styles were poles apart. We were both single but the way we organized our working hours and our social lives was completely different. I hated being on my own, so I went out a lot (every night of the week, sometimes with three different things in a night and often four things planned for the weekend). Jack was more solitary, he hardly ever planned social events in advance and would only call his friends at the last minute (shall we go out and eat somewhere in Paris, right away?), he rarely went out during the week and didn't exactly overdo it at weekends either. Anyway, when we first started living together, he started out trying to do things my way. For three months it was a real struggle for him. In the end he called a halt, and for the next three months we did things his way. At the end of those three months it was my turn to beg for mercy. After that we tried alternating for six months while we sorted things out. In the end we gradually reached a compromise: I often go out more than he does (evenings with girlfriends, activities of various sorts), and often during the week, and we go out together at weekends, but without trying to do four different things. . . . Sometimes I still go a bit over the top: there are months when I tend to plan too many nights out, meetings with friends, etc. Which, of course, Jack finds extremely irritating. So then we go back to a radical method (we don't go out at all for two weekends on the trot), to help us get back to a "normal" rhythm.' The process is still very much ongoing, governed by feelings of irritation on either side, which can result in abrupt changes of course. The solution which seems to be gradually emerging is based on a significant factor which we will be examining in more detail at a later stage, notably the use of personal time (nights out with the girls) as a means of absorbing irritation within the couple. 'I go out more often than Jack does, mostly during the week but sometimes Saturday afternoons as well, to see my colleagues and friends. But Friday nights, Saturday nights and Sundays are reserved for the two of us to go out together (on our own or with friends).'

The pattern of alternately going out / staying in, going out alone / as a couple, appears to be working well and is gradually becoming established. In other areas of their lives some thorny issues still need resolving. Take the cooking, for example. 'Deciding what we're going to have to eat every day is a source of irritation for us.' Small disagreements keep cropping up about, for example, the kind of meal (a quick bite on the go or something rather more fancy?), what they should eat, and, most significantly, who does what. 'I hate cooking', protests Eline; 'Jack loves it, but only when he's cooking for other people, not on an everyday basis.' So why, if he enjoys it so much, does he not do it more often? It is this incoherence that is most annoying. Irritation always arises from a conflict or a dissonance between different attitudes or approaches, whether these remain internal, within one individual, or divide the couple into two separate clans. In this case the irritation arises initially, in the simplest and most classic way, from the daily squabble between Eline and Jack over who does the cooking. But, more insidiously for Eline, the matter is further complicated by the additional irritation provoked by the incoherence she has spotted within the enemy camp. Since Jack is incoherent (he refuses to do more of something he enjoys), logically he should be the first one to feel irritated. However – and this is a new and subtle aspect of irritation – living as a couple provides an opportunity (provided the person concerned is sufficiently skilful to take advantage of it) to sneakily transfer irritation onto the partner.

The issue of cooking is, however, trivial in comparison with the exhausting problem of how to organize the housework. 'Our attitudes to housework are completely different and this is a constant source of irritation which still remains unresolved. Personally, I go for a fixed once a week solution, with both of us doing the housework together on a Saturday morning for example, so that in two hours it's all done and that's it for the week. Jack prefers a more random approach along the lines of – I do the housework on my own, when I feel like it or when I find time (if I'm first home during the week for example). As a result, I get irritated with him because I feel he doesn't want to commit himself and he gets irritated with me because he thinks I'm always going on about it all the time. At the moment we fluctuate between getting the housework done at the week-end (which he feels is forcibly imposed on him), and a random "as and when" approach (which I hate).' Jack's random approach tends to be a popular one with men. It usually brings the following advantage: since the availability and the desire (to do the housework) are generally (as if by magic) less present in men, the theory of sharing tasks equally between the two partners remains little more than a theory. Having only heard Eline's side of the story, there is insufficient evidence to accuse Jack of resorting to this subterfuge. Eline is irritated by the multiplicity of dissonances mixed up together: by the sight of things left lying around (offending her secret notion of how things should be), which is a constant source of annoyance; by the verbal confrontation between the two theories about housework; by the more pressing everyday conflict over who is going to sweep the floor or put the bins out. And, most of all, by the dreadful suspicion that Jack might just be deliberately adding a little pinch of treacherous insincerity.

They are both, however, good at facing up to issues. They discuss things together and negotiate a lot, adjusting and changing things constantly in response to irritation and arguments. Which means they have a fairly realistic vision of the way power struggles and opposing irritations come together in the setting-up of a domestic system. This process of determining the structure the couple will operate under is a historically recent one. It is a social phenomenon resulting from the disappearance of the previous hierarchy, handed down through tradition, which meant that each partner stepped into a clearly defined role (with men in a position of authority and doing relatively little in terms of household and family matters). This kind of pre-determined hierarchy of roles has now, in theory at least, been replaced by an opening up of domestic roles to two equal individuals, in other words by a situation where many activities can be carried out interchangeably by either party. This change involves a long process of adjustment, one in which irritations play a major role. Yet the manoeuvres over power have not entirely disappeared. They have simply become more secret and more subtle. It is not unknown for a crafty husband to exaggerate his feelings of irritation in order to obtain exemption from some particularly unappealing task. Such underhand behaviour is unlikely in Jack and Eline's case. I asked Eline if she thought Jack might be taking a little bit of advantage sometimes. This was her reply: 'No, that's not how it works with us – and that's an honest answer because we discussed the issue in the context of your questions. I think our relationship is generally well balanced, though still a bit precarious at times, because it's often challenged by everyday events and by the things life throws at you. For example, I was unemployed for a while and the power balance had to change: for me that meant a loss of boundaries, of confidence, a sense of being useless, in terms of the relationship as well. Jack took on the role of being the stronger half of the couple, representing stability, money, confidence. . . . For a while everything was thrown off balance: my independence, my financial stability, the bits of housework I was doing on my own during the day . . . even after I got my job back it took a long time and all kinds of crises and discussions before we were able to get back to a situation that we both felt happy with, especially me. But, one way or another, by discussing things and being aware of each other's feelings we always manage to balance things out in the end. In fact that's why we still get on each other's nerves quite a lot – neither of us wants to give in to the other, but it's all very amicable.'

Eline and Jack are not really typical in this respect. In the majority of couples the two protagonists have no scruples in feigning irritation, or at least exaggerating it, in order to influence a decision in their favour. Often without even being aware that they are doing so. Louis was genuinely irritated by the little table Anne's mother had picked up to help them furnish their first home. He felt it was too 'family' or too 'stuffy', that it made them seem old. Anne recalls his irritation. 'He suggested we get rid of it, because we didn't really like eating at a table. We felt a bit awkward . . . sitting down to dinner there.' She mimes the scene, laughing about it. 'I prefer eating at a low table, it's much nicer. The other day we looked in some Japanese shops and decided we'd like to buy a big solid square table.'[1] As often happens during the period in which the couple are establishing their system, the irritation felt (by one of them) pushed the couple into a decision about the future, a decision implying an ethos, a commitment to certain issues, a pattern for future actions. And in this case the revelation of an aesthetic code as well, which to their delight they discovered they both shared. As though by magic, a whole universe

[1] Comments recorded and quoted by Marie-Pascale Alhinc-Lorenzi (1997, p. 44).

of values and styles was suddenly mutually established and all kinds of dreams began to emerge: dreams of plain, low furniture, exotic without being fussy, sending out a discreet message of refined elegance. Anne was delighted. She had taken Louis's irritation to heart. It had given her the strength she needed to take the dream one step further and to make it reality. 'I went back to the Japanese shop at Christmas time, and spotted a beautiful teak table, untreated, square, with wonderful carved feet. It really was lovely and I couldn't wait for the January sales. I went back when the price had been reduced, Louis and I were supposed to be going to pick it up, I'd even phoned to reserve it, we were going one Saturday. . . . I remember, I was so thrilled. And then, that day, he mentioned some table that had belonged to his great-aunt . . . it was quite a valuable teak table. Then, one weekend in January, we went to see his mother and out of the blue she presented us with the mahogany table. It's a really nice one, very practical . . . you can lift it easily and it folds away . . . we've ended up saving some money.' Out goes the dream, the Japanese aesthetic is forgotten. Anne accepted her defeat without a struggle. The financial argument clouded the issue. Cleverly put, it disguised the fact that the very thing which had irritated them in the first place (having a family hand-down) had paradoxically come round full circle: the new table had also been handed down within the family. The only difference was that this time it was Louis's family who were doing the handing down.

A comparative analysis of the number of minor disputes within couples according to age, shows that the younger the couple are, the greater the number of rows they have (Brown, Jaspard, 2004). This number declines subsequently in accordance with the age of the couple and the amount of time they have been together. An observation which might seem surprising at first glance but is in fact perfectly logical, since the process of adjustment and the definition of a shared existence is extraordinarily complex in the early phase of the couple's life together and necessitates some major adjustments. Our perspective is in fact distorted because these little disputes tend not to have the tense and vindictive tone they later acquire. These early disputes are a fundamental part of the changing life-style. Irritation is relatively rare and is easily and quickly dealt with for the simple reason that it is not gratuitous: it triggers action, the discovery of new ways of doing things, the organization of a more appropriate system. 'These are the irritations you associate with the early days, the ones which cropped up when we first moved in together. Before that we each had our own way of organizing our living space and keeping things tidy, but we quickly reached some compromises. And it's got easier as time's gone on' (Eline). In contrast to the situation later in the couple's life, each day provides the opportunity to modify things in one domain or another, and the two partners tend to be open-minded and adaptable. Irritation has not yet had time to become rooted in repetitive and ongoing behaviour.

The comfort zone

The early stages of a couple's life are an adventure. A sentimental adventure, of course, marking a complete departure from the previous existence. But an everyday adventure too, with the creation of an intimate world which radically redefines the identities of both individuals. Attitudes and ways of doing things, likely to last for a very long time, are established as a result of minuscule events. Anne and Louis could have embraced a very specific aesthetic universe had they not acquired the old table. Instead, everything else was swept aside and the elegant exotic sobriety of that aesthetic is now nothing more than a forgotten dream.

The adventure of ordinary existence is inevitably full of emotions, which, whether agreeable or disagreeable, function as the dynamic that keeps things moving. Minor irritations scarcely have time to really irritate, no matter how frequently they occur. Then, when things gradually start to settle down, negative feelings surface only where there are sudden or persistent breakdowns in the system. Unfortunately, since the process of reform within the couple has by that stage slowed down, or even come to a halt altogether, these have a much greater and more damaging impact given the inertia which now prevails. Agnès had battled relentlessly to get Jean to put away the clothes he left lying around all over the place. Her outbursts, although sometimes violent, blew over quickly because her irritation melted away as she started to see signs of progress: Jean was clearly making an effort to change his ways. Today he has almost succeeded. Except for a few tell-tale signs, admittedly infrequent, but which nevertheless indicate that Jean is still not quite ready to abandon his freedom completely.

AGNÈS: That really used to get on my nerves at first, but now it doesn't happen so much. . . .
JEAN: It doesn't happen so much, but when it does, it irritates you even more!

22

Agnès has sensed imperceptibly that the situation has changed. The page of constant change has been turned and they are embarking on a new chapter of conjugal life, one dominated by a more stable everyday existence and the quest for comfort. This quest for comfort should not be condemned – indeed it is an inevitable process. Initially predominantly material and concrete as the shared home is equipped and decorated to become a cosy nest, the process is fundamentally a psychological one relating to identity (Kaufmann, 2004). Indeed, in our aggressive and destabilizing society, the couple increasingly functions as a source of comfort and reassurance. So, over the dinner table for example, each person will often begin by recounting all the little woes of his or her day, knowing they can count on their partner's sympathetic ear and therapeutic support (Kaufmann, 2005). But the quest is often a more basic and, sometimes, even regressive one. Home becomes the place where we can let ourselves go, safe from endless competition and away from critical eyes, where the simplest pleasures can be savoured unconditionally, where we can enjoy the comfort and the basic well-being to be had from just letting go. The first stage of being comfortable in one's identity comes as reference points are established, in the form of the routines which simplify existence. In addition, there is the simple pleasure to be had from 'natural' and regressive forms of behaviour. The temptation to regress is often much stronger in one of the two partners. As that person discovers the delights of being able to let themselves go a little at home, the other partner begins to see them in a completely new and hitherto unexpected light, and is surprised by the discrepancies between daily reality and the dream, which now form a rift between them. 'I love going out, going shopping, seeing friends. He's more of a stay-at-home type. He likes being at home, where nobody can bother him, and where his time is his own. Whereas for me, being at home all the time and not seeing anybody, really stresses me out' (Eliza).

The exaggerated exploitation of the couple for personal therapeutic ends radically alters the image each has of the other. Not only does the end of the process of conjugal reform mean that irritation focuses on issues which are all the more aggravating because they refuse to go away and keep cropping up, but also the person who previously had made such an effort to seduce now no longer seems interested in doing so. He (or she) pays more attention to what they wear when they go out, even just to buy a loaf of bread, than when they are alone together. Could it be that, by some strange twist, the partner has become the last person in the world worth seducing? Which leads one to wonder if this is not, after all, the inevitable outcome for the

23

couple? The increase in irritation suggests that a negative answer is in order: no! Enough is definitely enough, the boundaries have been overstepped. 'When we first met, ten years ago, we must have been quite modest and shy with each other because neither of us ever let ourselves go in front of the other. When I think about it, I reckon it was probably about five years before these little habits set in, at about the same time as routine took over! And yes, I do think routine is to blame. You don't take as much notice of each other, you know each other so well, so why bother?' Aphrodite is surprised and disappointed, but, above all, suddenly irritated when her husband forgets himself to the extent of 'picking his nose, biting his fingernails or picking at his toes! Never mind the fact that I'm curled up beside him watching the TV.' She gets it off her chest by shouting at him: 'OK! Would you like my nails too?' Francis apologizes (for the thousandth time), but Aphrodite, carried away by her irritation, continues to berate him. 'Those little tics of his really get on my nerves and I can't help commenting on them.' Then it's the husband's turn to be annoyed by these inopportune outbursts. 'That's probably what he finds most annoying about me!' Feeling justified in his response, he defends his behaviour on the grounds of freedom and happiness: why should a married couple have to hide things from each other, what is the point of being a couple if each partner is forced to keep up a pretence and constantly watch their behaviour? The tactics required to combat irritation are evidently not always straightforward. By going that bit too far, Aphrodite, until that point in a strong position from which to impose her model of behaviour (in the sense that the dissonance was lessened by the guilty partner being brought into line), ended up causing irritation in the enemy camp herself. The old roles of dominator and dominated have been replaced by the confrontation between conflicting theories. The dissonance previously associated with the difference between a theoretical model and its execution now stands between good manners and freer, more natural behaviour. A similar breakdown in understanding occurs in Zoe's case: 'Excuse the details, but when he clears his throat and then spits into the sink . . . Yet for him this kind of privileged intimacy isn't in the slightest bit shocking.'

Another stigmatized husband – 'HE' as Melody calls him – similarly pilloried for failing in his duty to seduce, probably feels the same. In their case, the little drama of everyday life is played out not on the sofa, in front of the television or at the bathroom sink but around the issue of table manners, which, as we shall see, are a much-cited source of irritation. 'At mealtimes, HE systematically "mops up" any sauce left on his plate as soon as he's finished eating, using bits of bread to thoroughly wipe every bit of the plate, and going over it repeatedly until not a speck is left, before guzzling down the dripping morsel. Honestly it's like watching someone with a floor cloth! I find it quite disgusting, and it takes me back to my bourgeois upbringing where I learned not to eat like that (at the very most you were allowed a tiny bit of bread on the end of your fork). I appreciate grace, elegance. My husband is a handsome man who could have tremendous presence, but he couldn't care less about all that. With this little gesture of his, in the space of thirty seconds, HE takes me back to the working classes and physical slovenliness (I'm talking beer, sausage, beer-bellies and a good post-beer belch). Seduction score minus 40!' For a long time Melody restricted herself to the odd discreet comment. Nowadays she has 'moved up a gear' and has taken to commenting 'loudly and clearly as soon as he starts his little circus', though not without certain reservations about the strength of her reaction. 'I suddenly see myself as some kind of grouchy, cantankerous, overbearingly bossy figure, but I know that it's important for us as a couple, for the fascination–admiration bit that the other can and must arouse if the sexual "flame" is to be kept alive. And too bad if it's not spontaneous.'

Doubly irritating objects

The objects of the little world that surrounds us play a major role in irritation. Precisely because this little world is not content simply to surround us. Familiar objects are not simply decorative. In the course of our everyday gestures they exercise a profound influence on who and what we are. As I pointed out earlier, irritation often results from a feeling of dissonance between the subconscious patterns which dictate ordinary routines and the 'abnormal' place occupied by substances and objects. Mary Douglas (1992) points out that there is no objective definition of dirtiness: it is a social convention established over a long period. Dirtiness refers simply to the fact that a particular substance is perceived as being in the wrong place. Soil is not in itself dirty; it becomes so only when it gets onto the floors or sticks to our shoes. The difficulty lies in the definition of what the right place really is, since it varies from one individual to another, including within the couple. The longer the couple are together, the more each partner discovers that what irritates them personally does not necessarily irritate their partner and vice versa. The most trivial details (the way a floor

25

is swept, the way a pile of clothes is stacked, a decision about decor) can suddenly reveal subtle and far-reaching clashes between cultures. The starting point is an object which provokes irritation in one of the two partners. From there, however, what happens next can vary considerably. When Louis was irritated by his mother-in-law's table, the couple could have developed a new mutual area of common interest (Japanese design). Irritation can set things in motion and intensify the couple's sense of unity. On the other hand, the object causing irritation can not only remain interminably in the same place, but can also send out extremely unwelcome messages spelling out the extent to which the partner we thought we knew so well is in fact living in a different (aesthetic or emotional) universe from our own, at least for some of the time. The object becomes doubly irritating. It offends us by its presence, in the same way as dirt or untidiness might. But it also upsets us because of the message it delivers each time it catches our eye, a message we would prefer not to hear. Witness the example of the sad story of the stuffed pike's head.

This research was conducted by Sofian Beldjerd,[2] who discussed the episode with Marie-Anne at great length. The interview is so telling I have chosen to quote from it extensively. It all started with a random event which would subsequently lead to a whole series of problems. 'We were about to go off on holiday and the . . . the day before we were leaving, he says: "Right, I'm going fishing." So off he goes and when he comes back, he tells me with great excitement . . . like a kid who's just been promised . . . I don't know . . . the whole world:

– "Look at this, look at this – I've caught a pike!"
– "OK, fine. Er, that's nice. . ."
– "Can you believe it – my first pike. . ."'

The husband is keen to remove the head and take it to a taxidermist. Marie-Anne is astonished by this strange passion, which, while it leaves her completely cold, transports her man into a totally alien emotional universe. Although immediately on the defensive, she cannot really see how she can stop him, especially as the fact they are about to go away on holiday makes the problem seem less pressing. 'I just couldn't see the point. Really for me, well, it's a fish, fine . . . but to keep a head like that . . . I mean when I see wild-boar's heads and that kind of thing, I think it's pretty horrible. . . . So, this, this really . . . well, . . . I wasn't very enthusiastic. . . . He started to say,

---

[2] Research as yet unpublished, conducted in the context of a sociology thesis, University Paris 5.

"Oh, no, OK, I'll. . .". At which point she gave in, thinking that, after all, it was up to him and not really an issue for them as a couple. "Go on then, it's your pike. . .".' But the story did not end there. 'So off we went on holiday. When we got back, off he goes to pick up the precious head, mounted on a nice bit of wood!

– "Where shall we put it?"

– "Ah. . .!!!"'

By accepting the plural used here ('we' as opposed to 'I'), Marie-Anne finds herself inextricably involved in this disagreeable conjugal adventure, from which she tries to extract herself in a diplomatic but firm way.

– "'So where shall we put it?"

– "I don't know, but I don't particularly want to see it myself . . . it doesn't really appeal to me. So see if you can put it somewhere a bit out of the way." So for a while it went into his workshop . . . and then, some time later, he said to me: "You know what, I'd like to bring it in here (the living room)". And he saw how thrilled I was with that idea! And then . . .'

And so began the interminable journey of the pike's head, from one room to the next, at the mercy of first one person's wishes and then the other's, and all in the name of an implausible but supposedly shared vision. 'He'd say "Oh, I wouldn't mind putting it here . . . I think he ended up trying it out on virtually every single wall in the house . . . certainly in the sitting room and the dining room. And then, I'd say "Um, well, no . . . I don't want it there! Hold on, it doesn't look right there . . .".' But the husband refused to admit defeat.

– "'Marie-Anne, come and have a look!"

– "Ah! Er, no, it doesn't look right. . . ." So, down comes the pike, back goes the picture!' Until eventually, overcome with longing and for once refusing to get involved in conjugal negotiations, he put the pike in pride of place in the living room. Marie-Anne had to settle for secret irritation, punctuated by angry comments 'I'd say to him "Oh, that thing is just so ugly!" Or I'd say things like, "Oh dear, that thing really gets to me. . . . I mean I just can't bear your . . . that head of yours. . . ." And he knew it, and sometimes he'd even say, "I know you don't like this head of mine!" But anyway, we didn't fall out over it. It was just that he could tell I wasn't very happy about it. But he liked it, so . . . we were . . . well we just didn't discuss it.' Fortunately, after many years of discreet domestic combats the sad story of the pike eventually resolved itself, initially with a compromise acceptable to both parties. 'One fine day, he took it down and said "where shall I put it?" So I replied: "Anywhere you like, as long as I don't have to

27

look at it." So he says "Oh, OK, I'll put it in the kitchen." To which I said "Well, that makes sense in a way, because after all it is more to do with food than . . . !" So, if it has to be somewhere, I suppose the kitchen will just about do. "But make sure you put it where I don't have to look at it."' So the husband put it up opposite his place at the table. For years Marie-Anne ate her meals with her back to the pike, avoiding any eye contact with the loathsome trophy. Until the real happy ending, a miracle she had given up hope of ever seeing happen. 'I think that eventually after all those meals with that head in front of him he just got fed up with seeing it! Because one day, he started to say: "I think I'll put my pike in my workshop." Well you can imagine my response! "Of course, that's fine . . . that's a great idea!" And then just like that . . . one fine day he took it into his room and it was gone.'

Key episodes

However discreet they may be, controversies over objects often high-light a confrontation between individual and couple. Each of the two partners retains certain aspects of identity which set them apart from the couple, at least in their thoughts. This tendency towards separate-ness is particularly apparent in relation to certain tangible spaces. When this happens the partner becomes aware that entire micro-territories remain resistant to the conjugalization of existence. Claudie knew perfectly well that Pierre's interests lay in politics.[3] The books and activist literature scattered all over the place were daily proof of that. 'I've always felt that Pierre would put all that before his family life and our relationship and I have to admit that in some ways that really bothers me.' Claudie's main concern was simply to keep things from getting out of hand. But when it came to their bedroom, she had no qualms about declaring a state of war. In this most intimate corner of the couple's life, the piles of books and, particularly, the posters stuck all over the walls were an affront threatening their relationship and even the family. 'I'm much more interested in normal, everyday life. I put up photos of the kids. [. . .] I'd like him to see the bedroom more as our own special place.'

Through the interplay between the conjugal, the individuality of one person and the individuality of the other, the war of objects has a certain linearity when looked at over a long period of time.

---

[3] Comments recorded and quoted by Karim Gacem (1996, p. 125).

For the logic of this process is that objects accumulate layer upon successive layer, in such a way that old layers are never erased, gradually becoming embedded and creating long-lasting reference points. This is why moving house, for example, is so mentally exhausting (Desjeux, Monjaret, Taponier, 1998): even more than any technical aspects of the move, deciding what to keep and what to throw away and arranging the new home entail a complete reorganization of identity. Other even more significant events and biographical upheavals disrupt the linearity. Some are dramatic and unexpected (divorce, accident, job loss); some are happy occasions; some, more predictable events corresponding to different times of life: the birth of a child, the children leaving home, retirement. The arrival of a child can have a more dramatic effect on the parents' existence than many people realize. There are suddenly so many things to do, all of them so urgent. The new parents stick together in the face of the domestic chaos which threatens to engulf them; they seem, more than ever, united. Once the worst of the crisis has passed, however, this frenzied period, which at the time had made the sacrifice of the old life-style seem less significant, can take its toll in the form of crises exacerbated by fatigue, sometimes even leading to break-up (Geberowicsz, Barroux, 2005). Such extremes aside, and in a more general sense, the expansion of the family brings about a paradoxical transformation. The presence of children and the pressing issue of their upbringing imposes a much stronger demand for a unified domestic group, with the parents needing to show the children how to behave and setting a good example. However (we are becoming familiar with this law of opposites), the more urgent the need for a united front becomes, the more scope there is for irritations to come to a head. Zoé's upbringing meant she inherited a 'little censor' which lurked somewhere at the back of her mind. In the early days of her relationship with Charles-Henri, the little censor seemed to be dormant. Admittedly, her partner's odd ways – spitting into the sink, licking his knife, leaving his clothes lying around – secretly took her by surprise. As time went on and these little habits persisted, she found herself reviving that 'little censor'. But things only really reached a head when the presence of a third party drew attention to the "unacceptable nature of his behaviour. Particularly with the arrival of the children. 'If he licks his knife when someone else is there, I could die of shame and sometimes I can even get quite aggressive. I couldn't bear the thought that my own children might behave like that. In fact the tension between us stems largely from the fact that he behaves in a way which totally conflicts with the way I'm teaching the children to behave (good table

29

manners, putting things away, language. . .)'. And when he spits in
the sink, 'the little censor nudges me and I can't bear the idea that my
children might take this kind of behaviour for granted. So I react by
explaining how I feel to my partner who promptly takes offence at my
comments. But then a few days later he does exactly the same again.
And the tension rises! Take the fact that he's always leaving his socks
lying around in the living room. I can't stand the fact that there we
are nagging the children to put away their socks, or their slippers, and
yet he leaves his all over the place. So I gently point out to him that, if
he expects the children to do something, he needs to begin by setting
a good example himself. I'm quite capable of stuffing his socks in his
coffee mug if I find them lying around in the morning.' In the name of
the family and of the children, war has been declared between the two
of them. Witness the violence of those socks in the coffee cup.

The arrival of children increases the tension as rhythms intensify
and a united front becomes even more necessary. Discussions about
the children turn out to be amongst the most frequent causes of
disagreement (Brown, Jaspard, 2004). Unfortunately, their departure
from the family home does not necessarily improve matters. This is
because one problem (the fatigue caused by family responsibilities
combined with conflicts about the children's upbringing) is suddenly
replaced by another equally delicate one as the couple find themselves thrown together again. While some of the intensity might have
gone out of their conversations (meal-times can even be threatened
with silence), the simple fact that the other person is always present,
and there is little or no means of escape, in itself provokes a certain
amount of friction. And the situation can often get worse when retirement comes along. More than ever before, the other person suddenly
seems intolerably different. 'Life just isn't the same anymore when
your tastes are just so completely opposite', observes an irritated
Mr Berg.[4] Nor does this other person confine themselves simply to
being different. Suspicious or over-attentive, the sheer fact of their
omnipresence can be suffocating. 'He'll say to me: "Where are you
going? How long will you be?" And that gets on my nerves a bit, that
kind of . . .' sighs Mrs Louis, who used to enjoy being able to go off
on little shopping trips without having to justify herself. Mrs Vannier
seems to echo her feelings: 'I can't have a chat, I can't phone anyone,
I can't do anything at all. . . . Before, well, I could do a bit of gardening, I mean I could potter about in my bit of garden . . . but now it's
"What are you doing?", "Where are you?", "Where've you been?".

[4] Comments recorded and quoted by Vincent Caradec (1996, p. 93).

It's . . .' And Mrs Blanc sums up the situation: 'That's what I can't stand about retirement.'[5] The law of opposites (togetherness provoking irritation) is again clearly in evidence, this time not because of a desire for ethical harmony, as in the issue of bringing up children, but simply because the couple find themselves sharing activities and physical space in a more intense way than was previously the case. Nor does reserving some time for yourself necessarily solve the problem. Francky, for example, is by no means a typical retired person. At the age of forty, after a very successful career, he chose to give up his professional activities in order to concentrate on leisure activities and family life. Yet this idyllic prospect only made the ensuing irritation experienced by the couple all the more unexpected and difficult. 'Ah! At last time for myself. Time for all the sports and leisure activities I'd been longing to do! At first it was idyllic. We even bought our dream holiday home in the South of France. What a change for me! No more early mornings, no more stress, lots of holidays, lots of free time for all kinds of activities: DIY, gardening, mountain-biking, trail-biking, shooting, body building, etc. The main problem with all this was the fact that I was suddenly spending so much time at home [. . .] Ah! I can hear you thinking: "Another of those macho types". Not at all. Just someone trying to organize the daily life of the family in the best possible way. But it was hopeless! We argued almost systematically over everything even to the point of out and out rebellion [. . .] It's not easy being a couple! And it's amazing how things irritate you even more as you get older!'

So far I have painted a rather depressing picture of the way conjugal life evolves: after the adventure of the early stages of discovery, the establishment of routines is accompanied with attendant irritations, or various key events in life bring with them, like plague or cholera, either an excess of fatigue and endless discussions about the children, or the confined emptiness of forced togetherness. Fortunately, however, this is only one version of events, and things can be very different indeed. Francesco Alberoni (1993), in spite of the quality of his analysis, in my opinion does little justice to reality by stressing the fact that the institutionalization of the couple automatically leads to a diminution of feelings. In fact, new emotional forms take the place of old ones; love is a living relationship, which changes day by day, and not necessarily in a negative sense. The tender generosity of old age is in no sense inferior to the youthful emotional roller-coaster of falling in love. Love is also a concrete relationship, deeply rooted in

---

[5] Comments collected and quoted by Vincent Caradec (1996, pp. 82–3).

the smallest gestures, thoughts and words of everyday life, rather than something reserved for specific occasions, separate from normality. On the contrary, it is often the capacity of the two partners to transform that normality, or at least to soften its rough edges, that brings about a rosier version of the picture. Routines, as I have pointed out, are inevitable. They are a response to a social necessity which has become increasingly pressing in the context of the contemporary emphasis on the individual. Yet, rather than taking over completely, they need to allow space for awareness of the other person, for surprise and inventiveness (Brenot, 2001). When this does not happen, the result can be an accumulation of irritation ultimately leading to a sense of dissatisfaction. In the third part of this book, we shall see how certain tactics employed to combat feelings of irritation can be a means of generating love on an everyday basis. Feelings of irritation are fundamental to the way a couple functions, an inevitable element in that process. It is knowing how to deal with them that shifts the relationship into one of loving complicity. And with each challenge successfully overcome the little group ends up more closely united.

There are, however, a great many obstacles along the path of ordinary happiness. There is insidious routine, when it starts to dominate to an unacceptable manner. Or the opposite, where a sudden change, such as the discovery of a new interest, transforms the partner. The most trivial and absurd detail can sometimes cause major disruption – witness the story of the pike's head. In some cases, however, people's interests can prove extremely invasive (Bromberger, 1998; Le Bart, 2000). Cindy sent me her comments by post. Her letter begins: 'I would never have believed that a motorbike could cause so much harm.' A reference not to a road accident but to the destruction of their relationship. She knew Fred had once dreamed of owning a motorbike. When he was younger he had wanted to get his licence but the opportunity had not arisen, and she thought that it was no more than a forgotten dream. In fact the dream was merely in hibernation. His passion flared up again when their neighbour bought himself a motorbike and began to put pressure on Fred: 'You ought to treat yourself from time to time; otherwise what's the point in working?' Yet the real reason probably lies within the couple themselves: Fred, as apathetic towards Cindy (he claims to be exhausted by his work) as he is passionate at the very mention of his bike, was really looking for a pretext to avoid spending time with her. 'Ever since he went out and bought the most expensive and powerful bike possible, that's all he thinks about.' Cindy feels as though she no longer even exists. Her irritation cannot be expressed in anger since such outbursts only make the motorcyclist more inclined to disappear on his bike. Instead she makes up for it by eating and has put on 21 kilos.

The change in a partner can also be a more gradual one. Over a period of time Yannis had become more and more interested in ecological issues. Today, however, what began as an interest has evolved into a vision. 'As a result, certain aspects of my behaviour have become much more radical.' Aspects that permeate his private life: he now campaigns to stop his wife using the car for little bits of shopping and keeps a close watch on how she does things round the house. 'The thing is that for the last two or three years now, I've been really keen on saving energy, and what I find most irritating about my partner is the fact that she "forgets" to turn off the lights – or the heating – whenever she leaves a room. So I let slip a little comment along the lines of: "Hey, this isn't the Palace of Versailles!"' Caught off guard, she responds with a surge of irritation which can at times be quite virulent. 'She either politely tells me where to go, or she gets really angry and I can tell by the look in her eyes that it's not worth insisting. . .' The subtle architecture of conjugal interaction can find itself seriously destabilized by a change in one of the two partners, almost amounting to a breach of contract. Some changes turn out to be for the better. Others, however, do not, and are all the harder to accept given that the former identity of the partner remains in the other person's memory and has left its mark on the automatic gestures collectively established in the past. This additional dissonance (between the old idea of the partner and the new one) further exacerbates irritation.

—— 2 ——

MEN AND WOMEN – DIFFERENT OR COMPLEMENTARY?

Today's couples start out as a blank page where everything seems possible. Their first foray into domesticity can even seem like a kind of game, steeped in the quaint charm of homely little scenes which it is impossible to imagine might one day seem oppressive. Every meal is like a doll's tea-party; sweeping the floor is quickly subverted into a game with jokes and peals of laughter. After a few days of this, however, the need for some minimal kind of joint organization becomes apparent. But what? And how? The traditional roles and ways of doing things no longer exist. There remains only the notion, widely adopted, albeit somewhat vaguely, that tasks should be equally shared by men and women. As in many other aspects of their lives (Dubet, 1994), today's couple will have to rely on experience, a gradual process of trial and error on both sides. Even though both try their hand at everything, it soon becomes obvious that each has a different culture where everyday matters are concerned. The dirt or untidiness which 'bothers' one person goes unnoticed by the other. Some people even turn out to be scarcely 'bothered' at all, at least not until they find themselves living in a complete tip. We know that what 'bothers' and automatically provokes irritation is when objects no longer conform to the secret blue-print which controls automatic reflexes through the subconscious. By observing the different levels of irritation when confronted with what each finds oppressive or accept-able, the two protagonists discover the extent of the gulf between them: Eliza 'notices' things (forcing her to take action) which her partner fails to notice. 'What I find most irritating are the household chores. We really don't see eye to eye about that. Sometimes I don't feel like doing the housework but then I think of the satisfaction I'll get once it's done and that motivates me to do it. My boyfriend on the

34

other hand couldn't care less whether the apartment is clean and tidy. He can live perfectly happily with a pile of dirty dishes. It's simply not an issue for him; he'll deal with it when he feels like it. It's even more frustrating when you can't do it yourself (I know, because twice I've had surgery on my leg and been in plaster). I notice things (the bins need to be put out, the floor needs sweeping, some item of clothing needs to be put away . . .) he simply doesn't see. "It doesn't bother me" is his usual reaction.' It is of course conceivable (one would need to investigate further in order to verify this) that he might be deliberately exaggerating his inability to notice or be bothered by things. Some men intuitively develop this handy tactic as a way of getting their wives to take things into their own hands. For, inevitably, the person who gets most irritated will be the first to do something about it, in order to re-establish harmony between those objects which are not in the right place, and which therefore cause irritation, and their own secret blue-print of where they ought to be. But, by doing this once, twice, three times, a system of complementary roles will gradually start to take shape, whereby the partner who is most irritated becomes the specialist in a particular task and ends up in charge of it. Leaving the least irritated in the role of mere spectator.

The secret blue-print brings together various elements, some of which, handed down from generation to generation, have a very long history, a history unknown to the person concerned. Dormant schema can be reactivated by the new domestic context. When this happens, each person 'discovers' themselves (and simultaneously discovers the difference, even strangeness, of the other). After two weeks of living together, Géraldine is astounded by Bernard's pernickety sophistication when it comes to the washing, especially since until then she has never ironed anything. She is relieved to discover she can compensate in another area. 'I realize I'm quite obsessive when it comes to the cooking.' Each person uncovers hitherto unknown aspects of themselves, discovering that they have high expectations when it comes to housework for example (along with the interest and the competence to go with it), or else cooking, or even simply just the barbecue. A complex tangle of specialist territories gradually emerges within the household. In spite of female dominance in many areas (due to the greater weight of historical memory), male micro-specialisms also emerge. So, for example, it remains to be seen whether Jack will indeed end up taking charge of sorting out the paperwork. We have seen that, in terms of more general domestic tidiness, his 'as and when' approach puts him firmly in the classic male position of remaining on the fringes when it comes to the housework. But, in the more specific area of the paperwork, the opposite seems to apply. 'We each have our own approach when it comes to dealing with it. I let things pile up until they start to get on my nerves (a fortnight to three weeks) and then I go through the whole lot and file what needs to be kept whereas Jack likes to sort things straight away' (Eline). Closer analysis of the two methods suggests, however, that it is by no means certain that things will end up going Jack's way. It turns out his irritation is short-lived and simply results in him carrying out a preliminary sorting. 'He puts the paperwork in a tin until such time as it can be properly put away into the appropriate box files. Which gets on my nerves, because it makes me feel nothing is ever really put away (not true) and that nothing ever gets dealt with (not entirely true). As a result we still haven't hit upon an efficient system for dealing with our joint paperwork.' The situation remains unresolved. And it is highly likely that whoever finds it most irritating will end up taking on the job of sorting out the paperwork, probably definitively.

The different approaches

Irritation is not born with the couple; the isolated individual is also beset by feelings of irritation which arise from their own internal dissonances. Yet such feelings tend to be multiplied in the early stages of life as a couple. 1 + 1 = 4. Eline and Jack are both irritated by their disorderly paperwork, but each in a separate and contradictory way. The increased irritation keeps things in motion: both partners try to find a new equilibrium, a process which favours specialization. This comes about as a result of irritation and at the same time, is also a way of absorbing it. By assuming the responsibility for a particular activity, the most irritated party aims to eliminate the dissonance and to re-establish their personal equilibrium. Of course, he or she also has to accept the increased workload involved. But the incentive is nevertheless considerable given that the alternative is to be doubly irritated: by the grating gestures of the partner and by the unavoidable injunction to take on a role they do not want.

The paradox is as follows: for the person who takes charge of a particular activity, the specialization both reinforces their conjugal integration and, at the same time, reaffirms their individuality as each expresses the particularities which restore their personal unity, but as an element of the greater entity of which they are now a part. We see from this that the construction of the conjugal state is an incredibly complex process. For, in addition to the task of forming a

MEN AND WOMEN – DIFFERENT OR COMPLEMENTARY?

unified group and establishing a common culture, notably through the medium of conversation (Berger, Kellner, 1988), the exact opposite is also happening, with the creation of internal oppositions which although functional and precisely regulated, are nevertheless triggered by the accentuation of differences. 'The more money he fritters away, the more I try to save', observes Marie-Lyse.[1]

The new partners allow themselves to be swept along and it is easy to understand why: complementarity is in fact psychologically comforting in that it reduces personal dissonances. What is more, the realization that this personal well-being is more likely to strengthen the couple than to harm it removes any lingering doubts on the subject. This is why, very often, life as a couple can be transformed into a veritable production line turning out contrasting identities. In the face of a general trend supporting the notion of equality and inter-changeability, experience suggests the opposite is happening. Carla, for example, intensely irritated by the intolerable differences between her and 'J-P' (of which more later), was astonished to discover that other differences between them, apparently of a similar nature, could be positively combined to produce an agreeable and productive complementarity. 'There are times when our differences "work together" fantastically and when we complement each other really harmoniously. For example, a little while ago we bought a flat and needed to do quite a lot of work on it. When it came to wallpapering, the two of us really worked as a team. J-P's way of organizing everything (you cut and measure, I paste, you bring the paper over to me, I hang it, you wipe off the paste . . .) really worked well and didn't bother me in the slightest. For me it was a kind of game in which I obeyed his orders and acted as his little apprentice! If I'd had to do it all on my own it would have been a total catastrophe! We would have wasted loads of paper and it would have taken ages . . . whereas for this par-ticular job J-P was just perfect. My contribution was to keep things more relaxed, which was important because J-P tends to start getting annoyed as soon as things don't go quite as he wants, and wallpaper can be rather awkward sometimes and doesn't always behave as you want it to. So I encouraged him by saying things like: "It'll be OK, you'll see . . . it'll smooth out as it dries" and I made him feel more relaxed by saying stupid little things, laughing at our clumsiness and giving him plenty of kisses and cuddles to help him relax. Our different approaches, brought together like that, really made those decorating sessions relaxed and productive. I didn't get at all irritated

---

[1] Comments recorded and quoted by Pascal Duret (2007).

by him wanting everything to be perfect and highly organized – in fact quite the opposite – it paid off and I could see why it was necessary.'

Over and above the use of complementarity as a technique for occasional decorating jobs, the gradual assignment of roles brings together, in a much broader sense, two contradictory universes (ethical, cultural, psychological). Faced with someone who is organized, punctual or stressed, generally responsible for the kinds of activities such people tend to take on, the other person can appear either irritatingly apathetic, or they can be seen as the epitome of the laid-back approach (a role which Carla subtly played on in order to calm J-P's excesses). Unlike what happened with Carla and J-P, it is often men who become specialists in this rather agreeable role. Alice puts her finger on the benefits of complementarity. 'His relaxed approach can sometimes have a positive effect in that he manages to de-dramatize certain situations, to see the positive side, and that means he helps me to be more relaxed, not to panic for no reason and it's really nice to have someone so laid back beside you when you start to get a bit stressed – he calms me down and at those times I really love and appreciate his capacity to stay relaxed.' A person living on their own is forced to constantly arbitrate themselves between the two opposing roles. Being part of a couple makes it possible to leave this double game behind and to attenuate the dissonance which results from it. But this can only happen on condition that a complete reshaping of identity takes place. Sometimes a radical change of personality is necessary in order to take on the expected role. As a young girl, Dorothée was beset by all kinds of fears. Nights haunted by nightmares (of assaults, accidents) left her exhausted by morning and further undermined her self-confidence. Then she fell madly in love with Roberto. His good looks, which had initially blinded her to any faults, narrowly disguised what she was later to discover was a pathological instability, a nervous agitation almost uncontrollable at times, and which meant he was incapable of dealing with the simplest everyday situations. Drawing on previously unsuspected strengths, Dorothée transformed herself to the extent that she was able to become the secure rock on which the couple were anchored. This responsibility, which initially focused on the details of running the household, gradually extended to a more systematic moral position, with the result that her own deep-seated anxieties were eventually completely obliterated. Now she is afraid of almost nothing and does not even bother to lock her door. She is proud of the fact that she recently walked around New York at night on her own. Her sleep is filled with new dreams. She sees herself in the guise of wild, muscular heroes who unfailingly triumph over the forces of evil. She wakes up full of energy.

Glitches

On paper, the method of complementary roles seems perfect. In practice, it turns out to be an extremely delicate process and the slightest glitch can clog up the entire mechanism. We have seen how Alice sometimes appreciated the calming presence of Aziz at her side. 'He helps me to be more relaxed, not to panic for no good reason.' But this kind of functional complementarity is unfortunately rather rare. In most cases the couple find themselves squabbling over the disciplined versus the relaxed approach, each trying to impose their philosophy onto the joint life-style. Aziz refuses to restrict himself to what (in Alice's opinion) his role should be. By trying to impose his vision as the unique reference point for both partners, he accentuates the dissonances rather than allowing them to be reabsorbed. To make matters worse, he is more than capable of resorting to the form of revenge which comes easily to advocates of the relaxed approach. In other words by (gently) teasing Alice who, trapped in her role, becomes even more irritated. 'Aziz definitely takes advantage of certain situations which he knows I find stressful to lay it on a bit thicker and he finds it's really entertaining to tease me in that way.' Double, even triple aggravation for Alice: Aziz, who already fails to comply with her own secret vision of how things should be, particularly with regard to punctuality (he is always late), has the nerve to deliberately 'lay it on a bit thicker', either purely for his own amusement or, more deviously, as a way of getting his own back. But worst of all is the internal dissonance all this provokes: she is unable to maintain what she feels is the perfect attitude. 'So naturally I feel angry with myself for falling for it, for not managing to stay calm and relaxed in the face of whatever is going on. That of course is what irritates me most about this whole thing.' Events follow on from each other so rapidly she finds herself unable to disentangle the various dissonances involved. This lack of clarity about the causes of her irritation makes it more intense and prevents her from responding in a more rational manner. A trivial event, perhaps initially no more than a joke on Aziz's part, has degenerated into genuine conflict.

We saw earlier how irritation can result from the kind of interchangeability which is common when the couple are first together. A situation which prompts the strengthening and institutionalization of differences which are complementary and an integral part of the way the couple functions. We now discover that failure to respect this system constitutes a further source of irritation. In the ideal model, the supporting role should be able to step back completely. They should have no personal opinion, make themselves invisible and only express themselves in the context of offering unconditional support to the person who has taken on the responsibility for the task. This kind of social invisibility in the context of the supporting role was a common feature in traditional society, and continued until after the Second World War, the era which marked the end of the first phase of modernity (Beck, Beck-Gernsheim, 1995; Dubet, 2002; Singly, 2005). Today, when everyone seeks every opportunity to assert themselves and to be their own person, the situation has become more complicated. The supporting role needs to be able to resist thinking and saying what they really think if the complementarity is not to cause friction. When Agnès was doing the ironing herself, Jean had to be constantly on his guard and took great care not to make his feelings known (except for those morning outbursts on the specific matter of the shirts). 'Obviously if the pile of ironing is one and a half metres high, I might say something, but only ironically, no more than that. I won't get angry about it because it's not my domain.' Yet keeping such thoughts to oneself can be so difficult! Since he retired, Madeleine's husband cannot resist lifting up the lids of dishes and pans in the kitchen to see what they contain. Although he does nothing himself, he has very definite ideas about everything and in particular about the cooking. Madeleine finds this intensely exasperating. 'Ah! That business! I can't stand him poking his nose everywhere. And making remarks like: Oh dear! That's a bit overcooked!' The intruder is sent packing and is instructed to wait until she is ready to serve him, his feet firmly tucked beneath the table as in the traditional model of conjugal life.

The partner who voices an opinion must be prepared to practise what they preach if they are to avoid irritating whoever has taken on that particular responsibility (unless, of course, the remarks are complimentary). But this is only possible if the supporting role can either cast off their previous identity entirely or suppress it efficiently. Anaïs and Pat are an example of the opposite scenario. In their case the dispute is over the correct temperature for washing clothes. 'This disagreement over temperature has been going on since we first met, which means we've been arguing over it for nine years. Our lives are completely dominated by this temperature business' (Anaïs). Anaïs washes everything at 30°. Pat is of the opinion that things need to be washed at a much higher temperature: a minimum of 60°. The 30/60 controversy has raged for nine years because they failed to reach agreement over a mutually acceptable system. Although technically complicated, they could have sorted some of their laundry into separate washes. Another possibility, unacceptable in the context of equality between the sexes, but more practical, would be for Pat to accept defeat and allow Anaïs to do things the way she wants, especially since she is more inclined to take the initiative in this particular domain. After nine years he still cannot bring himself to accept such a solution. Instead, he has taken to storing his own laundry separately, perhaps with the intention of washing it himself, but more likely in the hope that Anaïs will do two separate washes. Alas, as soon as she turns up, infuriated by the sight of this separate little pile, she snatches it up and with a liberating fury, adds it to hers and washes the whole lot at 30°. Realizing what has happened (a trivial but unacceptably frequent event), Pat still refuses to give in. Instead he resorts to an even more aggressive tactic in order to give vent to his own irritation: once the trousers have been washed, dried and ironed, he takes them out of the wardrobe and puts them back in the washing machine. In the course of their last interview, which took the form of a conjugal confrontation, all hell broke loose. Accused of being treacherous and obsessive, Pat retorted that he was simply trying to be instructive, in both their interests. It transpires he suspected Anaïs of acting out of a spirit of economy. For him such penny-pinching shows a lack of *savoir vivre*, and is a serious fault. Cut to the quick, Anaïs counterattacked with an argument along more technical lines. 'Oh! He washes everything much too hot. He creases things, he shrinks them. He ruins things – it drives me mad! The number of things he's ruined like that! He thinks they get cleaner – that's utter rubbish. I just put everything in together, at 30, and that's that! That's how it should be done!' Even more than the technical argument of 30 versus 60, the intensity of their mutual irritation is more to do with the inability to choose between two different ways of doing a specific activity. As Pat is neither completely involved nor completely detached from the activity in question, everything is thrown into confusion. Anaïs senses that she will eventually end up being the one responsible for the washing. Consequently she is looking for ways of marginalizing him and is rigorously imposing her way of doing things and her principles as being non-negotiable: 'That's how it should be done!' For her this aggressively blinkered approach is a way of dealing with her own internal dissonances and of restoring a sense of balance through action. But Pat, in choosing to remain very much in the forefront (both by giving voice to his dissenting opinions and by interfering in the activity itself) has allowed dissonance to creep in and it is now firmly rooted in the form of systematic hostility between the two sides: Pat versus Anaïs. Neither of them can win.

The supporting role must accept the prevailing method and refrain from expressing an opinion unless they are prepared to set in motion a chain of irritation. In addition to the fact that they may desperately want to assert their own individuality, this position of having to take a back seat is made even more difficult because of the frequent occasions when positions are briefly reversed. Jack is never in a hurry to put things away, except when it comes to paperwork. In this specific domain, he is by far the most efficient and so has ended up imposing his system on Eline. Their positions are reversed, according to whether it is paperwork or something else which needs to be put away. The same kind of sporadic change of position happens in the case of Aziz. This practitioner of all things 'cool' turns out to be not quite so 'cool' about everything. He is capable of becoming suddenly uptight over things which seem completely trivial to Alice who is then temporarily transformed into a champion of the relaxed approach. 'We're cool about different things. We have completely different notions about what is serious and important and what isn't.' After U-turns like these, which place them temporarily in the dominant position, it is clearly difficult for the person in the supporting role to stand back and say nothing when they have been the one imposing their point of view. Any area of uncertainty, any reversal of the rules, can potentially lead to irritation.

We shall see later that the supporting role is generally much less inclined to be irritated than the person in charge. Indeed it is often the differential in terms of irritation which led to them taking a back seat when the domestic routines were initially established. But this difference is further accentuated as time goes on, since the person who has assumed responsibility become increasingly susceptible to the risk of irritation, from a wide variety of sources. Firstly, since they are on the front line of the activity, their own dissonances are operational on a daily basis to ensure that order is established according to their own secret blue-print. This needs to apply to all the members of the family, some of whom may have their own, different, ideas on the subject. Where children are concerned, this is acceptable: an educational model is being imposed and some difficulties are inevitable. But when the person who has taken on the supporting role has the audacity to cunningly resist, and even openly rebel, all the additional irritations associated with the fact that dissonances are multiplied by this process rebound on the person in charge. Luc, typical of a supporting role, is a true hoarder who finds it extremely hard to get rid of anything, even when – in the case of his clothes for example – they have begun to look seriously worn.[2] Anita makes up for his failings, energetically forcing Luc to take action in order to avoid even more irritation. 'Aaargh . . . that . . . that really gets on my nerves, that does! Because with him it's a case of: "No! Don't throw those away; I'll wear them for gardening!"' In order to get round the problem, Anita gets rid of things behind his back. 'But in that case I don't tell him.' She gets away with doing this because she has sensed that, in spite of his official declarations, his resistance is fairly low. 'I'm not even sure if he's noticed.' Luc tries not to notice too much and lets her get on with it. He senses vaguely that he would have trouble dealing with all those superfluous objects on his own. Thanks to Anita he is spared that challenge, although he still feels she is unnecessarily brusque with him. 'If she has to take my stuff, I wish she'd at least ask me.' He has mixed feelings on the matter. This internal division could produce irritation. It does not have this effect in his case because he transfers the irritation to Anita, who then has the responsibility of deciding whether to tell him or not, in addition to that of deciding whether to get rid of things or not. The person in charge is not content to simply manage their own individual relationship with their surroundings. He (or she) also takes on responsibility for the collective model which involves individuals who disagree on certain aspects. And often that means inheriting their dissonances as well.

And it goes without saying that this person also needs to fully accept the role, however onerous, they are taking on. The slightest hesitation can provoke a new flurry of internal dissonances. In the name of women's liberation, Sabine disapproves of domestic stereotyping. She has, however, inherited a complex family history. Her mother was 'the last person to notice dust' and this was the source of violent clashes between her parents. Under her father's approving gaze, Sabine got into the habit of stepping into the deficient housewife's shoes, and as a result acquired a number of automatic reflexes. When she first met Romain, she was convinced that their romance would rescue her from this trap. Romain himself had grown up in an extremely orderly household but had no practical expertise himself nor any particular inclination when it came to housework. What would happen? There were internal conflicts on both sides. When they first moved in together, Sabine could not resist throwing herself wholeheartedly

---

[2] Comments recorded and quoted by Françoise Bartiaux (2002, pp. 145–6).

into action to prepare their little love nest. Romain was happy to allow this distribution of roles to take place, especially as it meant he could escape lightly and resolve his own internal dissonance. After a month, Sabine began to see her actions in a more critical light: this life-style did not really 'match up' to her philosophy. An increasingly insistent 'little voice' kept saying: 'But I'm turning into a proper little housewife.' Soon sparks started to fly. Maya was equally reluctant to take on the little housewife role. She had gradually taken charge of the tidying in their house. Igor was only too happy to let this happen: the position of supporting role is psychologically extremely comfortable. Perhaps a little too comfortable in his case, for Maya's irritation has reached such a point that it impacts on the amount of housework she ends up doing. 'One of the things that gets me about Igor is that he never knows where anything is. Whether it's papers, clothes, food, CDs, keys, etc., the phrase I hear all the year round is: "You don't know where such and such is do you?" At first I didn't take much notice and when we were just sharing the same place rather than really living as a couple, I thought perhaps he just didn't want to rummage around and wasn't quite sure where things were kept. But gradually, this habit of his has become more and more irritating (from my point of view) to the extent that I no longer answer the question! On reflection, I realized that what makes it even more irritating is the fact that he asks the question before he's even started looking for whatever it is. Which means that now, regardless of the circumstances (whether he's already started looking or not), the slightest question of that sort makes me fly completely off the handle.'

Women often find themselves caught in a trap. Irritated by the way men do things, they prefer to take charge of the activities themselves, only to realize later that their partner, protected by his reputation for incompetence, is lounging around comfortably without a care in the world while they have their nose to the grindstone, a realization that is in itself a new source of irritation. Akira is (voluntarily or not?) so 'unsuited to practical matters' (Gally) that his incompetence has become legendary and is a source of great amusement to his family and friends. Gally is no longer quite so amused. 'The other day the washing machine overflowed, yet he managed not to notice either the continuous sound of running water or the fact that water was starting to spread across the floor. It was only when water started to drip from the ceiling that I became aware (too late unfortunately) of the damage. I was beside myself: how can you be practically paddling about in water and not even notice? Being absent-minded to that extent is almost an illness! Hardly the dream husband.' Particularly with regard to the issue of housework (or, more broadly, the issue of where objects should be), the gap between the person in charge and the supporting role is very gender-led, with women often on the same side, taking on responsibility (and the associated irritations), and men on the other, clearly more comfortable, one. Evidently this is an issue which needs examining more closely.

Are men less irritated?

Thousands of little irritations add to the spice of life – all sorts of irritations, for all sorts of reasons, including some which are ridiculous or incongruous. They pit individuals against each other, each affected by their own personal trajectory and by the smallest details of their backgrounds, or, more generally, by the moral codes they have acquired. Where most of these details and rules with their potential to generate irritation are concerned, the fact that the individuals in question are men or women is not of any immediate significance. We shall see later, for example, that differences in attitude to punctuality are a common source of irritation, pitting punctual and organized people against unashamed latecomers vaunting their *cool* approach. There is, however, no evidence to suggest that either men or women are more likely to be associated with a particular side. To confine the study of irritation purely to the context of male–female relationships would in fact deprive us of some of the most interesting aspects of the subject and, notably, of the insight it gives into the way the couple and, by extension, the individual function. We need to be wary of the generalizations and hasty oversimplifications currently much in vogue. Imagining that men and women are so irretrievably and totally different that they originate from two separate planets (Mars and Venus for example) may be hugely reassuring, given the complexity of divergence that exists within the couple. It reduces everything to an argument so inevitable that any notion of future change might as well be abandoned immediately Witness these comments from Alphonsine, written in a satirically poetical form, and the perfect illustration of this state of affairs: 'If ever I come back on earth again I do not want to be a man. Men irritate me more and more. I feel we are not made to live together. Why do men urinate with the toilet door open? To paraphrase Verlaine the long sobs of flowing urine will never resemble the violins of autumn. Women never leave the door open.' With all due respect to Alphonsine, some women do indeed leave the door open (Kaufmann, 2002). The world (fortunately!) is not quite so radically divided, especially when it comes to the subject of irritation.

A large proportion of what we find irritating is not sexually determined. Nevertheless, it remains the case that a small core of it is indeed gender-related. This is after all quite logical, given that the issue of who does what within the household is, as we have seen, a crucial one. The issue is the legacy of a history which has divided men and women, and which continues to exert an influence today: how many women would identify with Maya's irritation when Igor asks: 'You don't know where . . . is, do you?' Without wanting to confine the study of irritation to male–female relationships, it is, however, important to mention those irritations which are specifically and structurally feminine.

Yet one question needs first to be resolved: does the existence of these specifically feminine irritations imply that men are generally less irritated than women? It is an interesting question and by no means easy to answer. To do so, we would need a statistical study, extremely difficult to envisage in this domain of emotional displays which are often minuscule and difficult to express. Initial reactions to my research on this subject, however, led me to suspect that men are indeed less inclined to be irritated. Or that they experience and express irritation in a different way. After an initial appeal inviting people to share their experiences, I received a huge quantity of replies from women, some virulent, many very detailed. And nothing at all from men. Admittedly several of the advertisements had appeared in publications aimed at women, which obviously affected the balance to some extent. Following on from this, I put out further appeals, this time specifically aimed at men. The response was disappointingly thin, and the accounts tended to be brief, to the point, and with very little emotional content. In the context of his research on domestic quarrels, François Flahault had encountered the same phenomenon. 'When it came to men, on the other hand, it was difficult to find volunteers. And, amongst those who did come forward, there was a tendency to avoid the use of the first person or to go into detail' (1987, p. 84).

There may be many reasons behind this feeble male response. Traditionally (again this is a historic legacy), men are less inclined than women to participate in intimate conversation; they are less willing to speak out in public, and they are also less likely to be forthcoming on such subjects within the couple. Danilo Martuccelli (2006, p. 188) confirms this in a recent piece of research, highlighting what he calls the 'dissymmetry of expectations' between men

and women on the subject of the couple: sexuality versus communication. The classic distribution of roles, still widely prevalent
today, reinforces this historic differential. Since women usually play
a leading role in family matters, they tend to be closely involved in
such issues, finding solutions and bringing problems into the open.
Male supporting roles, on the other hand, are more inclined to wait
until the storm blows over. They are unlikely to bring up such issues
since, more often than not, they are keen to put them aside and
forget about them. 'Look, I'm tired, leave me in peace, just drop
it, what's it got to do with you?. . .' snaps Eve's partner when she
tries to get him to talk.[3] Isabelle has got the message: 'We women
have plenty to say. I think that's true of men too but in general they
reply with: Um! Er, dunno . . . er . . .' Jack is much more involved
and forthcoming in his relationship. Yet even this 'above average'
man has reservations when Eline asks him to contribute alongside
her. 'He's not ready for that. He's the sort of person who doesn't
confide much anyway and *a fortiori* even less to someone he doesn't
know and in a context he can't really understand (he doesn't know
the first thing about sociological surveys – you have to excuse him,
he's an engineer). However, since we do discuss everything as a
couple (at least we try to!), it may be that I can sometimes give you
his point of view. Incidentally I already know what he finds really
irritating about me.' Subsequently he was to find having his opinion
interpreted by Eline (in his view, not exactly accurately) somewhat
irritating, to the extent that he made some attempt at a come-back,
before giving up again, still hesitant – ready to be involved in the
discussions, but without actually expressing his views directly. After
weeks of silence, Eline sent me a message which began like this:
'Here at last are my answers to your questions. It has taken a while
because we wanted time to discuss them together. As I said before,
your questions are pertinent and some of them are worth taking time
over. In particular, the issue of power within the couple. You will
however have to make do with just my answers to your questions.
While Jack was happy to take part in the initial stage of the survey,
he was less keen when it came to the follow-up. He has enjoyed
the discussions which have come out of this but is not prepared to
take it any further. Sorry. It's all part of his charm . . .' Kasiu sent
me a long list of grievances, all sources of serious irritation. The list
ends like this: 'Phew!!!! Apart from all that, everything is fine, he's
got lots of good qualities and I adore him. We met when we were

---

[3] Comments recorded and quoted by Danilo Martuccelli (2006, p. 187).

19 and we are now 33. I have my faults too and it's important to know how to compromise if you are going to succeed as a couple. I'm sending him a copy of this e-mail in the hope that he will write to tell you about what gets on *his* nerves about our relationship.' I never heard anything from him. Neither did I hear anything else from Eléonore, after her first message, written under supervision: 'Having discussed this with my husband and with his agreement, I am ready to embark on this new adventure with the stipulation that everything is completely totally open. My husband wants to read all correspondence between us.' Marital censorship was evidently in full swing.

The fact that they are more reserved about wanting to discuss the issue does not, of course, constitute an absolute proof that men are less subject to irritation. They may be secretly irritated without wishing to discuss it. This is certainly their preferred approach when it comes to dealing with the little crises and clashes that occur in every relationship, a model based on the art of evasion and altogether in keeping with the supporting role. This tactical element can be confirmed with considerably more certainty: men tend to deal with their feelings of irritation in a specific and less demonstrative way and to experience them in a different way to women. We have heard Melody tell us that she expresses herself 'loudly and clearly' when 'HE' irritates her by gulping down his soup. 'More often than not he pretends not to have heard my comment, avoids the issue, leaves the room or changes the subject, waits for it to be over.' None of which stops Melody. 'If I'm in the right mood, I'm certainly not going to let it drop as easily as that, so I reiterate my comments. If the wall of silence continues, then I start cold war tactics.' Cornered, 'HE' is then forced into expressing himself in a slightly more open manner. Usually in a way not dissimilar to the 'Er, um, dunno . . .' quoted by Isabelle. 'At that point, he either says something completely hypocritical along the lines: Sorry! I forgot! Oh, do you think so? How can that be possible? I did it, I didn't do it, I will do it, etc.' Or, when he's feeling on form, 'HE' will come up with some crafty tactic to distract Melody. 'Either, and this is mostly what happens, he tries a bit of distraction (a compliment, a joke) which stops me feeling irritated, without really resolving anything of course, but at least it offsets the negative effects a bit.' But sometimes, to her surprise, 'He counterattacks: "And what about you then?"' Before quickly retracting his remarks when Melody makes it clear that persisting with that kind of attitude could be 'a risky business, since open conflict can easily turn sour'. This brief moment of revolt is, however, an indication that irritation may indeed be seething in men too. Such irritation, undoubtedly kept tightly under control most of the time, can erupt, violently at times, when it has been suppressed for too long. Jade finds it difficult to understand how her boyfriend, normally so indifferent to her criticism and whose contribution to conversation is so minimal she feels as though she is living on her own, can suddenly explode. 'For someone with a lethargic temperament who is slow to the point of being almost spineless, he's also remarkably highly-strung and quick tempered.'

More reserved when it comes to expressing themselves, more inclined to suppress matters or change the subject, are men also basically less inclined to be irritated than women? While the context of this research does not permit me to reach a definitive conclusion, I will close the subject by quoting observations made by Markus expressing (a little over-dramatically it is true, but in a way that makes it even clearer to understand) what is undoubtedly a widely held male attitude. It is indeed quite conceivable that men are less inclined to irritation, or that they experience it less openly than women, given that the position of supporting role means that irritation is incorporated into a whole series of negative feelings (which are not the subject of this book), encompassing and diluting the irritation *stricto sensu,* though without eliminating it entirely. There is a strong sense of suppressed anger in Markus's comments. 'She doesn't just irritate me, she absolutely kills me! She's like a permanent tornado. An extremely irritated tornado at that, always on edge, just a bundle of nerves. All I hear is "Well do something! Say what you think! Surprise me!" The children for example – the worst possible things will happen to them if I don't move heaven and earth. I'm worn out, completely worn out! Fed up! Of course this whirlwind irritates me, it irritates me from one end of the day to the other, but mostly it wears me out. Life's too short, for goodness sake! You have to make the most of it. Cool, cool, sweetheart! What's the point of getting into such a state, often over nothing at all? I do what I can to minimize the damage, spread a bit of sunshine and light. And when I get irritated (which I often do), I think it over quietly and I get out of the way or else I go out for a jog, to calm myself down and stop the atmosphere getting any worse. What else can I do – I'm all for a peaceful life. But as for her, you'd think she enjoyed being irritated, that it gives her energy, and she's certainly capable of moving mountains when she needs to. It's like a drug; she's addicted to being irritated. Even if I don't do anything wrong, I can guarantee she'll still fly off the handle over something or other.'

Irritated by a spectre

As far as women are concerned, it is precisely this tactic of walking away and avoiding the issue that proves irritating. They are not interested in peace and calm in the relationship: what they want is communication and presence, a shared life. Yet at the slightest hurdle men are ready to escape, either physically or secretly in their thoughts. Caroline is reassured to observe that such behaviour is not confined simply to Marc but to men in general, even though she still fails to understand the reasons behind this male attitude. 'Another thing that irritates me is this almost autistic attitude, that moment where a man retreats into his own solitary little cave, even though physically he continues to be present. Actually that irritates me one time out of four – the rest of the time I understand. And what gets on my nerves is the fact that I've seen it all before and it's as though I recognize the tune but can't read the music because the score is closed. In fact my irritation isn't about him or me at all but about a typically male attitude which I just don't understand. So I just let him get on with it and try to carry on as though he wasn't there.'

This tactic has its limits, however, and is only effective if it is of short duration. Unfortunately for Clémentine, the spectral nature of Felix's presence is quite simply chronic, especially when it comes to hearing; she appears to have a husband who lacks ears. 'My husband is kind, charming . . . He has only one fault: he never listens to what you say to him!! Oh, it's not that he's deaf, there's nothing wrong with his hearing at all. He hears what you say but doesn't listen!! It's so irritating!!!' Living with a spectre is not easy at the best of times but when the ghost in question has the nerve to emerge from his limbo to make some reproachful comments, all that long-suppressed irritation can suddenly be transformed into anger. Take the classic scenario of meal preparation where an identical scene is re-enacted on a daily basis in many households (Kaufmann, 2005). 'Félix also irritates me because he never has an opinion about anything!! And I'm not talking about general knowledge . . . If I'm going shopping and I ask him what he wants for dinner, he'll say: "I don't know. . . ." Then when I get back, suddenly it's: "You should have got some mussels, some tabbouleh"!! And I find that so irritating, so irritating . . . just as irritating as the fact that he doesn't listen!!' But for Clémentine and Félix, the intolerable presence of the spectre (and a critical spectre at that) imposes itself systematically, not just over the simple question of what to eat. 'He never listens: "Félix you need to call the accountant about various things." Even if I tell him three or four times, he still doesn't listen and then the accountant ends up phoning him!! Result: "Clémentine, you should have told me that I needed to call the accountant"!! That's when I realize I've got two children at home; a two-year-old plus the one I'm married to!! I'm really fed up with that – I honestly feel as though I'm his mother!! I'd like to be able to tell him something once and be sure that he had really taken it in. It must be wonderful to know you're being listened to! Last Saturday we went off to see some friends who have just moved about 80 km away. I told him to have a look at the route while I sorted out some things for the baby. He knew perfectly well that he had to sort out the route and bring the road atlas, especially as I'd reminded him twice the night before. But – guess what! – no road atlas!! "Clémentine, you should have reminded me to put the atlas in the car"!! I could have hit him!!!'

Women generally tend to be far more closely involved when it comes to both the couple and the family. They have higher expectations of the relationship on a personal level, and they take the lead in terms of day-to-day organization, with the whole mental burden that involves. As a result, men irritate them twice as much because of their lack of presence. This emotional build-up inevitably leads to issues being blurred and confused. Yet this very specific area of irritation needs to be tightly regulated if a chain reaction of further irritations is to be avoided. Lorenzo (similar in this respect to Markus) comes across as a man who is completely exhausted, at the mercy of a 'housework maniac'. He feels incapable of keeping up with her excessively high demands and has deliberately placed himself in an extreme version of the supporting role, enjoying the psychologically comforting position of the person who never knows where anything is. His wife finds this extremely irritating, as he well knows. 'My constant "need for help" also gets on her nerves. For example: "Where's the such and such?": "Wherever you last had it, I haven't touched it" (I didn't mean to imply she had touched it, I was merely asking the question).' He could of course make more of an effort; but that is not always an easy matter. For, as we have seen earlier, the supporting role also needs to know how to stick to their role and resist getting too involved if they are to avoid accentuating any dissonances within the couple. For Lorenzo, whose own approach to tidiness is clearly very different, withdrawal is a way of avoiding the need to defend his ideas and thus potentially making things worse. Unfortunately for him, irritated by his 'need for help', his 'housework maniac' behaves in a way that ends up emphasizing the differences between them. Perhaps because she forgets about the existence of the spectre once she is in the midst of

51

her domestic frenzy, perhaps subconsciously as a sort of revenge, she moves things around without telling him. Lorenzo, already constantly out of his depth, feels even more lost and childishly helpless. 'She's got this habit which really gets on my nerves: every once in a while, she suddenly decides to move something to a new place. I get really irritated looking for it. For her, the new place is perfectly obvious and she moans about my lack of patience and about how little perseverance and effort I put into looking for the item in question.' Such minuscule elements can sometimes come to dominate our existences in a recurrent and irritating way. These inevitably reflect issues within the relationship. In their mini-war over where things should be kept, Lorenzo and his wife are effectively struggling to define their proper place within the couple.

Millions of Peter Pans?

Clémentine is 'fed up with that', fed up with having to be a mother to her husband, of having to look after him in the same way she looks after her baby. Not only are men sometimes little more than a spectre, they can also become an onerous responsibility. Gally is concerned about what will happen if they have a child and keeps deferring the decision. 'The only thing is, I'm worried I'd end up looking after the child more or less on my own. Not that Akira would want to end the relationship but I'm concerned he'll just carry on behaving the way he does now. I can just imagine the result! Which is what makes me think twice about taking on another child in addition to the one I already share my life with.' This assimilation of husband and child comes up time and time again in comments sent to me by women. Viràg is a typical case. 'We've got three children, and I honestly feel I've got a fourth one all to myself.' Like many of my correspondents, she began by listing all the things that irritated her. The beginning of the list refers in a very classic way to the insufficient presence of the man-spectre, which she refers to as 'immaturity'. 'The thing that irritates me most about him is his immaturity and I really think that is at the root of everything. Take these few random examples:

 – A constant lack of attention: I speak to him, he doesn't answer or else he replies a couple of minutes later with a distracted "mmm".
 – Those dirty socks left all over the house.
 – I ask him to do the shopping (he does it, which is at least something), I provide him with a detailed list (which aisle, which brand – to make it

easier): on average a quarter of what he buys needs to be either taken back or exchanged every time.
– When I criticize him, instead of defending himself he says, literally: "It's true, you're absolutely right." ARRRGHHH! I can't stand that phrase! I'd like to be wrong occasionally.
– He never knows what to get for me. Since he never listens, he has no idea what I might need, or what kind of things I like.'

The examples are indeed rather 'random'. Everything is jumbled up together: failure to pay enough attention to the partner, the tendency to switch off, the refusal to face up to things, lack of competence. But what Viràg finds most irritating is what she refers to as 'immaturity', the feeling that she is dealing with a child. The way she talks about her shopping list is typical: you could easily be under the impression that she is talking to a child. Subsequently she describes her situation in more detail, notably in this anecdote, where under the gaze of the child's teacher, irritation was transformed into shame.

'We were asked to attend a meeting with our eldest son's teacher who was worried about his distracted behaviour, his daydreaming, lack of concentration, etc. (does that ring a bell?) My husband sits there with a big grin on his face throughout the entire conversation. The teacher notices and makes the comment: "Like father, like son": which makes him laugh even more! So much for our credibility with our son.' The blurring of roles is what sickens her the most, the poor educational example given by this father-child.

Like Viràg, Zoé is irritated by the socks left lying around. When she gets really exasperated, she has been known to punish the guilty party by putting them in his breakfast mug. Conscious of the violence of her reaction, she sometimes responds in a more diplomatic way, explaining the situation to him so he can amend his behaviour. 'I refuse to put them in the washing basket myself. It's not as if I'm his mother after all! So how does he react? Like a little boy caught red-handed. He apologizes and heads sheepishly off in the direction of the bathroom. That gets on my nerves almost as much as finding his socks because he shouldn't be playing that role. I never wanted a third child.' Could it be that conjugal life turns men into children? Without wishing to jump to the wrong conclusions, the question is worth exploring and may throw up some unexpected answers. In a previous book, *La Trame conjugale* (Dirty Linen), I showed how the contemporary definition of domestic roles gives rise to a typical male figure, that of 'the guilty pupil'. In traditional society, the man held a position of power without so much as lifting a hand around the house. Today, men still do very little (progress has been real but slow), partly through lack of motivation and partly because there is a genuine technical difficulty associated with stepping out of the supporting role (as we have seen), a difficulty fuelled by a historically sexually differentiated memory. Although for the most part supportive of progress towards equality, men are caught in a contradictory injunction: that of trying (more or less sincerely) to do more, whilst at the same time being unable (or unwilling) to genuinely do what is expected of them. A situation which puts them in a position of latent guilt and drives them to make brief but imperfect attempts to learn, always remaining subordinate to whoever is in charge. Guilty pupils! It is in these terms that Suzette describes her husband, who is keen to learn to cook: 'He does help me sometimes. He'll make a dessert for example, or he'll help me prepare things, but nothing very complicated.' She lets him play with the pastry, as she would a child.

But there is more to it than this and we must not be afraid to probe further. Over and above the hard core of domestic issues, which tend to put men in a subordinate and childlike position (leaving women with an exhausting and irritating work load), it is undoubtedly the way the couple functions on the basis of contrasting complementarities which pushes men to behave in an apparently childish way. Childhood is characterized by immaturity, but also by the cultural aspects that go with that state: freedom from care, joy, playfulness. At the heart of the irritations and of the dynamic of the complementary roles within the couple, our research shows that the conflict between responsibility and relaxation, seriousness and pleasure seeking, etc., is omnipresent, and central. On the one hand is a pole A, responsible for the smooth running of domestic operations and vigilant against any risks, and, on the other, a pole B with a carefree, live-for-the-moment attitude. It is a necessary and functional opposition but one which tends to accentuate splits and personality traits. And it turns out that women tend to be on one side and men on the other. Not, it must be emphasized, because they originate from two different planets. But rather because of the enduring weight of historic memories, different according to gender, and because of the mechanism for generating opposites which lies at the very heart of the couple. These complementary differences do not emerge in an arbitrary manner. Each of the two partners seeks to reduce their own internal dissonances, to achieve unity. In the most varied aspects of existence therefore, each individual tends to take a position consistent with his or her habitual cultural characteristics. Without, of course, as we have seen, ever fully succeeding: there are frequent one-off reversals, even within a specific domain such as tidying. Nevertheless, a clear general tendency does emerge, and the quest for personal coherence produces a global opposition between two fairly distinct cultural universes. It is reasonable to conclude that the kernel of the way (household) roles are allocated reinforces the tendency, amongst men who are already disposed to do so, to adopt attitudes characteristic of childhood and youth.

A significant number of elements pointing in this direction came out of our research. Although disparate and often insignificant in themselves, looked at as a whole these tend to confirm the hypothesis. The fact that men, like children and adolescents, are far more inclined than women to play, for example with balls or screens. And statistical studies certainly show that they have the additional personal leisure time to make this possible. But, time being equal, they still play more. 'My boyfriend plays a lot (internet games, war games . . .), it helps him to be more balanced (he was an only child, needs freedom, time to himself . . .) I don't feel able, in the name of the couple, to forbid him from playing just so we can spend time "together". Some of my friends can't understand the fact that he can play for hours on end, that he comes to bed two or three hours after I do.' After ten years together, Eliza is still struggling to reconcile herself to this husband who ignores her in favour of his toys. More significant still is the use of jokes and irony (incidentally a favourite male tactic to try to diffuse adverse irritations). Take the case of family discussions around the meal table, where all manner of different subjects and types of conversation criss-cross endlessly, each attempting to dominate the others (Kaufmann, 2005). Often parents bring up a serious subject (in particular relating to school issues) involving recrimination or negotiation, at which point the children attempt to inject a bit of humour as a diversionary tactic. Exactly the same thing happens between husband and wife. In some cases, the mother finds herself the only serious, responsible person in the family, faced with this alliance of flippant father–children. A final illustration, undoubtedly the most important: men are great advocates of the laid-back approach, favouring a 'cool' attitude in the face of stress and excessive discipline. But the 'little god of cool' is a characteristic icon of adolescence and youth (Bouchat, 2005, p. 27). Indeed, there is nothing surprising about this male attraction for the youthful cult of *cool*, associated as it is with another structural element: not the systems of roles this time but the manner in which both sexes embark on their adult life. Whereas young men increasingly put off family commitments in order to preserve a young life-style for as long as possible, women, although they behave similarly at first, are affected by the pressing need to think in advance about the cut-off age for child bearing (Kaufmann, 1999). They are forced to leave their youth behind them and start taking on responsibilities at a much earlier stage. Men, on the other hand, are not affected by this biological time-bomb and are able to prolong their carefree existence much longer. As Caroline says, perhaps generalizing a little unfairly: 'In fact, even when he's thirty-six, a man is still a teenager.'

The fact that Dan Kiley's book, *Le Syndrome de Peter Pan*, provoked the response it did is yet another indication that something is indeed brewing somewhere in the depths of society. The book, however, has a number of limitations. It focuses on a pathological psychological profile dominated by anxiety, by the refusal to accept reality and by an incapacity to establish relationships with other people. While this type of personality undoubtedly exists, the male behaviour we are exploring here is in no way pathological and is on a considerably broader scale. These men-children rarely find it difficult to establish bonds – quite the opposite in fact, particularly through games and sport. Nor do they experience difficulty when it comes to forming relationships with their own children. They are even capable of developing extraordinary bonds which are affectionate and playful. A lot has been said, and with good reason, on the subject of the new fathers. The transformation has indeed been a huge one, over a period of a few decades and within the context of a profound change in the concept of masculinity (Castelain-Meunier, 2005; Welzer-Lang, 2004). A change that is all the more striking given that the same progress cannot be observed when it comes to the concrete issue of domestic tasks. Men, still almost as likely to be occupying supporting roles as they were in the past, are now much closer to their children, forming intimate relationships with them. Hence their distress and incomprehension when they find themselves separated from them by a legal decision in the wake of a divorce.

From a historical point of view, this apparent shake-up, in the form of an overturning of alliances, is astonishing to say the least. Faced with a male-dominated universe, women have always been seen to be on the same side as children. A situation resulting from their physical proximity, the consequence of a childrearing tradition centred on the mother figure (Knibielher, Fouquet, 1982). And because they were long perceived as inferior by the men in power who considered them in a similar category to children. So could it be that we are witnessing a genuine historical inversion? The answer is no. In spite of the progress made, men still hold dominant positions in a number of key (economic and political) sectors of society. They have also retained part of the power they traditionally exercised within the family (Glaude, Singly, 1986), either in terms of their role in major decisions or by retaining a more comfortable status for themselves. For their part, women continue to form special bonds with their children. Their involvement at the forefront of family issues gives them a pivotal role, particularly when relationships between the couple are under threat. In the context of the growing fragility of relationships, this role is likely to become even more important (Kaufmann, 1999). The increase in childlike male attitudes within the family must therefore be regarded as a significant (and surprising) but limited phenomenon. Men only become childlike in specific contexts or circumstances, allowing themselves to slip temporarily into this regressive carefree state, often regarded as compensation for their heavy investment in the world of work. Women begin to get irritated when their Peter Pan oversteps the limits and lingers too long in this childish bubble. They get annoyed too, when, although outwardly favouring the notion of equality, they continue to entertain secret dreams of a superior man, capable of guiding them and protecting them at all times. Finally, they get irritated because of the dissonances caused by the grey areas in the distribution of roles, which are the result of occasional reversals. Like when the man, barely out of his regressive phase, takes the liberty of adopting macho attitudes worthy of the good old days.

Stubborn macho reactions

Between yesterday's patriarchy and the childlike regressions of today, the shift in male–female relationships within the couple, even if confined to certain specific contexts, is nevertheless spectacular. This is not necessarily always perceived as being a break with the past. Finding themselves comfortably installed with their areas of personal autonomy effectively means many men are able to continue as before. The legacy of a dominant status enables them to impose a power (the power to enjoy moments to oneself) and at the same time allows them to play like children. Machos and kids rolled into one. Women would find it easier to tolerate this behaviour if only the activities it involved were not quite such a threat; both to themselves and to conjugal life. The screens which take over the home (televisions, computers) are windows opening on to escape routes into imaginary worlds and other possible lives. 'It often seems as though for these men it's all just a fabulous machine for wasting time and not getting involved with family life. You see them chatting for hours on end with complete strangers without addressing a single word to their wives for the entire evening, unless it's to ask if she's going out since she's got her coat on. No. She's not going out; she's coming in, having spent her entire Saturday afternoon out of the house because she's so fed up with talking to a blank wall! He hadn't even noticed. And I'm not exaggerating!' (Isabelle). Malvina is extremely irritated by the fact that, as soon as he gets home from work, Richard 'immediately goes straight onto a chat room with his fishing friends'. Caroline is at the end of her tether: Marc is permanently glued to the TV. She sits down beside him so that at least they are doing something together. Sadly, Marc is too busy with the remote control and his frenzied zapping sends out all kinds of subliminal messages, each of an equally unattractive nature: I'm the boss here and I do what I like; this zapping is intended to wear you down and drive you away, etc. Caroline persists, regardless. When she feels irritation levels are dangerously high, 'then I get up and I give up on the TV completely, because I don't want to fall out with him'. But sometimes she does not have time to organize a diplomatic retreat – irritation overwhelms her without warning: like when he goes off to the toilet with the remote safely in his trouser pocket, where Caroline cannot get her hands on it. 'As though he didn't trust me at all (and that I would change channels at the first chance I got . . . which I have to admit, I do) or as if I simply didn't exist.' To make matters worse, it is not unknown for the remote to end up falling out of his pocket onto the bathroom floor. They have had to replace it twice recently. Irritation guaranteed.

Marc is undeniably guilty of a blatant macho abuse of power: imposing his choice of programme, even when he is not in the room! The majority of displays of strength are less overt, and can sometimes go almost unnoticed in the give-and-take between the couple. Indeed, the perpetrator is barely aware of his action. And the victim puts up no resistance. In what was clearly intended to show his sincerity and desire to do the right thing, Lorenzo sent me (of his own accord) a list of what he supposed to be the main things his wife found irritating about him. The list included the fact that he likes to have music blaring from the speakers in the car whereas she prefers quiet background music. In response I sent him a question, to which I received this extremely pertinent reply:

This issue of music in the car sounds like a mini power struggle. Which of you wins?
– Me. She often complains about that by the way.

A telling response, both in terms of the usual masculine brevity, and especially because of his conviction that the outcome is an inevitable one. Such small-scale seizures of power by men are commonplace. We must, however, also touch on the less trivial ones: on the continued existence in certain couples of power structures which are frankly archaic. When the rules of the game are clear and women accept them, as is sometimes the case in a working-class environment (Schwartz, 1990), this accepted submission does not cause any major irritation. But where any kind of dissonance exists (between the dream and the reality, between the declarations of principle and the actual practice, between a glorious before and a pitiful after, etc.), such resurgences of archaism are all the more irritating in that they often take the victim by surprise. Malvina's story is a perfect illustration. 'I was single for thirty years [. . .] For a long time, while I was still militantly single, there were things about some of the couples I saw around me, including my own parents, that I found unacceptable. For example, the way roles were allocated according to gender (along the lines of men go out hunting and women do everything else), in other words the failure to share tasks. Anyway, I was on a bit of a high horse over all that, then once I got into my thirties, the hormones kicked in and I wanted to settle down. Which suited him too [. . .] In his eyes I was the perfect woman to bring up his children – I'm a teacher. I liked him because he didn't run a mile when I talked about commitment – I wanted a child quickly – and his views were very much in line with my own principles: "I don't see why you should iron my shirts. You're not my maid."' Sadly, four and a half years after these fine seductive declarations, her prince has turned into an ugly toad. 'What I find most irritating is his slobbish narrow-minded attitude. Things like: "What? My green shirt hasn't been ironed and I wanted to wear it today" (never mind the fact that the other fifteen are clean and ironed and this is the only one in the laundry basket!!). Or "This place is a tip!! You could at least have tidied up a bit!! You've been at home all day!" (the fact that I've marked thirty-five books, prepared the meal and done two loads of washing goes unnoticed because I happen to have left the rubbish outside the front door).' Richard's behaviour is becoming increasingly ultra-macho. Malvina has been relegated to the rank of domestic slave without the slightest twinge of remorse on his part. He seems to belong to another century, one where the mere fact of being a man permits him to do what he likes. 'And the worst thing about all this is that he regularly goes out with his mates while I stay at home and look after our daughter. Yet if I want to go to the cinema or to some evening thing at school he kicks up a huge fuss designed purely and simply to put me off wanting to go.' And to top this display of outrageous male chauvinism, he also puts on superior airs and throws his weight around like a little tyrant. 'The other thing that annoys me is the way he thinks he's some kind of superman: in the maternity hospital (when he was talking to the paediatrician you'd have sworn he was talking to a colleague, whereas once we got home his enthusiasm waned rather quickly); in restaurants (he tells the owner of the restaurant to change his menu); at home (he's determined to prove that he can do all the cleaning in two hours but he doesn't vacuum under the bed or behind the doors); with his daughter (he's the one that looks after her!! And to prove it he claims it's him that takes her to school every day!! Unfortunately that's about all he can say! Even then, if he has to go and collect her every evening for a week, he "makes up for it" at the weekend by staying out until midnight). What's more, when we fall out over something, his way of punishing me is to say: "If that's how it is, I'm not going to pick her up for two days!!" As though that would affect me!! Don't even get me on to what happens when we talk about our respective jobs: whereas I have to listen religiously to everything he says, preferably when I'm trying to watch the news on TV, whenever I mention anything about my school, he interrupts me and goes off into long tirades about how the system needs reforming. For example when a teacher is absent because his or her children are ill, that's not on: he should have made other arrangements!! But when our daughter had chickenpox, I had to take compassionate leave to look after her. He didn't even offer to go to the chemists. Which, by the way, brings me to the subject of shopping: he works opposite the supermarket, yet when he runs out of wine (which as it happens is the only thing we ever run out of) he asks me to go and get some for him!!' Between his puffed-up, over-blown speeches and the hollow phrases so far removed from reality, Malvina is hard put to say which irritates her most. No doubt the fact that she has been tricked into a life so completely different from the one she dreamt of. This, incidentally, is how she ends her long list of woes. 'I think what irritates me most about him is that our relationship is so archaic that my grandmother said to me: "What do you think my life with granddad was like? Men cut the logs and women look after men – that's perfectly normal!" As though our education and our hard work had done nothing whatsoever to break with this determinism!! Help!'

A male-chauvinist situation as caricatured as this one takes us beyond the strict context of irritation. Malvina is certainly irritated – acutely so – from morning to night, with a constant nagging irritation punctuated by sudden flare-ups. But these continual feelings of irritation are part of a deeper-rooted feeling which goes further and redefines them. It is the feeling of deep dissatisfaction.[4] The same feeling emerges in the statements sent by many women, complaining of being irritated because their husbands turned out to be "mean", constantly scrutinizing and criticizing their slightest expenditure. These women were both extremely irritated by these petty calculations and deeply dissatisfied with their relationship. The husband might indeed be a bit macho, when it came to sharing household tasks for example. But if you are going to live in an archaic way, you should at least benefit from the few compensations that it ought to offer (Singly, 1987). For example, being able to enjoy the money he earns. Yet, even without being marvellous providers, some contrive to have all the failings rolled into one; they are macho, immature and mean. In such situations irritation turns to exasperation, despair sets in, anger erupts.

---

[4] Some months later, the situation had, however, slightly improved. See 'Stop press' in the appendix.

Part Two

In the Eye of the Storm

― 3 ―

THE CAUSES

It is perfectly normal to feel irritated within the couple, even in the most successful relationships. Indeed irritation is a central element given that the functioning of the conjugal relationship is based on associations of opposites which give rise to dissonances. This is the underlying mechanism: irritation always arises as a result of dissonance. On the surface, however, it erupts for reasons which are far more specific and sometimes even absurd. We have already seen numerous examples of one of the most common: the proper place for certain objects. The two partners fail to agree on the proper place for a particular object (a stuffed pike's head) or about a particular substance (the quantity of dust which is considered acceptable). One of them, the dominant one, imposes their way of doing things. The other, forced to comply, whether they like it or not, experiences a sudden rush of emotion when the sight of the offending object makes it clear that they are not, after all, prepared to accept the situation imposed on them. If the irritation is intense, they may at this point attempt an individual rebellion. This clash of everyday micro-cultures is particularly evident when household tasks are being shared out, each partner having their own very precise conception of how things should be done (provided roles are not too cut-and-dried). The correct place for objects and the division of household tasks are not, however, the only things to provoke irritation. We shall now focus on some of the others, selected from amongst those most frequently cited in the course of our research. These should be regarded purely as illustrations without any representative value, since a statistical study would be needed to establish a truly representative and comprehensive picture.

The symbolic toothpaste tube

To give honour where honour is due: I shall start by focusing on certain key objects which most dramatically symbolize irritation within the couple. Returning to the theme of the correct place for things, keys are a classic example. In many households there is a designated place for these. Yet the two protagonists in the little drama about to unfold rarely respect this to the same degree. The resulting irritation is all the greater in that the person who 'forgets' to put the keys in the right place usually admits to being in the wrong and vows not to do it again. Which, of course, they then proceed to do. 'We have two cars which both of us use. I always leave the key on the key-rack on the wall. She always leaves it in her bag, which she takes up to our bedroom. . . .' In addition to the irritation of having to hunt for the key in a hurry, rooting frantically in her bag or shouting out angrily to give vent to his feelings, Lorenzo just cannot understand this irrationality in his partner's behaviour. It would be so much simpler just to put the keys in the right place. The irritating dissonance directly associated with the object not being in the right place is aggravated by a split within the couple. Two cultural universes clash. A minor detail like the proper place for the keys can end up emphasizing the incomprehensible strangeness of the partner.

Objects are made familiar by the person who looks at them or handles them, to the extent that they end up forming a kind of individual culture. We invest part of ourselves in our material surroundings and these in turn define who we are in terms of our everyday existence (Thévenot, 1994; 2006). The couple are constantly striving to construct a shared familiarization. Through discussion, they formulate plans aimed at establishing a common way of doing things, plans which extend well beyond the simple question of where things should go (extending, for example, to the way they should be used). Within the minutiae of gestures, however, the individual secretly adjusts their behaviour as they see fit, generally guided more by their own inclination than by the official rule. Sometimes to the extent of deliberately adopting a mode of behaviour that they feel is appropriate (or one which is too deeply physically inherent to change), even though they are well aware it is likely to cause irritation in their partner. In such cases, a single object can end up crystallizing all the anger and incomprehension involved. Each couple has its own little bones of contention, discreet or flagrant, which crop up regularly and tenaciously. Some of these are so common as to be almost universal. Where the keys are kept for example. But also, in pride of place, that ultimate symbol of the shock of discovering other people's intimate habits: the humble toothpaste tube. Along with the toothbrush, this is no ordinary object. It is, after all, the first item to be introduced into the new partner's home, indicating by its presence the beginning of the domestic phase of this conjugal adventure. From this significant moment onwards, already a highly symbolic object, the toothpaste tube represents the different micro-culture that is attempting to find its place within the new conjugal entity. In this context it can surprise, and even shock, before (at a much later stage in the couple's life) becoming the focus of "incontrollable irritation". The world is split into two separate camps when it comes to the toothpaste tube. In one camp, the rather particular people who have precise ideas on the correct way of rolling the tube, of replacing the lid, and of squeezing in order to extract the paste. And, in the other camp, the freer, more relaxed individuals who do not give the matter much thought at all. The problem is not so much in the precise definition of one or the other way of doing something as in the differential separating them. A minuscule detail can sometimes be enough to make the difference seem unacceptable. Even the good intentions of the partner, or some technical strategies aimed at reducing the observable discrepancy, are powerless to resolve the problem once attention has started to be drawn obsessively to that irritating difference. 'You'd think that having two separate tubes would solve the problem. My father thought so. But the mere sight of that "squidged" tube is enough to send him into a blind rage. And mayonnaise, paint tubes, chilli sauce, all come in for exactly the same treatment. I for one started by trying some diversionary tactics and opted for the solid toothpaste tube which stands upright and gives a really smooth flow of toothpaste. Or at least it would, provided it's kept in the right position. Which NEVER happens.' The toothpaste tube plays a significant role in Isabelle's life. Here is her commentary, delivered in a delightfully witty style which threatens to disguise the true extent of her feelings: laughter can often conceal genuine anger. 'The "to squidge or not to squidge" debate has nothing to do with gender. To prove my point, my mother is an adept "squidger" much to the annoyance of my father who is anti-squidge. I, their daughter, on the other hand, am also anti-squidge; my dear partner is a squidger, as was my ex-husband, who probably still is. Who are this strange sect? Let me explain: take a tube, of toothpaste for example. That's the one that annoys you most, because it's the one you see on a daily basis. Anyway, it's OK the first time, but when you see it for the thousandth time something snaps. So, the tube can be delicately squeezed at the far end, even rolled up a little so as to ease out some of the contents.

67

Joy, bliss, sheer pleasure. Mmmmm! Alternatively, the poor thing can be brutally squeezed somewhere in the middle producing a sinister squidge of paste before being abandoned in a lamentable state. Cue the early morning cry of distress of the anti-squidger as he or she struggles to sort out the mess and extract a blob of toothpaste. Often the struggle lasts a full five minutes only to yield a huge blob of toothpaste, half of which drops into the sink. Arrrgghh!' When attention becomes focused in this excessive way on an apparently derisory object, redolent with multiple irritations and dissatisfaction, the tiny object can spark off a gigantic reaction. Isabelle's ex-husband, a confirmed 'squidger', played on her irritation over the tube. It all became just too much. 'Of course I didn't get divorced over a tube of toothpaste, but the smug little smile of someone who knows they are about to irritate the other person was certainly a revelation.' Although her current partner is also a 'squidger' the irritation seems much more localized. Which is why she can now see the funny side of it all.

Forced proximity

The couple live under the illusion that they have constructed a shared culture. And indeed, *grosso modo*, they have, at least in general terms regarding the hierarchy of values, ethical principle, etc. A result obtained thanks to an ongoing work of unification, in which day-to-day conversation between partners plays a crucial role (Berger, Kellner, 1988), particularly through criticism of friends or family. It is indeed this habit of analysing why their choice of holidays, their financial decisions, are not the right ones that the couple determine, by contrast, what unites them. In general terms only though, since certain key issues continue to be argued over on a regular basis, in particular those relating to bringing up the children (Brown, Jaspard, 2004), where the contradictory roles occupied within the couple exacerbate the divergence between them.

Even when a consensus appears to have been reached through discussion, the resulting unity is in reality merely theoretical, applying in broad, general terms only. Far removed from the profound ordinariness of reflex gestures and the personalized micro-culture they express. The person who 'forgets' to put the keys in the right place is perfectly well aware where they should be kept. Gestures, specific contexts, objects themselves, are all signs of the enduring survival of the difference. They manifest themselves when the interchangeability between the two partners is at its strongest and when they are forced into very close social proximity. Divergence diminishes with distance or when the need for unity is less urgent. It flares up, on the contrary, in the heat of the action, when the two partners are supposedly united and acting in accordance with the same set of rules. Keys come fairly high in the charts of minor causes of irritation because they are used on a daily basis and are used separately by each individual but belong in a mutually agreed place. However, it is unusual for there not to be some degree of friction between the various systems possible (between each individual's own idea and the official joint theory). This is all the more inevitable in that this kind of dissonance can just as easily affect the lone individual (between action and theory, even though implemented on their own): keys are just as irritating to the single person who cannot find them because he or she failed to put them in the place they had previously designated as the correct one. In the couple, where two individual cultures are more or less successfully combined, the probability of irritation occurring is infinitely greater. All kinds of objects, appliances, areas, both individual and collective like the keys, have the potential to become the focus of irritation or other outbursts on a regular basis. Each with their own specific features, worthy of an individual analysis. The keys, for example, have the particularity that they often have a clearly identified official place, in theory agreed on by all parties. With other objects the situation is less clear-cut, some being assigned to a specific spot and others drifting from one place to another. Scissors, another frequently mentioned object, are a good example. Géraldine has a very simple arrangement. After use she systematically puts the scissors away in a kitchen drawer. When the couple first lived together she tried to ensure this arrangement was adopted as the model for both of them to use. Bernard went through the motions of going along with this, while at the same time continuing to do things his own way (he has lived in the flat for longer). Once he has used them, he prefers to put them away somewhere close to hand, rather than have to go back to the kitchen each time. As a result he has a number of different places where they can be put, some of them used on a regular basis and easy for Géraldine to find, others much vaguer and less obvious. 'She gets so annoyed, you should see her! She accuses me of just leaving them anywhere, which isn't true at all: I do put them away. It's not as if I'm going to take them all the way to the kitchen when I'm in my office, that would be ridiculous! I find it irritating that she gets so irritated about it. It's completely ridiculous to fly off the handle like that over a pair of scissors.' Questioned independently, Géraldine explains her exasperation over this absurd story. 'They are never put back in the right place. Every time I need some scissors I end up shrieking and shouting!! Surely it can't be that difficult to put them back in the proper place!' Sometimes the scissors, which have apparently been 'put away', are nowhere to be found. Bernard cannot remember where he has put them, but manages not to get annoyed himself. 'He has the nerve to laugh at me and tease me. I could almost kill him sometimes!' A few months later, the joint interview which had been scheduled was unable to take place; Bernard was still alive but the couple had separated.

Irritation focuses in particular on objects which are (badly) shared, or in contexts where two people are brought into forced proximity. Proximity is, of course, not necessarily problematic for the couple! Romantic desire magically eliminates the potential for irritation which differences can otherwise cause. Other forms of love (complicity, tenderness, mutual generosity) can also suffice to ensure that contact and proximity bring nothing but sweetness and pleasure. When the sentimental impulse is not quite so strong, on the other hand, or in circumstances where the confrontation of differences is particularly intractable, proximity can prove explosive. In bed, at the table, in the bathroom: in any circumstances where two people find themselves intimately close without necessarily wanting to be. Particular mention should be made of the car, a tiny closed-in world in which tensions can be dramatically magnified. Inexorably, over a period of several weeks, the tension had been rising between Mimie and Mickaël. And it was in the car that things finally came to a head. Mimi was driving. Mickaël, very tense, lit a cigarette, which she immediately asked him to put out. He told her she was driving dangerously, that she needed to do something about it, or he would have to ask her to let him get out. Which is what he did, before hitting the car violently and setting off, muttering angrily the entire time, to walk the 10 kilometres on foot. Forced proximity is capable of bringing out both the best and the worst in people.

Often, in theory, jointly owned, the car inevitably ends up being mainly appropriated by one of the two protagonists, who is then anxious to impose their ideas concerning its appearance and cleanliness. The resulting conflicts are much like those over any other shared object. Except that, inside the car, with sir and madam sat side by side, they can be even more intense. In this closed-in little world, the two people need to agree on a whole series of parameters: the temperature, choice of radio programme and volume, etc. Yet another culture shock. Lorenzo irritates his wife by having the radio on full volume. For Eline and Jack, the 'car-wars' revolve round the issue of heating.

'As for the car, it's a source of irritation every time the two of us have to be in it together: I can't stand air conditioning, he hates having the heating on . . . We still regularly fall out over the issue.' A favourite tactic involves using the driver's seat as a position of strength. But Eline's aversion to feeling cold means that, even when she is not at the wheel, she still intervenes. 'Often the driver has priority when it comes to the temperature inside the car, but I admit that I systematically refuse to have any air conditioning on and that always gets on Jack's nerves.'

Whether at the wheel or in the passenger seat, roles are never neutral inside the car. Particularly when it comes to the thorny issue of driving styles, which we shall now examine. If, as in the good old days, it is always the man who drives, the situation is perfectly straightforward. In such cases, madam need not concern herself with what is going on and can happily sit back and think her own thoughts. But, for some considerable time now, women have had their driving licences too, and refuse to take a back seat, in any circumstances. Often they have their own cars which they look after and drive just as they choose. The problem arises in circumstances where the couple need to travel together since, in theory, either of them can do the driving. In reality, however, things are not quite so straightforward, given that each has their own style of driving and continues to drive in their heads even when they are occupying the passenger seat, picturing how *they* would do things and unable to refrain from making comments. Two cultural universes collide (Hoyau, Le Pape, 2006). Driving style is one of the rare examples where men appear to be more susceptible to irritation than women. This can be easily explained in terms of a throwback to the time when the man took sole charge of the driving. Being in the passenger seat is still something of a novelty for him, and he finds it extremely difficult to step back and let his partner take over. He cannot help keeping an eye on the road and is ready to criticize at the slightest opportunity. We have already seen how incidents of childlike behaviour in men can lead women to make hasty generalizations: men are all the same and will never change. Conversely, the loss of the dominant role as driver has led some men to take the rather excessive view that women in general will never make good drivers. Pedro is of this persuasion, which is why he always drives when they take the car together. Except in exceptional circumstances, such as this particular occasion, described by Fidelia. 'Here's one hot off the press: today I'm acting as chauffeur for my husband – his car is in the garage – even though I've got a very busy schedule. To be fair, Pedro was booked in for a medical procedure, something painful but not

71

serious. So I made sure I was available and ready to look after him. Unfortunately, he can't resist commenting on my driving and telling me what to do. Both of which really annoy me, especially as neither of us are bad drivers – it's just that we drive differently. When he drives, I force myself not to say anything even if he does things I don't like. Anyway this morning, after five or six comments, I ended up sending him packing. I just dropped him outside the clinic without offering to go in with him, though I did phone him afterwards to find out how he had got on. I really get the impression that, in this particular area, I'm the victim of a deeply rooted old stereotype – women drivers – coupled with a lack of confidence and a need to dominate.'

Situations where proximity is uncomfortable, forced or inharmonious are breeding grounds for irritation, including the most unexpected and intimate contexts such as the shared bed (either going to sleep or when engaged in another of its prime functions), around the subject of hygiene habits, or mealtimes. Lorenzo evokes the endless 'battle over the sheets' which disrupts their nights. 'Especially when someone can't stop tossing about all over the place. There are fights over the cover or the duvet in the heat of the "battle".' Agitation which leads to a new source of irritation when they wake up. 'The sight of the bed in such a mess at the start of the day . . . the sheets all over the place, the cover half off the bed, the duvet rolled into a ball, when the other person likes things to be neat and tidy and wants to be able to slip into a crisply made bed in the evening!' Caroline, like many others, generalizes unreasonably, and in a sexist way, basing her views on Marc's behaviour. 'Men are so irritating when they're getting up for work in the morning (bleary eyed, hair sticking up all over the place, not a trace of a smile, nor of any manners either).' The same might just as easily be said about women, given that waking behaviour and rhythms can vary so much from one person to another, independently of gender (Kaufmann, 2002). Mealtimes are frequently cited and turn out to be a hot spot of irritation between the couple. It is here, for example, that the difference in rhythm between Gally and Akira leads to most misunderstandings and clashes. 'I eat more quickly than he does (when we were first together, I tried to eat at his speed, but I had to give up because I like to eat my food while it's hot!), and usually I end up doing the washing-up while he's still finishing off his meal. And then I have to remind him to bring his dirty plate through to the kitchen when he comes to get a dessert, because otherwise he'd just leave it on the table. He thinks he should be allowed to finish his meal before clearing away his dirty stuff. Which means I either have to go and get it myself (which is a bit much considering I'm the one doing

72

the washing-up) or I have to wait until "sir" deigns to finish his meal before I can finish the washing-up' (Gally). Irritation associated with mealtimes has the particular characteristic of being closely linked to another negative emotion (disgust), similarly provoked where close proximity is unwelcome, as we shall see later.

A waltz in double time

The couple is a dance (Hefez, Laufer, 2002), an endless dance of opposites, bringing together hot and cold, intensity and calm, order and disorder, discipline and spontaneity. For better or for worse, two opposing cultural universes simultaneously confront and embrace each other. Particularly as far as time is concerned. Time is not a neutral element. It can be empty or full, light or dense, slow or rhythmic – characteristics which vary even within one individual. But, most importantly, characteristics which, over and above individual variations, come together in a relatively coherent form in each of us, defining a sort of temporal personality profile: the punctual–stressed type, or the laid-back – don't-know-what-time-it-is type; the organized plan-ahead type living more in their plans than in the present, the improvising spur-of-the-moment type, etc. Jack sees time as an abundant and generous commodity whereas Eline is conscious of it running away like sand between her fingers. She calculates meticulously to assess the little time that is left, coming up with all sorts of tactics to try and persuade Jack to share her view, none of which are successful.

'We each have a very different notion of time: Jack thinks he's always got plenty of time to do things and to make plans, even up to the last minute, whereas I like things to be organized and planned in advance. For example, when we're getting ready to go out somewhere, Jack is first in the shower but then spends hours getting dressed: he puts some paperwork away, puts his socks on, looks something up on the internet, searches for the particular pair of jeans he wants to wear (he has a wardrobe worthy of a girl), zaps through the TV channels . . . I can shower, get dressed and put my make-up on before he's even got dressed. Now I'm the "get ready and go immediately" type: I can't stand hanging around for two hours before we actually leave. . . . My strategy to avoid getting irritated is to let Jack know that I'll be ready in ten minutes (at that stage I'm not even dressed or made-up, but I tell him anyway), then I keep reiterating the info until I'm sat there on the sofa all dressed up and waiting for him. And there he is, still fiddling around, so I inform him that I'm ready: "Now!" (i.e. – I'm beginning to get annoyed!). At which point he says: but I've been waiting for you all this time (?!?!?!). . . . That really gets on my nerves! It's the same when we're leaving somewhere after an evening out or when we've been visiting family, etc. For me, "we're going" means we're going *now*, we put our coats on, pick up our bag and we're off . . . but with Jack it can take hours, he introduces some new topic of conversation, he goes off and inspects some changes that have been made in the house, he makes an appointment for ten years time . . . Ahhggrrrr!'

Eline is aware, however, that for the other party, with their very different philosophy of life, things may well be equally incomprehensible and annoying. 'I admit that what gets on *his* nerves is precisely the fact that I don't like taking my time and waiting around: I like things to be done immediately, as soon as they've been mentioned. Which I agree doesn't leave much scope for chilling out and relaxing . . .' The idea of a more relaxed attitude to time is not without appeal. But it quickly goes out of the window as soon as Jack starts dawdling and dilly-dallying, and is swiftly replaced by irritation, confirming the truth that in reality she prefers a strictly organized approach to any fine ideas.

The more punctual of the two is often correlatively the one who favours a disciplined and programmed approach as opposed to a more relaxed attitude, in terms of both time and organization: two completely different outlooks in direct confrontation. For Eline, Jack is both always late and disorganized, allowing himself to be distracted by endless digressions, whereas she herself sticks rigorously to her plans.

Robert is guilty of similar crimes in Elsa's eyes. 'What irritates me too is the fact that he never thinks ahead, whereas I like to plan things and anticipate (for example, we're going to have to do a massive shop on Saturday because there's nothing left in the fridge). Unlike me, he doesn't think ahead at all, so when he realizes on a Saturday that the shopping needs doing, he's not "psychologically" prepared to spend two hours in a shop (with the result that we end up eating convenience food all weekend). And another thing that irritates me is that he's never on time, for him there's always plenty of time. As I've got wise to this little defect, I've got a few tricks up my sleeve, like bringing forward the time we have to be somewhere, so as not to be "too" late.'

The couple is a dance which, for better or for worse, constantly brings opposites together. For worse when the difference crystallizes around confrontations likely to provoke irritation, such as shared objects, forced proximity or zones of interchangeability. For better when the difference leads to the couple taking on complementary roles which make their lives easier. Eline and Jack, as we have seen, are in that initial phase of life as a couple where differences are indeed worked on energetically in order to define a satisfactory domestic arrangement. Absorbed in this complex process, they are not yet in a position to distinguish between productive irritation and sterile irritation. Between what they should hold on to and what needs to be resolved. Eline intuitively senses that her man's digressions and dawdling have no useful purpose and simply generate gratuitous irritation. But when it comes to time management, things are less clear-cut. The problem is as follows. Irritated by the tranquil improvisations of her beloved opponent, Eline is tempted to take over any general organization needed, doing so in an almost authoritarian manner, clarifying and tightening the existing complementary roles. 'When it comes to holidays, weekends, free-time, I like things to be planned meticulously in advance, so I know exactly where I'm going, at what time, where we're staying, how to get there, why . . . So, I plan everything (in terms of what time we leave and what time we get there. When it comes to the rest, what we do once we're there, that can be sorted out on a day-to-day basis). I only plan a month in advance, and I sort out all the details the week before we go – there's no point in getting too carried away. . . . Incidentally, I am capable of last-minute trips too, provided I know exactly what I'm doing (whether we're staying with friends or family, what kind of accommodation, etc.).' Jack finds all this a bit much. 'When we're stressed or tired I have to admit this is what gets to us most: I seem to be constantly on Jack's back and he gets more and more annoyed by my insistence on organizing everything.' Jack finds it a bit much because his whole attitude to organization is turned upside-down: not that it makes much difference to his life, at least as far as this aspect of it is concerned. But the upheaval, mentally exhausting like all such changes relating to identity, is in fact less painful than might be supposed. He is effectively spared from having to do something he is not particularly good at. He can relax all the more: Eline will organize everything. 'Jack finds that a bit irritating because he feels it leaves no scope for spontaneity (he's right). But in general he's more than happy for me to deal with everything.' Eline also has mixed feelings. Sometimes she regrets the free and easy early days of the relationship ('he's right'). This notion of freedom, is however, no more than a vague nostalgia, which quickly turns out to be intolerable and irritating whenever it becomes concrete; Jack is wrong, irremediably wrong. The strongest proof of this comes from those occasions when they have swapped roles and Jack has had to organize things. Sadly, Eline is incapable of taking this opportunity to relax a little. 'What irritates me though is that when he's in charge of organizing anything, nothing gets done until after 9 o'clock the previous evening. We're supposed to be going to see his parents: he forgets to tell them we're coming, or to let them know if we're getting there on Friday evening or Saturday morning. That really irritates me because as far as I'm concerned that shows lack of respect and bad manners!' For her, having to put up with this kind of sloppy organization is even more irritating than having to constantly spur him into action. This occasional reversal of roles does not seem destined to have much of a future. Their existing roles will probably end up being further reinforced.

Differences can also manifest themselves in relation to other time-related issues, that of rhythm for example. Some people do things quickly, others are much slower. Some are particularly good at one activity, others at another. Some like to get up early while others prefer to sleep in. 'I'm a morning person, he's an evening person. So in the morning he's desperate to stay in bed (when he's not working). We've got very different temperaments. The worst thing about it (and this is when I really hit the roof!) is that on Saturday mornings, when he's had a good lie-in, the first thing he says is something along the lines of: "I haven't slept long enough, or well enough, I'm tired, I've got a headache, a bad back, a stomach ache . . . You're making too much noise, you've woken me up." After all the years we've been together (eight and half years), things have got worse. Suffice it to say that if, after getting up late and taking a leisurely shower, he then eats slowly, I can quite easily find myself shouting at him because he's buttering a piece of bread as though it was a work of art' (Nicole). A difference in rhythms can be even more explosive in situations of enforced intimacy, such as in bed or at the table. And as soon as the irritation crystal-lizes around certain gestures, attitudes or ritual phrases, these focus points for irritation turn into triggers which highlight the cultural rift between the two parties. An innocent slice of bread, meticulously buttered as though it was a work of art, is suddenly perceived as the most intolerable thing in the world and provokes immediate conflict. At first, Nicole would retaliate by answering back aggressively, claim-ing her own right to sleep in. 'And what about me, don't I have the right too?' An unfortunate tactic, since she has not the slightest desire to do so. Unable to come to terms with this irritation, her feelings are now more akin to those associated with conjugal dissatisfaction. 'I feel rejected, with an increasing sense of physical malaise.'

Differences in rhythm are often merely the visible manifestation of

far wider cultural conflicts, extending to relationships with others or
to the way the world is perceived. Gally cannot bear Akira's slowness
because it makes her feel he is not as involved in life as he should be,
that he is not as alive as she is. 'We certainly don't have the same
rhythms, or the same characters. I think of myself as a very active
person (I do a lot of sport, my job is extremely demanding, I've got
lots of different interests), whereas Akira is very passive. Well, what
you might describe as slow. He's completely incapable of doing two
things at the same time. Unlike me. I quite often do three things at
the same time, and plan a fourth while I'm at it.' Akira, for his part,
thinks his wife does far too much and misses out on the wisdom of the
moment lived to the full. 'I know that seeing me wandering round the
house with the telephone wedged to my ear really gets on his nerves.
He thinks it shows disrespect to the person I'm phoning if I hang the
washing out while I'm talking to them' (Gally).

Traces of the self

Within the couple, the partner will always be a stranger, someone
profoundly different in spite of the ongoing process of unification.
These differences are usually forgotten, pushed aside by the simple
familiarity which settles into place, or, better still, by attraction
and desire. Then, without warning, they surface again, forcing the
two opposing sides to confront each other once again, divided just
as easily over ethical issues or broad general principles (education,
relationship to time) as over trivial matters (a stuffed pike's head,
a slice of bread buttered as though it was a work of art). The other
person is a stranger because their story is a different one, because
they bring with them a long and complex memory, multiple or even
contradictory, but which belongs only to them. Even though the
individual is malleable, and increasingly so, he or she is still at the
mercy of this memory which marks them for ever. The determining
factors are sometimes even more pressing, close to biological ones.
Being sensitive to heat or cold is not simply a matter of upbringing
and background culture. Yet differences such as these, even more
involuntary than others, can irritate just as much, as though the other
side is somehow to blame. Remember Eline and Jack in their car; the
confrontation between how warm or cool it should be is a constant
issue. 'I'm always cold. Even in a heat-wave I'm quite capable of
putting on a jumper in the evening. Which Jack finds really irritating
because he's always hot. So we argue over temperature a lot.' Sarah,

77

on the other hand, is irritated by Peter's laugh. A laugh which she no longer finds the least bit funny. 'He laughs after every single phrase. He laughs at all sorts of odd moments, over nothing. That laugh gets on my nerves and embarrasses me in public. He can't finish a single phrase without that little laugh! So I look at him as if to say "what's so funny?"' I asked Sarah if she really thought Peter should be held to blame for something which is clearly so deeply rooted in him. Since nothing can be done about it, should she not try to find ways of controlling her feelings? She admitted it was simply a reflex. Yet so profound is her irritation that she continues to act as though, wild dream though it is, she could actually do something about it. 'No, I just can't get used to that laugh punctuating every single sentence, even when it's about something sad. I agree with you, it's become a reflex he can't do anything about. If I look at him in that way, it's like saying "what's so funny?" precisely to show him that it isn't funny and that he's laughing over nothing. Of course I've mentioned it to him on various occasions and he just says that's how he is and he can't do anything about it. I'm worried I'll end up being really horrible to him, just because he gets on my nerves.'

A stuffed pike's head, a buttered slice of bread, a disagreement over temperature, a laugh: the circumstances causing irritation to crystal- lize are extraordinarily diverse. The list of grievances people sent me is a glorious hotchpotch of all kinds of examples: little gestures, a way of speaking or of not speaking, a whole range of different objects. Pets too are cited with some frequency. Particularly when chosen by only one of the partners. Isabelle's partner, for example, had I questioned him, would have had plenty to say on the subject of the cat. 'My cat stretches out on the bed next to me. But never next to my boyfriend, because he knows he might end up being the first cat on the moon if he ever takes that risk.' Enforced togetherness and negatively experi- enced intimate proximity can lead to a surge of intolerance, even sometimes culminating in the irritated refusal of the most physical attributes. Conversely, even when the adversary has left the scene, the problem is not necessarily resolved. For traces of his or her passage and gestures remain behind, like so many reminders of their unac- ceptable and irritating way of doing things. The tiniest fingerprint can be enough to suddenly reawaken the irritation. As can much more obvious signs like when the husband, convinced his technique was the right one, decided to clean everything with acid in spite of objec- tions to the contrary. 'Not a single day goes by without the sight of the marks left on the windowpanes and the rusted-away locks and iron-work catching my eye and irritating me profoundly' (Lamia).

Money matters

Amongst the major recurrent themes, such as where things should be kept and attitudes to time, money is often a source of gnawing irritation which can eventually turn into dissatisfaction. As in other areas, roles are generally defined within the couple. On one side is the calculator, careful with money and in charge of the household finances, and on the other, the exponent of happy-go-lucky attitudes, of generosity and of living from one moment to the next without thought of the future. It appears that in this area the usual distribution of complementary roles tends to be reversed, with men more often veering to the side of asceticism and discipline and women to hedonism and the relaxed approach. Hence, the large number of cases where irritation results from male meanness over money. This rule is, however, subject to many exceptions. Take the case of Isabelle, who in addition to her combat against the insouciant tube 'squidgers', is also militant in this field, waging war against extravagance, especially when money is tight. 'I've had painful experience of the latter, with a joint account as dry as the Gobi desert by the middle of the month, and no way of knowing where the money had gone. We both ended up feeling irritated, he because of having to account for his spending and me because I had to dip into our savings to pay the phone bill. The same bill he'd stashed away somewhere so I wouldn't shout at him (it was at a time when internet use was charged per connection and was very expensive). I'll spare you the number of rows we've had on the subject. His approach was to bury his head in the sand, mine was to be the accountant: not very compatible. Unless things are very comfortable, we both need to tighten our belts to a greater or a lesser degree. And when one does and the other doesn't, there are inevitably going to be some frictions.'

Two different approaches, two opposing views of saving and spending the same sum of money make for an extremely volatile situation. In order to minimize the impact, the two adversaries frequently resort to a placatory tactic which involves attempting to define as their personal money (included in a little sphere of individual liberty) anything that might cause too much offence to the more penny-pinching party. Marie-Agnès has stopped shopping for clothes when she is with Marc for this very reason.[1] Because she (like Isabelle) is very careful with money, whereas he is a fan of designer labels. 'He throws money away. On anything at all.' It became just too irritating. Now

---

[1] Comment recorded and quoted by Johanne Mons (1998, p. 107).

she prefers to let him get on with it without knowing what he is up to. Until he gets home, that is, when she enquires about the cost of his latest fit of extravagance, and cannot help remarking that it is far too high. 'But that's all, we don't argue about it.' She keeps a grip on herself and has accepted this discrepancy in their relationship in a way few people would be capable of. In most cases, the dissonance is transferred to the definition of frontiers which guarantee some personal rights outside what is strictly communal. Rights which are just about tolerated as long as things are relatively calm. At the slightest rise in temperature, however, they shrivel away entirely and the spendthrift is called to account. Nothing is worse for irritation levels than this kind of double language and these recurrent fluctuations which give rise to all sorts of dissonances. For both sides. 'Honestly, the clothes!!! You should see the bulging wardrobes and the piles of shopping bags she still brings home with a huge smile on her face!! Her eyes are glistening with excitement and I'm supposed to tell her how wonderful all of it is!! She does her little fashion parade for me, and I know I have to make the effort to look enthusiastic!! I stick to the basic minimum: "Yes, not bad." And even that's a huge effort because I'm really just about ready to explode. It makes my blood boil!! You should see the money she spends, sometimes for some stupid thing she'll only wear once. Yes I know that when it comes to clothes it's a personal matter. But it is our housekeeping money after all. And there's me being incredibly careful, and buying a hundred times less stuff for myself. It really is a case of double standards. I just can't bear to see that satisfied little smile of hers any longer' (Markus). Markus's girlfriend is probably none too happy either. That flat-voiced 'Yes, not bad' must fall a long way short of the admiring gazes she hoped to attract. But, in a confused way, they both sense that it is better to stick with this vague compromise. The "basic minimum" is a small but necessary price to pay. A little vagueness can be a way of avoiding confrontation and a few small irritations are worth the price.

Isabelle too needs a little vagueness to mask some troubling contradictions in her own situation. As the thrifty one of the household she gets extremely irritated when her boyfriend spends unnecessarily large amounts on the internet. Yet she regards the money she spends on herself as an entirely separate matter which ought not to be subjected to the joint rule of austerity. 'A man throws up his hands at his wife's hairdresser's bill, blissfully unaware that for women even a simple cut is bound to cost twice as much, because that's how hairdressing prices are fixed and there's nothing she can do about it.' Evidently some little financial secrets are best kept to oneself.

Secret worlds

A certain reserve is also advisable in a number of other domains; political ideas, for example. In cases where the two partners see eye to eye, or differ only over minor points which make for some pleasantly animated discussions, conversation about politics is one way of constructing a shared world. But where there are major differences in their way of thinking, our research indicates that couples prefer not to talk politics so as to avoid irritation and preserve harmony, each choosing instead to discuss such subjects elsewhere, with friends (Stevens, 1996).

Eline and Jack are not prepared to accept any such conjugal compromises based on silence. They want to discuss things, to hear what each other has to say and attempt to understand it, to open up to each other, driven by the desire to battle everything out and impose their point of view. Yet they find themselves constantly stumbling over some persistent differences of opinion. In their case, the object of discord is not politics but their attitude to their jobs. 'Discussions about our relative commitment towards the companies we work for often leave both of us feeling irritated. Jack simply cannot understand that I don't have that long-term commitment to a company, and that I don't "believe" in all that type of thing. And I can't understand his sense of loyalty and the effect that this "team spirit" stuff can have on him . . . Plus a year and a half of being unemployed has rather undermined my "team spirit". Anyway, we each have a different opinion on the subject and neither of us is going to change our minds.' And this subject turns out to be even more explosive than politics in that it can switch without warning from being a general discussion about ideas, where both of them manage to 'respect the other person's point of view and to listen to what they have to say', to much more concrete discussions about the relationship. 'We often get irritated with each other when we try to discuss the future.'

To what extent is it possible, and indeed preferable, for each individual within a relationship to cultivate their own secret garden? Faced with the risk of irritation and crises on the one hand, and duplicity and betrayal on the other, there is no easy answer. Those drawn to autonomy and secrecy are plagued by a guilty conscience. Melody felt obliged to compensate (as a way of making up for what were not even faults in the first place) by being open with 'HIM'. The result was catastrophic. 'I wanted to share something from my private world, something he wouldn't normally be involved in unless I told him about it (things like your e-mails, a dance workshop, my friends, the sports I do, etc.). Anyway, on this particular occasion I felt more or less obliged to tell him about it, so as not to keep something secret from him which would make it look as if I didn't trust him. At the same time, not being quite clear about the situation myself, I didn't really feel like talking about it very much. Very quickly, because of how he reacted in what I felt was an inappropriate way, I could feel irritation beginning to mount ("He's no help at all. He doesn't know anything about it and doesn't understand it").' Double irritation in fact, arising from the confusion of two dissonances: the idealized version of the scene in contrast with the pathetic reality ('HE' is not all she thought he might be), and the precise extent of her sphere of autonomy. Her attempt to share a secret area of her life with her partner had failed; the resulting irritation was worse than the preceding guilt.

'HE', for his part, would no doubt define autonomy somewhat differently, seeing it as less to do with having secrets and more to with the importance of personal comfort. As we have heard, Melody finds it extremely irritating when he dips his bread in the sauce before 'guzzling down the dripping morsel'. For her, mealtimes are an integral part of their life as a couple, and her husband needs to put good manners (indeed, though she hardly dare even dream of it anymore, seduction) above his own comfort. 'HE' simply cannot understand this notion. What is the point of being a couple if you cannot relax and enjoy the simple pleasures of life? For those seeking just to luxuriate in the pleasures of personal comfort, the partner can seem to take on the role of domestic tyrant, constantly on the war-path to stamp out guilty pleasures and other liberties, and all in the interests of the higher cause of shared life.

Too close

Out of domestic tyranny, or love or simple familiarity, the partner intrudes on areas the other person would prefer to keep private. He or she simply wants to get closer, never imagining for a second that the other person may feel aggressed, suffocated, trapped or spied on. Once again two different philosophies come into conflict, each attempting to re-define the boundaries of personal space. In my book *Premier matin*, I discovered how anything connected to the intimate gestures of personal hygiene was capable of causing a culture shock. On one side, the advocates of an authentic, natural (nothing to hide from each other) approach, and, on the other, those more in favour

of modesty and mystery. As a result, much anxiety and embarrassment that first morning, a great deal of irritation later on. For such
habits are particularly tenacious and tend to change little over the
course of time. They are the cause of irritations, generally more likely
to be experienced by those desperately seeking an unattainable level
of privacy. In her now familiar style, Isabelle describes what happens.
'The brusque opening of the bathroom door when the other person
is on the throne is also not necessarily well received, especially if the
intention is to have a bit of a chat about something that could perfectly well wait. No, this is not the place for a conversation. And you
thought this appalling behaviour was confined to children? Not in
the least. Adults are equally guilty of it, much to the despair of their
partners. Then there are those who like to leave the door open and
carry on with their conversation against a background of all manner
of noises, or, if the topology of the room allows, carry on watching
the match or whatever programme is on. Bring on the smells! That's
really annoying as well. The invention of the hands-free phone,
undoubtedly a great blessing in its way, can also be a curse when you
are busy in this normally solitary spot and someone hands you the
receiver with a cursory: "It's your mother." Since you can't exactly
hang-up on your mother, you end up feeling embarrassed as though
you were on a video-phone where smells could also be transmitted.
Even more so when she asks: "What's that strange noise?" Whereas
all that needed to be said was: "She's busy at the moment, I'll tell her
to call back as soon as possible. Good-bye, mother in law." It's not
exactly complicated!'

The person guilty of profaning personal space in this way sometimes
deliberately persists with their crime, exercising a tyrant's power, even
to the extent, in the case of Kasiu's husband, of resorting to espionage
techniques. 'When I'm on the phone, my husband spies on me, from
a distance initially, but gradually getting nearer and nearer. And his
speciality is to participate in the conversation by trying to guess who
I'm talking to and what we're talking about.' Generally, however,
the person in question has no intention of causing offence, acting
on the contrary out of a desire for friendly, or loving, proximity. I
was struck, during my research on that first morning couples spend
together, by the little battle of 'too close' versus 'too far apart' in the
bed. Other aspects are understandably awkward for obvious reasons
(waking up to a barrage of questions, matters of personal hygiene in
the toilet or the bathroom, exposing one's nudity in the cold light of
day, etc.), whereas beneath the duvet all should be pleasure, warmth
and caresses. Too many caresses it transpired, for one of them, who

83

felt suffocated and overwhelmed by this outpouring of love. His only thought was how to put a bit of distance between the two of them in order to have a little more personal breathing space. By going to get the croissants for example. Two conflicting visions of what constituted a correct distance were emerging in this very first instance of conjugal life, already setting in motion a process of balancing contradictory desires, and establishing the rough outline of patterns of behaviour which will inevitably be reinforced with the passage of time. Patterns focusing on bringing them closer on the part of women, inclined to give themselves up to intimate contact, and to retaining their independence in the case of men, afraid of losing control of their existence and their little spheres of personal comfort. A case of 'I' becoming 'we' versus 'I' remaining obstinately 'I'; the battle of 'we-I' versus 'I-I'. A major war of passion or daily skirmishes over all kinds of minuscule details. 'Annette is very sweet, says Alex, but she has no sense of "yours" and "mine". Or rather, what is mine is hers – that's her interpretation of "ours". I spend my time looking for my pen, my note-book, my lighter . . .'[2] Marie-Edith cannot resist wearing Éric's sweaters which remind her of his warmth and presence. Much to Éric's annoyance. Irritated, he comes up with arguments to justify imposing boundaries around his own private universe. 'He says I ruin them, I make holes, snags, cigarette burns, all kinds of stuff that he's not very happy about.' Yet the boundaries between 'I' and 'we' shift constantly and are impossible to stabilize and clarify. Aurélie's boyfriend thinks it is acceptable for him to poke his nose into the pans when she is cooking because, in his view, this is a joint activity, simply delegated to Aurélie at the time the tasks were allocated. An allocation which, as it happens, she finds somewhat irritating. Nevertheless, once in the kitchen, she puts her heart into the task, determined to master it thoroughly. His remarks are therefore doubly irritating. 'He made a comment the other day that I didn't appreciate. He said, "The heat's too high, it'll get burnt." So I said to him, "Why don't you cook it yourself then! Since you can obviously do it better than I can, I'll let you get on with it." I went outside to have a cigarette and returned a quarter of an hour later.'[3]

Irritation provoked by the excessive proximity of a partner can be experienced by both parties. By the victim of course, who feels over-suffocated, trapped and spied on, and is desperate to find refuge in their own personal space but lacks the courage to voice that desire.

[2] Comments collected and quoted by Maurice Maschino (1995, p. 90).
[3] Comments recorded and quoted by Isabelle Garabuau-Moussaoui (2002, p. 191).

But also by the other person who sees themselves not as an aggressor but rather as the exponent of authenticity and naturalness, of togetherness and loving contact. The rebuffs from their partner are therefore experienced as a rejection of themselves, of the couple, of love. Such withdrawals are incomprehensible, intolerable even. Whereas, for one person, the partner is too close, for the other, he or she is too distant.

Too distant

The partner who is too distant does not cause irritation in the same way as the partner who is too close. The latter, cornered and without the advantage of distance, is generally condemned to dwell on their irritation or to devise some cunning strategies to avoid open confrontation. The person irritated from 'a distance' is not subject to the same pressure. We shall even see that the definition of personal spheres is a technique frequently resorted to (by both sides) as a means of limiting irritation. He or she hesitates to intervene, like Eliza, who, although very irritated by the long hours Robert spends on his video games when he could be joining her in bed, dare not intervene any more forcibly. 'I cannot, for the sake of the relationship, stop him playing just so we can be "together".' However, this failure to intervene exacerbates the sense of irritation, which, though less violent than that experienced by someone who feels their intimacy is under attack, nevertheless becomes a nagging presence, shifting uncomfortably close to what can potentially turn into conjugal dissatisfaction. An irritation constantly fuelled by the dissonance between an ideal schema, dreamed up in spite of everything as a possibility (the loving couple, united in intimate closeness), and the sad reality of individualistic resistance. The more noticeable withdrawals inevitably always come as something of a shock.

François de Singly has studied the shifting balance between the individual self and the shared identification within the couple, with all its frictions and lack of synchronization, pulling the little group to and fro with a 'pendulum swing – the "tick" of the individual "alone", and the "tock" of the individual "together "' (2000, p. 14). A number of everyday scenes are particularly telling in this respect, especially those involving use of the telephone. The phone is generally tolerated for use within the family, for work purposes, and even as a way of keeping in touch with personal friends. But everything hinges on the degree of threat posed by this call coming from outside and offering a pretext for escape. For example if the person speaking on the phone

85

becomes noticeably more animated (laughing, lots of exclamations) than they were only minutes before within the family context, where the tone was sometimes monotonous and the eyes lacked sparkle. Everything depends too on getting the right balance. 'What do I do if my partner spends the entire evening on the phone? Oh, I really sulk about it, I can't stand that. I don't like it because, during the week, the evenings are the only time we get to see each other. So if, on top of that, he spends more than twenty minutes on the phone, I'll go and ask if he doesn't have better things to do than to spend his evening on the phone. In fact what annoys me about it is that it makes me feel I might as well be on my own when in fact there are things I want to discuss with him plus I want him to be more a part of what goes on at home. I don't mind him making a few calls, but not spending the whole evening on the phone.'[4] Without fully realizing it, the two adversaries are attempting to define the red line beyond which over-usage of the phone or the television is likely to cause a surge of irritation (in the person who finds it hard to accept such individualistic behaviour). A slight disagreement provokes modest irritation; a more blatant disagreement can lead to real anger. As it does for Caroline who will no longer tolerate Bernard falling asleep in front of the TV and only coming to bed at two or three in the morning. 'What irritates me is the TV. He's always got to be changing channels and just sitting in front of the TV all the time. Even if it's rubbish, he sits there. The meal's ready, I call him. There he is glued to the TV. I have to call him at least ten times, and after about the tenth time, he finally gets up. He doesn't even notice that he's being called.'

Irritation erupts when simple autonomy degenerates into deliberate autism and selfishness, effectively a declaration of war on the couple. Take, for example, the scene of this Sunday morning breakfast, which Gally finds so irritating. The shift into selfishness, although apparently relatively restrained, is in reality extremely dramatic since it strikes at the heart of the romantic experience. It transpires that initially they both saw this Sunday breakfast as a moment of togetherness: the two of them preparing a tray of delights together. Alas, thanks to some chauvinist churlishness, their Sundays have become extremely highly charged. 'We often have Sunday breakfast together in front of the TV. It's the only time in the week we have breakfast together, as I get up earlier than he does. And for me breakfast is a really important meal. During the week it's copious enough, but at

---

[4] Comments recorded and quoted by François de Singly and Claire-Anne Boukaïa (Singly, 2000, p. 62).

the weekend it can easily be enough to take the place of lunch. So we prepare a tray of all kinds of food to take up to where the TV is. I always drink tea, so I boil the water, and then I put in the tea to infuse. Systematically, Akira, who takes ages over everything (but only actually takes charge of preparing his orange juice, while I in the meanwhile toast the bread, pour out the milk, get out the jams and the butter . . . and everything else, since if I don't, he forgets half the stuff) finishes loading the tray and takes it upstairs before my tea is ready. This really gets on my nerves because it makes me feel he only cares about what he's going to eat and drink rather than what I still want to put on the tray. Whereas from his point of view, since the tray is full anyway and there isn't room for anything else, he might just as well take it up. Which would be fine if he then took the trouble to come down again to help me bring up the rest of the things. But no, instead he switches on the DVD player.' He starts watching the film without even waiting for her.

Sharing everyday life is never an easy matter. It is about much more than mere decor. The perimeters relating to identity (what makes sense at a given moment) are not fixed and are constantly changing: private individual bubble or involvement with other worlds (friends, work, fiction) via the telephone, the computer, the TV; transcending the self in conjugal moments, little personal passions, etc. It is impossible to be truly synchronized. And when it does happen, our ways of doing things or our underlying moral viewpoints are not the same: everything is a pretext for irritation. Thousands and thousands of dissonances are at work, in every couple. Not a couple exists that is not based on such dissonances, with their potential for irritation. We are scarcely even aware of most of them, precisely because the art of living as a couple involves knowing how to deal with them, in a thousand different ways, with suppression being the simplest and most frequently used. Irritations remain below the surface of conjugal life. Yet they are still very much in evidence, ready to erupt at the slightest friction, or where love's defences show any signs of weakening. When that happens, daily life can become a nightmare of aggravating or angry emotions. Faced with this situation, an increasing number of couples who have the means to be able to live apart are opting to do so in order to share only the best moments (social life, leisure, sex, emotions) and keep the more ordinary ones, often the source of friction, separate. Unfortunately this is not always enough. Irritation has a nasty tendency to swiftly transfer itself to new objects, always managing to find some difference or other on which to fix itself. And living apart can sometimes accentuate differences. Rosy has become a complete bundle of nerves, ready to explode. Charly lives only 10 minutes away, but they see very little of each other, far less than she would like. He does not even phone her very often. 'I'm afraid for me the bare minimum is slightly more than 21h until 7h a few times a week.' She waits. Waits for him. Dreaming of the pleasure of sharing a meal with him. Charly prefers to eat alone. He will come and join her afterwards, late in the evening, sometimes without notice. The style of Rosy's message is understandably raw and violent. 'An on the spot reaction: it's 7.30 p.m. and I don't know if he's coming here, if I'm going there, if he's on the way to go and pick up his daughter . . . As usual, I'm getting uptight . . . What's the use of having free calls at the weekend (and it must have been a woman who first thought that one up)? Even that doesn't help. As my father used to say: "You can lead a horse to water . . ." Stupid idiot![5] I'm starving.[6] I' m sat here waiting for him and I bet he's going to tell me he's already eaten.'

---

[5] This insult is meant for Charly and not for her father.
[6] Rosy is hungry on two levels: physiologically, for food, and, more emotionally, for Charly's presence.

— 4 —

THE MECHANICS

The list

I asked my contributors to express themselves with total freedom and in whatever way suited them. And, if they were not sure where to start, to tell me about one or two specific things they found irritating so as to enable me to ask some initial questions. Some of them did exactly that. Many others chose to start by drawing up a detailed inventory and then sending me a list of all the things that irritated them. This approach is in itself extremely revealing. Before we begin our analysis, let us pause to see exactly what was included in these lists of conjugal woes. Clearly I cannot possibly quote them all in full. Nor would quoting a few extracts do justice to what such lists have to tell us. Instead, I have decided to select four fairly typical examples and to quote these in full. All of them (along with those I have not been able to include) have a similar structure: a matter-of-fact list of reasons which are both extraordinarily varied and often minuscule. Let us hear what Kasiu, Alice, Zoé and Cassiopée have to say.

Kasiu

A propos of your survey about what causes irritation within the couple:
– it drives me mad when I've just spent two hours doing the ironing on a Wednesday or a Friday, on top of two hours doing the shopping, an hour tidying my daughter's room, to say nothing of various other things as well . . . and my husband comes home, sees a scarf or something that hasn't been put away, and announces 'I've got to tidy the house.' It makes no difference if I say something, he just carries on. He wants to show that he's doing his bit;

89

– when he chooses the worst possible moment to embark on an interesting discussion or to bring up some issue that needs to be sorted out;
– when he interrupts when I'm talking to a friend;
– when he hangs around in the kitchen when he's feeling hungry, and gets in the way when I'm preparing the meal but is nowhere to be seen once we've finished eating;
– when he sits there calmly reading his magazines even though I haven't had a single minute to myself all day;
– when he comes home and gets into a rage if I dare to mention that I'm tired or don't feel well. I'm looking for a sympathetic ear and a bit of support but he can't stand seeing me 'below par';
– when we both go on the same diet and he loses 5 kilos in a week while I struggle to lose 3 in two weeks;
– when he decides it's time to think ahead about our daughter's education – even though she's still only five years old! And everyone knows that the best way of guaranteeing a child's failure at school is to pile on the pressure;
– when he's eating and sometimes his jaw makes a kind of clicking noise;
– when he acts as if he owns the whole building (he's on the management committee and wants to be in charge of everything);
Whew!!!! Apart from that everything is fine, he has lots of great qualities and I adore him.

Alice

Here is a list, by no means complete, of the 'big' and 'little' things that can get on my nerves about the person I love very much in spite of it all!

– when we're just about to got out and he says 'Right, are you ready? Let's go!' so I get myself ready in two minutes only to find he's still got all sorts of things to do and I end up waiting for him for ten or fifteen minutes. And then often, the minute the door's closed and we're outside the flat he'll say 'Hold on, I forgot to go for a pee, or I just need to put some cream on my hands';
– the fact that even after four years of being told he still doesn't understand the difference between cooked ham and Parma ham, or between garlic and shallots;
– that he is incapable of watching anything on the TV without analysing, criticizing, getting into a state, losing his temper, whereas for me it's just a nice relaxing time when I don't have to think;
– the way he takes so long over everything – eating, washing-up, ironing, getting ready, in fact it seems to me he wastes a ridiculous amount of time over the simplest things!

(I should point out that I am also quite capable, depending on the mood I'm in or my frame of mind, of finding all four of these irritating habits endearing and sweet and of feeling a sort of rush of love for him when he does any of these things)

– when he announces in the morning that he went to bed very late the previous night, that he feels exhausted and will have an early night but then ends up going to bed late again and being even more tired the next day and moaning about it!

– when he says in the most serious tone: 'Tonight you absolutely must remind me to call my dad, do a virus check on the computer, etc.' and then when I duly remind him that evening he just says: 'Oh, yeah, I'll do it tomorrow';

– this thing he does with his mouth whenever he's about to say something mean or when he's annoyed: I find it horrible and stupid;

– the fact that he gets himself so incredibly stressed and worked up when he's playing a computer game and fails to carry out some mission or other, whereas I see it as just a game and a game as far as I'm concerned is supposed to be relaxing and fun;

– he doesn't pay any attention to things which he regards as trivial but which he knows perfectly well are important to me, like playing with food for example or making jokes about subjects like death or illness;

– when we're catching a train together, he always manages to make us late and we end up being in a terrible rush to get to the station and then not getting decent seats on the train whereas I like to get to the station in plenty of time and be able to go off and buy a magazine for myself;

– his paranoia. He always assumes the worst, he's far too suspicious whereas I'm just the opposite, and I think he's stupid to get in such a state;

- when I say something to him and it's several seconds (which seem so-ooo long to me) before he answers or even notices I've spoken, even though he heard me perfectly well but was just too busy thinking about something else or watching something on the TV, yet when he wants to tell me something I'm ready to give him my full attention immediately even if I'm in the middle of something else.

There, that's all I can think of at the moment but I'm sure if I think about it over the next few days the list will probably get longer!

Zoé

I've been in a real state of 'crisis' for several months now and there are a number of things that irritate me all the time. To the extent that I sometimes find myself wondering if I still love my partner. I know I do really, but if I put my feelings to one side, I really think we'd be better

91

off living apart so as to avoid what I call 'the dead hand of daily life' which for me is all the little things we didn't notice at the beginning of our relationship . . . The things that I find most irritating tend to be associated with mealtimes:

– he puts so much food in his mouth that his whole face is completely misshapen;
– sometimes he licks his fingers really noisily;
– he makes loud 'slurping' noises when he drinks anything hot or even lukewarm. Just like his mother;
– instead of biting a piece of bread like a civilized person, he sticks his nose in his plate and tears off an (oversized) chunk like some sort of caveman;
– he always crumples his napkin into a ball;
– he talks with his mouth full, even though no one can understand what he's saying (something I'm always telling the children not to do);
– he licks the spoon and puts it back in the jam jar;
– he licks his knife;
– he licks his knife and then takes the butter with it (PS: this all sounds so comical and ridiculous when I re-read it that I wonder how such little things can possibly get on my nerves so much).

Here are some of the other things he does which I also find irritating:
– when we're in town and he wants to say something to me, he stops in the middle of the street to explain whatever it is (whereas he could perfectly well do so while we're walking along);
– also when we're in town he talks at the top of his voice and shouts as if he was the only person in the world;
- as soon as he's in company with a few other people, especially ones he doesn't know very well, he stands really stiffly and it looks as if he's puffing out his chest like a little cockerel;
– and on that subject, as soon as there's a female present he starts to strut around like a cockerel!
– he leaves his socks in the middle of the living room floor every evening;
– he has a way of clearing his throat that really gets on my nerves. And I'm sure he didn't do it when we first met . . .
– when he gets into bed, he lifts the duvet up and lets cold air in;
– when he comes to bed after me, he takes his trousers off in the bedroom and drops them on the floor. The belt buckle makes a loud 'clang' on the floor . . . it drives me mad;
– when he comes to bed after me, he always manages to somehow make the landing light shine right in my eyes;
– when the cats want to come in and he doesn't want them to, he kicks the bay window;
– he leaves little piles of various things (keys, nails, pen, papers) lying on the sideboard;

– he always manages to leave dirty finger-marks on the windows or on the white walls.
These are just a few examples.

Cassiopée

– he always criticizes everything I do and then the next day he does exactly the same thing but I'm not allowed to say anything: leaving the kitchen in a mess, not putting the shower head back in its place, leaving things lying around, not cleaning marks off the walls;
– we've got a cleaning lady who doesn't always do everything he thinks needs doing: he seems to think she ought to know what to do without him telling her and then he moans and expects me to phone her because he doesn't want to say anything to her face; sometimes it's quicker if I just do whatever it is myself!
– whenever it's anyone's birthday, it's always me that has to make any phone calls to friends or relatives;
– it's up to me to organize arrangements for holidays, leisure time, the kids' activities, otherwise nothing would get done;
– he pees on the toilet floor and doesn't clean it up;
– he criticizes everything but never questions his own judgement;
– if anyone wants anything he doesn't like, it's just to annoy him;
– he uses quite a lot of bad language himself and, of course, the kids copy him but he doesn't do anything about it;
– he won't use public transport or take charter flights;
– he gets dressed up to go and do the shopping at weekends whereas most people who work all week and have to think about what they wear do exactly the opposite;
– he won't let the children stay at their friends' houses overnight (they are 3 and 10);
– he's never positive or optimistic;
– he doesn't like parties, or going to the cinema;
– he doesn't have any hobbies or any friends;
– he's always glued to the TV.

Kasiu, Alice, Zoé, Cassiopée and many others were surprised themselves by what this process revealed. They were very keen to clarify this matter of irritation. They knew it was something they experienced but had never really identified what caused it or taken the time to think about it more precisely. The chance to be involved in the research was the opportunity to do exactly that and they imagined it would be a relatively simple matter. Equipped with paper and pencil (or installed at a keyboard), they began to ponder the subject. Sometimes with little initial success. 'I'm trying to come up with some examples but none come to mind this morning, even though I know there are plenty!!' (Clémentine). Lorenzo even wondered if he had anything much to say at all. 'When I first started thinking about it I couldn't think of anything that irritated me, but then I realised that I was actually sorting out in my mind the things that irritated me enormously, a little, a lot, often, depending on my mood, etc. So here they are, in no particular order . . .' A long list followed. Many correspondents told me of similar experiences: after a laborious start, where the notion of irritation was no more than a vague one, the setting down of the first lines of the list seemed to open a bottomless Pandora's Box. Perhaps exhausted by the effort of writing it all down, more likely disturbed by the new vision of their relationship which was emerging as they wrote, some ended abruptly with a short phrase that suggested that, although they could continue, they had decided to end their list there. 'I'll stop there for now' (Caroline). For some, the list ended up being the only evidence available. It is highly likely that the mere fact of writing it was in itself enough to provoke fears about the potential repercussions of such an exercise. The very act of compiling the list inevitably led to a whole series of discoveries, with one idea leading on to another and, in some cases, existential questions being raised, even to the extent of the relationship itself being called into question. Which is why some people found it preferable to stop at that point.[1] 'I'm sorry I've had to drop out, but recently my irritation levels have reached the point that writing about it would have ended up making me feel even more irritated' (Viràg).

The lists are an extremely rich source of information. Particularly because of the Pandora's box phenomenon. They demonstrate that the dissonances, potentially likely to cause irritation, are infinite, even though the couple are usually unaware of them. (Which is precisely what makes this a dangerous exercise.) In most cases, only a few trivial things cause serious irritation and even then the two partners can sometimes see the funny side. Yet this tranquil surface is the result of a constant and ongoing task of dealing with such dissonances, using a wide range of techniques, amongst which suppression is by far the most common. The act of making a list effectively opens a breach in the normally un-addressed issue of irritation.

The lists are also a rich source of information because of the extraordinary jumble of reasons, often minuscule, which they contain

---

[1] I was surprised myself by the contentious nature the subject of irritation proved to be within the couple as participants opened the Pandora's Box of endless lists. As a result I often found myself urging them to caution and moderation, and even, in a few cases, calling a halt.

– proof of the way dissonances crystallize around little details which then become triggers.

Crystallization

The term crystallization has been associated with the domain of emotions ever since the famous pages Stendhal devoted to it on the subject of love: the romantic crystallization marks a sudden break with the past and brings a new vision of the object of desire, suddenly as pure as a diamond. Yet this beautiful picture has its dark side, the black diamond of irritation, capable of suddenly breaking the spell between the two people, with a compelling and disagreeable emotional shift: an abrupt falling out of love, retreating into oneself, against the couple, against the partner who (for a time) has become an enemy.

Just as love has its preliminaries, the tentative movements leading gradually to the full emotional outpouring (which transports the individual out of their old self), so irritation also goes through a series of stages before a crescendo is reached. The first of these involves forgetting about the incident in favour of superficial peace – total suppression. At a slightly higher level it involves feelings being kept to oneself, so that nothing is said. Daniel was astonished to discover, as a result of our research, that for years Christine had felt irritated each time she found the cardboard centre of the toilet roll left lying around in the bathroom. 'But you never said anything! If you don't say anything, how is anyone to know?'[2] The step up to a deliberate action in order to reinforce the suppression is a clear indication that a dissonance is already at work beneath the surface and that irritation threatens. 'You keep it to yourself, you say to yourself: "Don't look for trouble." Then, inevitably, it all blows up' (Alain).[3] Crystallization, the third and final stage, happens quite suddenly. Irritation is no longer simply a faintly discordant music that grates secretly on the ear, but a violent liberating blast.

From the total suppression to the liberating blast, the process can sometimes follow a regular pattern. Laurence Le Douarin (2005, p. 171) cites the case of a father irritated by the sight of his son constantly 'glued' to his video-game screen. His irritation comes in waves which, at their peak, force him into making a clearer verbal

[2] Comments recorded and quoted by Johanne Mons (1998, p. 99).
[3] Comments recorded and quoted by Céline Bouchat (2005, p. 80).

intervention. In the evening, for example, his simmering irritation grows in intensity as it gets later. Once it gets to 11 o'clock, the time when the father is starting to think about sleep and darkness, the flashes of light from the screen are enough to abruptly open the sluice-gates and release an outpouring of anger. 'It gets on my nerves. Enough's enough!' More often though, the final emotional outburst comes as a surprise. Even when the irritated person is a victim for the hundredth, even thousandth, time, of the same ridiculous but unacceptable difference. They had forgotten all about it. They would not even have thought to add it to a list had they been asked to produce one. And yet they know it so well. It is indeed the intimate familiarity of this strangeness, strangely forgotten, that makes it most shocking. The crystallization thrusts the individual into a completely new sequence of life, one which is both familiar and different at the same time. So rapid is this transition that it scarcely allows more than the briefest glimpse of the mysteries of suppression. Which is much more a transfer of identity than a simple relegation into the unconscious (the individual identifies with the couple by concealing his or her more personal identity), the transfer of identity accentuating the erasure of the source of irritation.

How could all of that have been forgotten? The irritated person had forgotten it because he or she had become another, the individual socialized by the couple. This other self could face the difference without it having any unpleasant effect. Or very little, nothing more than a scarcely audible and faintly discordant music. Heard but not listened to. How many times must Isabelle have contemplated the mangled toothpaste tubes without reacting? How many times must Nicole have observed the slices of bread buttered like works of art without exploding? In spite of Madeleine's reiterated requests, Léon stubbornly refuses to participate in the household tasks (to his wife's great irritation). 'That kind of thing is all very well for young people. We belong to the old regime.' He does, however, occasionally dry the dishes. Léon is regularly irritated by the half-hearted way things are tidied and cleaned around the house. But he is condemned to say nothing, and to ignore it as far as is possible since he has no intention of participating himself. Yet when he picks up a plate to dry it, he is often horrified and disgusted to find it greasy to the touch, which immediately sets off an emotional reaction. Revulsion and anger. 'I don't know how I restrain myself from smashing it onto the floor and shouting at the top of my voice!'

Letting off steam

The scene of the plate is a perfect example of crystallization, both sudden and intense. Léon and Madeleine play out many other scenes of irritation, a rich repertoire which leaves them with little time on their hands. Especially as (with the exception of the plate incident where the outburst of emotion is virulent and potentially aggressive) most of their repertoire has long been carefully kept under control. They perform, and watch each other perform, a series of carefully controlled domestic scenes, as though on stage, except that the irritation they express is all too real. Take, for example, the saga of the two chairs. For years now, this little battle has been re-enacted every night. They have two chairs, one on either side of the bed, on which they each put their clothes once they have got undressed. The result is a similarly untidy heap of clothes on each side. This irritates both of them, but for different reasons. When Léon looks at his wife's chair, it reminds him of the general state of untidiness of the house and therefore irritates him. Madeleine finds her husband's sidelong glances and cutting comments extremely annoying. She can put up with them as long as they remain general, but she regards her chair as her personal space. 'It's none of his business.' Léon is also irritated by his own chair, entertaining secret fantasies that Madeleine will suddenly turn into a domestic goddess. But the distinctly undomesticated goddess Madeleine resents this and finds it intolerable. 'If he doesn't like it, why doesn't he do something about it himself?' A rebuff which reminds Léon of the contradiction in his own mind, torn as he is between wanting everything to be neat and tidy and not wanting to do anything about it himself. The ensuing imbroglio is so complicated that they never succeed in untangling it satisfactorily. Indeed angry phrases are rarely conducive to lucid discussions. Yet the ritual endures. 'We get it off our chests' (Léon). Some evenings it veers towards light comedy. Léon and Madeleine exchange their usual replies in a good-humoured manner, without paying too much attention to each other's remarks, ready to laugh at the situation themselves. On other evenings, passions run deeper and things can take a more dramatic turn, though without ever degenerating into tragedy or being dragged out into endless angry exchanges. For these two are old hands at the game and are careful not to stray beyond certain limits. Although they fail to agree over the fundamental issues, the little verbal duel calms them down, and has no long-lasting consequences. Since there is clearly no real risk of any catastrophic outcome, they can indulge in it whenever they choose.

Crystallization is not a random process; it selects a catalyst which is usually extremely telling. If they could calmly disentangle the issues instead of getting annoyed as they do, Léon and Madeleine could profitably use the scene of the two chairs to gain a better understanding of their differences. In certain cases, however, the purely liberating element dominates, manifesting itself all the more forcibly precisely because the pretext appears to be gratuitous and unwarranted. It is extremely difficult and very risky to release one's irritation by engaging in complex explanations. Hence those lists with their litany of extremely concrete and diverse reasons. Crystallization can only occur in the presence of very precise circumstances. Moreover, the random nature of some of these can make the resulting act of liberation even more satisfying. Remember Jean, massively irritated over the shirts and the shirt-buttons but trapped by the inadmissible dream of a more relaxed domestic regime. 'Often it really irritates him and gets on his nerves when I say: "Put your stuff away!"' (Agnès). Many of the things he feels strongly about cannot be said openly, or only in a carefully controlled way. The issue of 'the hiding place' for the key can, however, be more easily taken out of context, and the resentment it provokes can therefore be exacerbated. Although Jean may claim that his anger is provoked by a specific incident, in reality he is giving Agnès an example of the kind of obsessiveness he hates. Listen to them:

JEAN: You get there and bang! You find the door's locked. Why lock it like that every five minutes? It's completely pointless. And that's when you really lose your temper! And then, in a complete rage by this time, you look for the key – which turns out to have been hidden!

AGNÈS: It hasn't been hidden, it's in the hiding place.

JEAN: The hiding place!! Just the mention of it makes my blood boil, it annoys me so much.

Such episodes of ritual letting off steam clear the air and get things back onto an even keel. So much (whether minor background annoyances or more virulent irritations) finds itself relegated to the realms of oblivion without ever disappearing completely. This type of ritual is a compensation which, as the popular expression so clearly puts it, enables people to 'get things off their chests' (even if the things in question turn out neither the most important nor the most explicit). In some cases, no sooner are the angry phrases off the tip of the tongue than the speaker regrets having spoken in such a forceful and hurtful way. He, or she, is anxious to return to conjugal routine. But the opposite can also happen. For not everyone plays their little role as skilfully as Léon and Madeleine over their chairs. The fact that feelings have been aired and that angry words have been thrown in the partner's face can cause matters to escalate with lasting consequences. 'The smallest incident can spark things off', Alex explains. 'I only have to do something the tiniest bit "stupid", and Annette seizes the opportunity to throw at me all the things she doesn't like about me: the way I eat – I'm "greedy" and "disgusting", the way I sit, with my shoulders hunched, "like a criminal", my "rudeness" (when one of her ancient aunts turns up, I clear off).'[4]

Pascal is clearly looking for a pretext which would enable him to let off steam. He is constantly irritated by Ninette's untidiness, but dare not say so. He is even more irritated ('That really gets on my nerves') by the dirty handkerchiefs 'left lying about all over the place'. 'It's our major bone of contention. I rant on and on and on about it . . . I've been ranting on about it for ages . . . and it doesn't make the slightest difference'. In reality he probably 'rants' about it more in his head than out loud. For Ninette, who admits to having a permanent cold, claims to have heard nothing, or virtually nothing, on the subject. It is another matter entirely, however, when it comes to their 'butter war'. They agreed that they would take turns to clear the breakfast table. In practice their respective approaches to the task turn out to be very different. Pascal is disciplined and efficient; the table is cleared within minutes. Ninette, on the other hand, often leaves it until later. Pascal, extremely irritated by this, is particularly obsessed by the butter which, if he did not intervene, would sit there, getting softer and softer, until lunchtime. 'There are some stupid little things like that which really annoy me, I mean really annoy me! And it annoys me that I have to keep going on about them.' The disagreement is a violent one in which Ninette also responds angrily, annoyed over what she sees as his over-reaction. The 'butter war' is the opposite of a good cathartic ritual in that it fans the fire instead of damping it down. Nor are the handkerchiefs any more effective either (probably because Ninette cannot after all be held to blame for her cold and also because the subject touches too closely on intimate physical matters). So Pascal will have to continue his quest, perhaps to no avail. Letting off steam through irritation is in fact only possible when the internal turmoil is not too strong. Those more seriously afflicted are unable to benefit from a technique which requires enormous self-control, an impossibility where irritation is intense.

In general, the scene which enables someone to 'get things off their chest' comes at a certain cost, and what is said cannot be unsaid.

---

[4] Comments recorded and quoted by Maurice Maschino (1995, p. 91).

Although it serves to relieve feelings and calm emotions at the time, in the long term it tends to exacerbate the conflict. Rosy is extremely annoyed by Charly, who in her view comes to see her too infrequently, without letting her know, after dinner. She fantasizes about eating with him more often . . . yet at the same time finds his eating habits irritating, notably his addiction to mayonnaise (which is why he prefers to eat in his own place where he is safe from her comments). It is, moreover, to drive this point home that she chooses to end the e-mail in which she tells Charly she has decided to break up with him: 'Enjoy your mayonnaise!' In fact the break-up only lasted a few weeks. Today Rosy is still waiting for her Charly. But it will not be easy to create the conditions for a calm tête-à-tête over the dinner table after what has been said.

Aspects of identity

The pleasure of using irritation to let off steam in this way stems not just from 'getting something off your chest' by abruptly liberating yourself of something that had been imperfectly suppressed. It comes too from the rediscovery of aspects of identity which have also lain hidden for a while. The general consensus is that living together as a couple is an exercise in compromise. In reality it is much more than this. For the notion of compromise presupposes that the individual remains unchanged, even while accepting concessions. In fact the transformation is a much more profound one: it is the individual himself who changes identity. The fewer irritations there are and the less intense these are, the more complete the metamorphosis of identity: the degree of irritation acts as a barometer indicating the extent to which the individual has become socialized by the couple. The angry emotional outburst, however, causes him or her to step outside this context, and reveals the 'other' lying dormant within. An 'other' who is by no means a stranger but someone all too familiar: the old self from before the relationship began, the autonomous self, refusing to disappear whenever the 'compromise' proves too much, when the conjugal identity no longer appears to give meaning to life. This explains why, in the heat of the moment, many people respond as they do, typically characterized by some sort of autistic withdrawal, such as sulking for example. The irritated individual takes refuge in the familiar safety of their own little world. Carried away by their feelings and buttressed by their own certainties, they can allow themselves – for a while at least – to ignore concrete reality and cut themselves off from the little world that surrounds them. Especially as by doing so, they are going back a long way, to the time before the relationship, and to subsequent biographical episodes similar to what is now being experienced. The way we recount our own life stories (Ricœur, 1990) is not organized in a single and homogeneous manner. We tell ourselves a number of life stories simultaneously or successively, beginning each time by renewing the link with the preceding, sometimes distant, episode (Kaufmann, 2004). When it comes to irritation, the options are limited to two very distinct stories. Depending on whether they are in the midst of a crisis or not, the individual tells himself two almost contradictory life stories.

It is extraordinary how little we are aware of such changes in identity, abrupt as they often are, and how we bask in the soothing illusion of the continuity of the self. In reality, we swing from one aspect of identity to another very different one, with astonishing fluidity, whether it be autistic withdrawal or, at the other extreme, conjugal reintegration. In the first case, emotion takes over, leaving no time to even think about the change of identity, and the result is the simple pleasure of letting off steam. In the second case, there is more scope for reflection, for a realization of the difficulty and the inconveniences of persisting with an individualistic revolt. Added to this there may be feelings of remorse or malaise, all incentives for the pragmatic resumption of the conjugal identity, which, in spite of its flaws, is perceived as the only viable one. Eline, for example, allows herself to be uncharacteristically carried away by this cathartic irritation. 'Let's be honest, we also have the most terrible rows (they clear the air too).' I ask whether these do not sometimes get a little out of hand. In her answer she makes a distinction between the rows which are simply cathartic, generally over matters of little significance, and the others. 'If we're talking about a major irritation, the sort that affects the couple's everyday life, in that case, yes, it can make for a difficult atmosphere (which can last up to two days, but not much longer because I tend to give in).' Two days: in which time that other identity, the other vision of the self and of existence, has ample time to become firmly rooted. During this period Eline's position is less solid than would appear. In spite of appearances (her hostile expression) giving Jack the clear signal that she is still on the offensive, her own thoughts are in turmoil. 'Then it's up to me to calm down so we can talk it over in a more constructive way.' Even though her irritation takes a long time to subside, she finds herself longing to get back to the normality of the relationship as quickly as possible. An extreme irritation, provoking an unreasonably strong reaction in spite

101

of oneself, often induces the desire not only to return to normality but also to over-compensate. The person responsible for the irritation can also make a similarly abrupt about-turn. Pedro couldn't help criticizing Fidelia's driving when she was taking him to the clinic. Extremely irritated by this, she abandoned him outside the clinic to manage on his own. But, only a short time later, she called him to ask how he was, just as though nothing had happened. Pedro pretended not to remember either and the whole thing seemed to have blown over, with their respective forays into individualistic behaviour forgotten. Long before the incident, Fidelia had planned a trip with her girl-friends and without Pedro. The trip (although not originally intended in this way) became a form of revenge for the irritation she had had to put up with. 'Anyway, I got back on Wednesday after this little trip: a new woman!' A new man too. 'Pedro came to meet me and we had a fantastic reunion: he gave me a present of some beautiful skin cream and massaged my shoulders, which is an EVENT in itself: he hardly ever buys me presents and his "free" massages are even rarer. He told me he'd missed me; I think he knew he hadn't been very nice to me before I went away. I was really pleased to see him too. When we're apart, he always seems much more on my wave-length.'

The loving about-turn is always pleasing to the partner. The abrupt autistic withdrawal with its accompanying sullen expression is, on the contrary, an extremely disagreeable experience. The sense of liberation it brings to the irritated party is matched by the irritation it causes to the person responsible (who is rarely conscious of their offence). Whereas the change of identity takes place within the illusion of continuity for the person concerned, the experience is an extremely unpleasant one for the partner, who is doubly irritated. Directly, by the unexpectedly hostile expression in front of them; more deeply, because of the apparent incoherence in identity displayed by the partner, with the resulting dissonance. Trapped in this way, the ultimate tactic is to retaliate. An eye for an eye, a tooth for a tooth. With the proviso that the situation does not escalate too rapidly, the important thing being to make it quite clear to the adversary that resorting to an exaggerated autistic withdrawal carries a certain degree of risk.

'Passion killers' and the magic of love

The tendency to go along with events is clear, whether in the individualistic sense of irritation or its opposite, the romantic reunion. Pedro and Fidelia put all negative thoughts aside when they are reunited; they switch from being enemies to being lovers in a more or less synchronized way. Fortunately it appears that love's magic works as powerfully to bring two people together as irritation does to separate them. Merely going along with events cannot alone explain this result. The happy ending (alas, always provisional) is only possible because the romantic scenario, always held in reserve, is revived.

Life as a couple is a constant battle in which what cements and attracts needs to outshine what repels and irritates. A variety of techniques are used to achieve this. The easiest of these (though not one everyone can avail themselves of) is to simply allow oneself to be carried along by life, accepting whatever comes along without making too many demands or asking too many questions, much as couples did in the past. Often a more deliberate strategy is needed, however, taking the form of little loving counter-attacks, as Zoé explains: 'For me, love has to be more important than everyday life, or I feel as if I'm suffocating. Yet everyday life is full of "passion killers". The ideal balance is one where the things that destroy love can be wiped out by a really powerful dose of love. This powerful dose allows you to deal with irritations and move on to other things.' We will be examining some of the techniques used to combat irritation in more detail in Part Three. One point is, however, worth considering at this stage: irritation and loving reunion rarely take place on the same stage. Of course this can happen, with a simple, direct application of a 'magic dose' to wipe out any irritations, as recommended by Zoé. In most cases, however, the counter-attack is an indirect one, focusing attention elsewhere, away from everyday life: a universe of relatively abstract feelings. Zoé resorts to this strategy too, for over-frequent use of the dose diminishes its magic powers and allows irritation to start building up. She has already indicated as much in the introduction to her list. 'I've been in a real state of "crisis" for several months now and there are a number of things that irritate me all the time. To the extent that I sometimes find myself wondering if I still love my partner. I know I do really, but if I put my feelings to one side, I really think we'd be better off living apart so as to avoid what I call 'the dead hand of daily life' which for me is all the little things we didn't notice at the beginning of our relationship.' What can be meant by '. . .put my feelings aside'? Can feelings be separated from real life? It is easy to see how this happens when the couple first meets, when the emotional upheaval sweeps all before it; love is blind, as the proverb says. But this disjunction from the real world seems much less likely once the couple have been together for a while. Less attention is given to the reality of everyday life since this is somehow obscured by an idealized image, a dream sequence: the intangible world of feelings has its reasons which go beyond reason. Many of those we interviewed expressed their astonishment on this matter: when comparing the various partners with whom they had shared their lives, it seemed love was by no means inversely proportional to the scale of irritation. The person who should have been irritating turned out not to be, because he or she was loved; and the person who was all consideration and attention found themselves rebuffed over the slightest discrepancy. Sarah is amazed to find that she gets annoyed over the most trivial things (like the fact that he laughs too often). 'I don't think I really love him, not enough to put up with him. Because if you really love someone, those little things shouldn't matter. I was married to the father of my children for twenty-three years and he had all sorts of faults, none of which I noticed. All because I was madly in love with him.' Even though he was 'extremely cold, not at all affectionate and even, towards the end of the relationship, really nasty to me', in contrast to her current partner who is 'the complete opposite – a really affectionate man'. Affectionate, but irritating. The more kind and tender he tries to be, the more irritating she finds him.

Feelings transport the conjugal relationship into another world. A process which again demonstrates the power of those abrupt reversals of identity. Caroline, even when clearly extremely angry with Marc, forgets all his irritating features in a split second. 'I am so lucky, I've got a man who is incredibly sensitive and who knows how to apologize if he's gone a bit too far. And then, when he says "you're right, I'll try harder", I just melt.' Rosy is also capable of melting when confronted with her mayonnaise eater, even after sending him an e-mail to break off the relationship. 'He calls me and because he's so sweet, I just melt.' Only to lose her temper all over again when he arrives later than promised. These moments of romantic bonding are like little magical interludes, bubbles of intimate communion, neither truly outside reality nor truly within it. Not outside it since they are firmly rooted in reality, and the ultimate physical expression of desire. Nor truly within it either, since this version of the real is less about ordinary moments than about exceptional ones.

Normal life is somewhere in the middle, weighed down with the repetitive reality which gives it structure. At its opposite extremes (the height of irritation and the romantic bonding process), the two partners escape from the burdensome context of social interaction to play out a much more volatile scenario. They choose from two conflicting versions by either preparing for battle, one against the other and everyman for himself, or giving themselves up to love, and becoming one. Neither extreme is tenable for long. As for striking a balance between calm stability and emotional volatility, there is considerable variety. Some couples function on the basis of the tranquil repetition of normal life (a tendency especially favoured by males), whereas others prefer improvisation, intensity and emotion (a tendency more favoured by females). In the latter case, conflicting emotions balance each other out; there is more shouting and more demonstrative out-pouring too. Frequent irritations do not, it seems, necessarily indicate any less love.

Confused feelings

The couple is the result of an infinitely complex emotional alchemy. The two partners need to be in tune, at all times, whether in the throes of those little cathartic skirmishes or in moments of loving peace. Yet allowing oneself to be carried along by events, in one direction or the other, often leads to only partial harmony. Facts can, after all, be interpreted in widely divergent ways. Emotional rapprochements do not prevent there being a dialogue of the deaf over the usual sources of discord, since love merely pushes these temporarily to one side without ever completely eradicating them. Yet close bonding creates the illusion of intimate mutual understanding. Hence the feeling of surprise when an irritation resurfaces, proof of the continued exist-ence of an entrenched difference. 'You get an idea in your head about something, you imagine the other person is inevitably thinking the same thing, and sometimes it's hard to accept that it hasn't even entered their heads' (Marie-Edith).[5]

Various factors blur the perception of divergences. The main one is the continual process of conjugal socialization, especially when love still casts its spell: anything capable of causing irritation is pushed aside, provisionally forgotten. But there is also the fact that the points of contention, complex and tangled as they often are, are not always easily identified, especially since the person experiencing irritation does not stop to undertake a detailed analysis. The crystallizations which form around a few specific details are the trees (of clarity) which hide the wood of tangled causes. Even when the facts seem

[5] Comments recorded in the context of the documentary *Amour et chaussettes sales*, pro-duced by Bertrand Van Effenterre, with the collaboration of Danièle Laufer, based on *La Trame conjugale* (Gaumont Television / Canal +, 1994).

relatively simple. Jack, for example, gets irritated when Eline is on the telephone for too long, as she is all too aware. 'I spend ages on the telephone in the evenings, especially on a Sunday evening between 5 and 9 o'clock. Jack finds this irritating, because it often means I end up eating something cold, while chatting to someone or other, and I'm not really free until after 10 or 11 o'clock on a weekday evening.' The main reason for his irritation is clear (the threat of competition to the relationship), and has already been discussed. But there is also the fact that Jack himself hates using the phone. 'Jack hates the telephone and I always have to remind him to call his sister, his parents, his cousins, his aunts . . . Sometimes for weeks at a time.' Not only is Eline abandoning him, but she is doing so in a way which is incomprehensible to him. Jack is irritated by the combination of these two elements, unable to disentangle which of the two irritates him most. This is a relatively straightforward case involving only two factors, one superimposed on the other. Often, however, such cases involve a number of different factors, subtly interwoven (remember Léon and Madeleine and the two chairs). The situation needs only to be turned on its head once for matters to become blurred (Jack is generally untidy yet he is the first to put away any paperwork). The blurring is even more pronounced when the reversal in question relates not to a mere point of detail but to much broader issues. Eline is indisputably in charge when it comes to organizing and programming, planning the smallest details of their trips a month in advance. 'I'm always nagging Jack, and he finds it harder and harder to accept the fact that I insist on organizing everything.' Yet when it comes to her own evenings out during the week, she favours intensity and surprise, always doing new things. In contrast to this frenzied flitting about, Jack seems a pillar of regularity. 'Jack is very stable, and I'm all over the place: I move house every year, I change jobs regularly, I talk about moving abroad, or going to live in another region, etc. All of which is much more irritating to Jack than it is to me, because I'm the one wanting to change our life, to "move it on". But although I do introduce a certain number of changes, I often overdo it, at which point Jack steps in with arguments in favour of a certain amount of stability.' Each of them upholds their own idea of order, in their own way and in relation to the things they care most deeply about (Eline makes plans for the future whereas Jack is more rooted to the present and how things are). The desire for order is not therefore all on one side, but fluctuates according to the precise question which is being addressed.

Again this case hinges on the purely technical aspects of two conflicting cultures, in themselves already difficult enough to untangle.

But this is nothing in comparison with the complexity of what comes next: interpreting the thoughts of the person causing irritation. Are they simply irredeemably naïve, causing irritation without realizing it, incapable of doing anything about it? Isabelle thinks this is the most likely explanation as far as her current partner is concerned. 'My present boyfriend genuinely forgets, even though occasionally, when things get really exasperating, you can't help thinking Oh my god he must be a complete idiot, or else he must be doing it on purpose. But you only have to look at that pathetic little drowned rat expression when you moan at him to realize he is genuinely sorry. That's the difference between irritation and blind rage. You can't be angry for long with someone who just forgets.' Or could it be that he is deliberately refusing to make the slightest effort, that he is playing the innocent in order to cause even more irritation? The manner in which someone irritates can become even more irritating than the initial cause. As Isabelle found with her ex, the tube-squidging husband. 'The squidger is especially irritating when you know it's quite unnecessary. In fact, that's the only thing that makes you really angry. He knows, we know he knows, he knows that we know he knows and yet he still does it.' The 'squidge' itself had been relegated to the background. It was the underhand nature of the attack that made her scream with rage. And the same reaction can also result from an attitude that was not aggressive in the first place. Marc, for example, feels vaguely guilty about not helping Caroline more than he does. Reluctantly he mumbles various promises which, while not without sincerity, rarely come to anything. And it is precisely this duplicity which makes Caroline so angry: 'What irritates me too is when he says: "Why don't you take a break! You do too much! Let me do it!" all with such conviction. Yet the man saying it remains slumped on the sofa even though there are all sorts of things that need doing around the house.' The individual is not a fixed entity, but is constantly working to balance his or her internal multiplicity. Albeit imperfectly, and never more than provisionally. The resulting contradictions and sudden changes of mood fuel the irritations of the other person, while blurring the perception of the reasons for these irritations. Nothing is more likely to trigger anger than that lack of clarity.

A certain notion of the truth

However, irritation is not just about lack of clarity. On the contrary, the irritated party is often convinced that their truth is THE truth, the absolute, obvious, universal, rational truth. Nor are they necessarily completely wrong: fragments of rationality can intervene to arbitrate the clash between cultures. When the two partners have agreed where the keys should be kept, for example, the one who fails to respect the agreement feels a sense of inferiority and is usually reluctant to discuss the matter. But most of the time the inner conviction of possessing the universal truth is based entirely on a personal approach, which is no more legitimate than that of the opposite side. Hence the endless discussions, mostly falling on deaf ears, about the advantages of one technique over another. And the acute sense of irritation, intensified by the conviction of being in the right. Lamia is deeply exasperated because, after years and years, her husband still does things wrong and refuses to change his ways. She has taken on the role of teacher and nags him constantly. I questioned her to find out if she ever has doubts concerning the validity of her efforts. None whatsoever. 'I think I am in the right and that he's completely out of touch with practical matters.' Nor is she entirely in the wrong, particularly in the context of their arguments about driving. 'In the car, my husband has absolutely no sense of direction and insists on going round the block ten times rather than listen to me and taking the right route (and I know that I've got a very good sense of direction because I've proved it to him I don't know how many times on our trips abroad). His attitude really makes my blood boil because not only do we waste time but we also use twice as much fuel. Yet he can't stand me saying anything about it and complains that I'm telling him how he should be driving.' But her meddling has the opposite effect from the one she intends: her husband becomes tense and refuses to change a single iota. The same applies to the issue of the towels and tea-towels, another ongoing battle. Lamia just cannot understand that her husband lives in a different universe from hers, where things are neatly put away in separate categories. 'When my husband walks into the kitchen and sees a spill that needs clearing up, he grabs hold of any old tea-towel or cloth to wipe it up. Now as it happens I've got hand towels, cleaning cloths, and sponges, and all of them have a different function. More often than not, he grabs the best tea-towel (which happens to be the first thing he sees) to wipe up some drops of oil or ketchup or some sticky mess whereas I would have used a sponge (easily washed afterwards). I spend my time explaining to him that I don't want to stain my nice tea-towels with dirty stuff and that a sponge is there for that very purpose, that it makes extra washing for me and that sometimes I even have to boil the tea-towels to get them clean. He doesn't take any notice and does exactly the same thing on a regular basis. The same with the bath towels which he uses indiscriminately to dry his face or to stand on when he gets out of the bath and there's no bath mat!!! I find that scandalous because we've got perfectly good bath mats and if there isn't one there, all he has to do is go and get one or else ask me for one.'

Each person clings to their own way of doing things as though it were the only way possible, anxious to try to convince the other whenever an argument breaks out. In this context the claim of rationality is massively deployed to throw the adversary off balance. Sadly, more often than not, it is a relative and partial rationality, to which the other person, equally adamant, retaliates with similar arguments of their own. Isabelle eventually came to the realization that she was not right in any absolute way but was simply seeing things from a particular viewpoint. A first step towards wisdom. 'Our stumbling block is quantity: I'm really careful about the price per kilo, or metre or litre, depending on what it is, and I won't buy something that costs 2 euros a litre in a little bottle if I can get it for 1 euro in a big one, especially if it's something that won't go off. I'm a great one for bulk buying. My beloved cannot understand this obsession and will buy a single packet of washing powder on the grounds that he only needs one, not three of them. It's something we fall out about regularly: he goes on about having to store bulky things, and I go on about saving money, and the worst of it is that we're both right in a way because we've got a small flat and low salaries, so we need to save both money and space. We end up taking turns to give in: sometimes it's me with a tear in my eyes putting back the super-cheap pack of twelve packets of biscuits, and another time it's him moaning like hell as he tries to find a place in the store cupboard for the ten cartons of fabric conditioner I bought on special offer.'

Dissonance

Two opposing views separate Isabelle and her husband. They cannot agree on the subject and this dissonance is a source of mutual irritation. For half a century, particularly following the pioneering research conducted by Leon Festinger (1957), social psychology has found more and more evidence to demonstrate the extent to which 'cognitive dissonance' is unacceptable for the individual (Poitou, 1974). A series of laboratory studies have demonstrated that the introduction of an idea in conflict with a pre-existing ethical or behavioural pattern leads to a situation of psychological discomfort which forces the individual concerned to somehow or other absorb the dissonance, even at the risk of lying to themselves. This is because one over-riding imperative dominates the quest for the truth and filters everything to its advantage: the unification of the self (Kaufmann, 2004). Many of these studies are both extremely convincing and limited in certain aspects. Too often they consider dissonance as an exceptional situation, whereas in fact it is an integral part of ordinary life. And they give too much emphasis to rational arguments and conscious ideas. Yet the irritation produced by the conflict over the shopping between Isabelle and her husband occurs in an everyday context. Although irritation is always caused by a dissonance, it is only in rare circumstances that this is based on explicit ideas with a rational foundation. Most of the time it arises from conflicts between underlying behavioural patterns in an unconscious or scarcely conscious model, these conflicts operating on a number of very different levels (reflex gestures, intuitive idealized models, etc.).

The irritated person does not undertake a detailed analysis of the reasons for irritation; he or she is suddenly in the grips of an emotion sparked off by a trivial incident, sometimes simply driven by the need to let off steam. Between the objective nature of the gap between the two positions (already very difficult to establish because of its extremely complex nature) and the question of precisely why irritation suddenly erupts, the link is sometimes tenuous. Even if dissonance always lies behind irritation, it does not in itself explain why and how this is triggered. Couples are perfectly conscious that they go through all sorts of very different phases, marked by emotional atmospheres conducive either to irritation or to its suppression. All it takes is the slightest feeling of fatigue for the squidged tube to turn into 'the straw that breaks the camel's back in a life already overburdened with drudgery' (Isabelle). All it takes is 'a bad day at the office' and a tantrum from her two-year-old daughter for Caroline to lose control. 'Then I really lose it in a big way – I'm looking for a fight as a way of letting off steam in actual fact.' All it takes is the threat of an imminent visitor for Yannis's wife to undergo a total metamorphosis which turns the atmosphere electric. 'Last Friday one of her friends was supposed to be coming round to take her shopping. But, before the friend arrived, she's completely "beside herself" because the house is "a tip" and needs to be tidied from top to bottom. At which point, I'm not joking, she goes ballistic and nothing is safe: books, CDs, socks, jackets, bags, empty cups left next to the computer or on the living room table, toys our daughter "forgot to put away herself", etc. Personally I couldn't really care less, but well, to keep her happy

110

and for the sake of "a quiet life" I agree with her and let her have it her way . . .' Fortunately the change of atmosphere can also be more positive. Caroline, for example, contacted me after a peroid of silence with this explanation: 'For the last few months, my partner hasn't irritated me at all, and I mean that, because at the moment we're on a kind of high where we just feel really close and tender and romantic (even if at times I feel like strangling him, as usual!).' For Malvina, the switch between war and peace follows a regular pattern. There's the happiness of autumn. 'Because he's away a lot at this time of the year, so he doesn't get on my nerves as much.' And the much more difficult periods such as the summer holidays ('Top of the irritation charts ever since we first met!!!') and Christmas time ('Where the notion of the perfect Christmas sets the bar very high in terms of harmony; I've never managed to live up to it'). Contexts associated with happiness are all the harder to deal with when happiness is absent. Irritation will out, come rain or shine.

— 5 —

THE WIDER PICTURE

A gesture, a word, fail to live up to our expectations and we are suddenly overwhelmed by a negative surge of emotion, sweeping us out of the couple, into a universe where the self finds itself alone once more, secure in its certainties, reviving forgotten guidelines from its past. The partner becomes the enemy of the moment, usually for a relatively short period of time, before the contrite return of the temporarily irritated party to the conjugal fold. As though nothing had happened. Such is the basic schema of ordinary irritation. But the repetition of the event, the intensification of such emotional outbursts, the words let fly in the midst of the crisis, can lead to all sorts of wider repercussions, which add new modalities and dimensions to the negative feelings. While continuing to crystallize in more or less the same manner, irritation can in these circumstances find itself expressing many other things.

Family baggage

Often provoked by something perfectly trivial, the feeling of irritation originates from the multiple confrontations between the rival schemas which constitute the couple. 1 + 1 = 4. Four . . . or eight, or sixteen or even thirty-two! For, in addition to a long personal history, the loved one brings with them a whole collection of unknown people who are part of their lives. Work colleagues, friends and 'a whole troupe of uncles, aunts, brothers, sisters-in-law, cousins by marriage and grand-parents. You might as well accept once and for all that not all of these are going to like you' (Isabelle). And, by the same token, that we are not necessarily going to like all of them either. Alain is exasperated by the invasion of photos of his family-in-law on the little table in the living room.[1] True, he has made his own little statement on another table, with his display of bonsai plants. 'Yes, that's me. I like designer stuff. Chinese stuff as well. And I like Japanese art.' He has no objection to Béatrice displaying her own tastes, as indeed both of them do on the big shelf unit with its extremely ecumenical collection of things. Unfortunately, the little altar of icons is less about personal tastes and more to do with an ostentatious and, in his view, immodest, unappealing and extremely irritating parade of relations who have no right to be there. 'Displaying them like that when people are coming!' (Alain). All of which is even more irritating since Béatrice takes delight in vaunting her aristocratic connections, making him feel inferior by comparison. 'In fact I come from an aristocratic family.' Without meaning to, she uses her family origins as a weapon. 'I like it. And what's more I'd like to display a lot more photos; of my grand-parents when they were young for example, whole walls covered in photos' (Béatrice). She dreams of a new and much bigger table for her display, covered in a cloth with a flounced border. Just like her mother's which she admires so much.

Clearly the greatest threat comes from those closest and most likely to exercise an influence over the couple: the parents-in-law. 'Is there any point in bringing up yet again the inexhaustible subject of mothers-in-law? They never fail to irritate, they are invasive, prone to preach, they poison the atmosphere, they criticize everything and are frankly unbearable' (Isabelle). Isabelle exaggerates – not all mothers-in-law fit her description. Clotilde Lemarchant (1999) has even highlighted the very close bond that can form between daughter-in-law and mother-in-law, sometimes even to the detriment of their own families. In three out of four cases, relationships are neutral or even good. In the remaining quarter of cases, however (which includes Isabelle's), they are indeed particularly sour. The most important element in the face of this new source of potential irritation is the couple's capacity to negotiate. In our society, where relationships with relatives have become increasingly a matter of choice, it is unusual for a couple to have exactly the same relationship with both families; in most cases they feel closer to one of the two. This privileged position emerges as a result of a long process of adjustment, through the medium of ordinary conversation (Berger, Kellner, 1988), in the context of the quest for conjugal unity and concerning all aspects of private life: their general moral code, their way of speaking or of

---

[1] Comments recorded and quoted by Monique Eleb (2002).

conducting relationships, the food they eat, the decorative style, etc. Even their attitudes to order and cleanliness. Remember Agnès and Jean, for example, with those shirts ironed at the last minute and the buttons which were forever coming unstitched. Agnès begins with a sweeping attack. 'My mother would never have tolerated an untidy room, whereas in his house, they just closed the door on it, you see!' Killing several birds with one stone, she exonerates poor Jean, whose disastrous family background has done him no favours, takes the opportunity of re-stating the main principles according to which their own household is run, and finally attempts to steer the couple towards a privileged alliance with her own family. Initially Jean seems to be launching a counter-attack along much the same lines. 'Agnès is a bit . . . well; she gets it from her mother too. She's kept that habit of being a bit obsessive, if you know what I mean! In her mother's case it was very, very restrictive.' But then, quite unexpectedly, he continues with an extraordinary about-turn. 'I could never have lived with someone who was completely untidy, someone incapable of running a household.' Jean is caught in the crossfire. Secretly he thinks Agnès's domestic standards are disproportionally high and resents her criticism of his parents' attitude to tidiness. But in a more concrete and practical way, though still very much in a position typical of the supporting role, he now wants a well-kept house, neatly ironed shirts, buttons properly sewn on. For better or worse, he has therefore taken his wife's side (even to the extent of criticizing her for her shortcomings with regard to his shirts), while attempting nevertheless to soften the criticisms aimed at his upbringing. Conjugal unity, in favour of Agnes's family against Jean's, is therefore only superficial. At the slightest crisis, moreover, the system of alliances is turned on its head: at the height of his irritation, Jean went off to get his buttons sewn on by his grandmother, the paragon of all virtues.

'Mummy's boy'

Nowadays, setting up as a couple is a progressive process, with a shared system taking shape over a period of time as the two love-birds gradually shake off their links with their respective families. Holding onto these links is, moreover, often a form of personal reassurance and a way of controlling a commitment they are not yet entirely sure about. When such resistance goes on for longer than is considered acceptable by the other party, the family tie can be perceived as an obstacle, in direct competition to the relationship itself. Men in particular (once again, acting like children) sometimes appear to favour their mothers over their wives and partners. Pénélope is extremely exasperated. At thirty-one, her husband (three years her junior) allows his mother to refer to him as 'my baby' without a word of protest. 'My husband is an only child, so he's her "baby": she said as much to him last time we went to see her. I'm fed up of my mother-in-law talking to her son in front of me as if I wasn't there: if mummy's little boy wants some wine, I'll order him some, if mummy's little boy wants to go on holiday" And what about me? Will mummy's little boy be going on holiday on his own?' Especially galling is the fact that this intolerable familiarity goes hand in hand with vicious attacks on the daughter-in-law. 'Because I've put on weight, she says to me: "Yes, you'll have to be careful because it runs in your family", in other words because my mother is practically obese: that's really charming!!! Next time I'm going to tell her my family is just as good as hers. She's constantly trying to undermine me. Luckily my father-in-law sticks up for me. In fact I don't know if there really is a good solution to the problem of an over intrusive mother-in-law (because that's exactly what she is). They make out to be all sweet and kind and then suddenly they lash out at you (I play a game now. It's called "cutting remark of the weekend": when we go there I just wait for the inevitable cutting remark to be made). It was the same with the jokes I had to put up with when we were about to get married: she was always saying to my future husband: "You can always change your mind you know . . . " Anyway, I'd really had enough of it so I looked her straight in the eye and I said: "I can change my mind too you know." She didn't like that much, but apparently it was supposed to have been "a joke". Funny how she didn't find the joke funny when it was turned on her. . . . It's like that all the time. . . . She's weird, really sweet one minute, then suddenly incredibly hurtful. Once she gave me some perfume and when I'd thanked her because I was really touched and I thought it was really kind of her, she said: "Oh well, I thought I might as well give it to you as anyone. . . ."'

Pénélope is developing techniques for getting her own back now and is especially keen to persuade her husband to stick up for her against these outbursts of misplaced maternal affection, and aggression towards her. When they are safely alone together, 'baby' seems to be on her side. 'I'm worried about the effect all this will end up having on us. My husband is kind, he says he loves me, that he wants to have a baby with me and that his mother has always had a habit of making a fuss over nothing.' Sadly, in the presence of the said mother, it is another story altogether as he fades into the background,

115

abandoning her to face the dragon alone. 'I constantly have to spell it out to my husband to get him to step in on my behalf instead of standing by while his mother treats me like an idiot.' Irritation breaks out in all directions. The game of alliances that will determine the future is not yet cut-and-dried. At this point in the crisis – open warfare between daughter-in-law and mother-in-law – we are beyond the limits of irritation *stricto sensu*: Pénélope quite simply hates her. It is nevertheless an interesting example in that it demonstrates the extent to which rifts provoked by certain members of a partner's own family can have repercussions on the couple themselves. Pénélope hates her mother-in-law and adores her husband. Unfortunately, 'baby' cannot quite bring himself to cut the umbilical cord and the feebleness of his reaction is beginning to seriously irritate her. The issue hovers over them, as yet unresolved.

Irritation provoked by families-in-law generally follows a typical cycle. It is potentially at its strongest in the early days, during the period of mutual adjustment, an adjustment rendered many times more complex by the confrontation between these two sets of relationships. It begins right from the very first time they meet: when the intended partner is introduced to in-laws, who cannot help secretly exchanging some commentary on his or her odd ways (Cosson, 1990; Perrot, 2000). Yet, at the same time, irritation is relatively easily kept at bay at this stage thanks to the intensity of the emotions associated with the period and the constant evolution in the guidelines for this new life together. Certain irritations do nevertheless emerge, in a variety of different contexts. Malvina, for example, suddenly discovers a different Richard, seen in the context of his family, someone intent on resisting the whole process of conjugal socialization. 'When we were first together, we were constantly getting on each other's nerves and it was to do with the fact that we were spending one weekend in three at his parents' place. On his own "territory" he's completely different; the only thing that matters is what his mother and his friends think.' Malvina begins her commentary in the past tense and ends it in the present. She would still like to believe that his behaviour was a feature of his age, something which would gradually change with time as the relationship became stronger; hence that first phrase in the past tense. Sadly, after four and a half years together, she is forced to admit that the way things are now is the way they are likely to stay: Richard shows no sign of changing. Thanks to his family or his friends, he even goes out of his way to seek situations allowing him to express other facets of his identity. The couple struggles to take precedence. Carla, on the other hand, in spite of the serious irritation she experiences, is in the early stages of a cycle which promises the possibility of a more positive outcome. 'Luckily, this tendency to consult his mother about certain things, or to ask his parents for their advice, seems to be wearing off as time goes on. After all, we've only been together for six months and before that he had never lived with anyone. So I think he sometimes just needs a bit of reassurance from the person who's been beside him all his life: his mum.' Carla does not have any particular issue with her mother-in-law who is very kind and considerate towards her. The difficulty comes from 'J-P'. Perturbed by the shock of being confronted with a whole new way of doing things as he embarks on the early stages of the relationship, he clings to the values of his own family as a reference point, giving them a symbolic value and at the same time holding up his mother as a perfect example in contrast with the critical view he takes of Carla. In her description, the latter emphasizes two aspects (mutually linked) which she finds particularly irritating about 'J-P': his lack of confidence and of consideration, and his 'almost "instinctive" reflex to ask for his mother's opinion. I think that's the worst thing, even just thinking about it makes me feel annoyed. I remember one day when we were at his parents' place. He asked me something to do with a recipe. I gave him the answer and he immediately asked: "But are you sure?" (which was already irritating enough in itself because if I'm not sure, I say so). "Yes, I am sure" I said. At which point he got up and said, "Hang on, I'll ask my mother." For a start, that shows his lack of confidence, but on top of that there's that insistence on seeking confirmation from his mother, which I find intolerable. It makes me feel jealous as well as annoyed. Jealous of his mother, of how much store he sets by her advice and the fact that it means much more to him than anything I say. I hold it against him, against both him and his mother (who I admit has done nothing). I know that when something like that happens, I'm no longer the person at the centre of his life, the one everything revolves around. I am quite possessive and jealous, I know that, but for me there's nothing worse than being compared and contrasted with your partner's mother. Sometimes, for example, in much the same way, I'll be cooking something and he'll say, "No, that's not how my mother does it", or recently I was hanging out the washing and he said: "My mother hangs it like this and it's better because then it's easier to iron afterwards." At which point, even though I knew what he was telling me was actually right, I just said: "Fine, but I do it this way!" And I didn't take his advice (because it was effectively his advice but if he hadn't mentioned the bit about his mother doing it that way, I would

117

have followed it). Yet I adore his mother and we get on well, only that's not the issue, it's far more complicated than that. I want to be the only woman in his life, or at least the most important one, the one who comes first, even in little things.'

For Carla, the main source of irritation comes not from the clash between two different cultures, but from another dissonance, contrasting her notion of a relationship – based on confidence and mutual respect and, while not excluding others, heavily weighted in favour of the two partners – with the reality of being forced into rivalry (unfavourable at that) with another woman. She and her partner are divided, hopefully only provisionally, by two very different underlying approaches to the relationship. Most cases of irritation associated with in-law issues involve these two aspects: the clash of cultures and preference in terms of relationships. The conflict over the right way of doing things (which applies to the most diverse aspects of daily life) is the most frequent of these, but generally gives rise to relatively discreet irritations. Rivalries with other relationships outside the couple, however (where an emotional closeness, in itself perfectly legitimate of course, is felt to be in competition with the conjugal bond, sometimes even to the extent of sharing intimate secrets), although less common, are also far more dangerous. Especially when a son is unable to detach himself from his mother, and exploits the complicity between them as a way of criticizing and distancing himself from his partner.

The crucial element in such cases is that there should be a sense of progress. A bond between mother and son may indeed be important in the early stages, for example, where she continues to do his washing even though he is already living in a couple (Kaufmann, 1992). But a readjustment of the priorities between relationships generally follows, in a series of stages, using those very feelings of irritation to regulate and define the new system on which the couple's relationship is based. The couple then enters the second and usually much calmer phase in its cycle, following on from the feverish initial period of adjustment, and before attention has had time to focus on the presence of certain constantly repeated irritations, which can sometimes prove oppressive and lead to renewed tensions. Now it is precisely at this critical point that in-laws can re-enter the dance and fan the flames still higher. Hence, this rough rule: when dissonances are small or well managed within the couple, relationships with the in-laws are relatively free from irritation; as soon as more substantial rifts become evident, on the other hand, the cohorts of relatives turn into the rear-guard of the battle zone and end up supplying the

118

front-line with ammunition, inflaming the conflict to such an extent that it will subsequently be extremely difficult to negotiate a peaceful resolution.

A context of open warfare, fortunately relatively rare, provides the opportunity for a better understanding of how dissonances are interwoven in normal circumstances. The couple and the two families are engaged in a constant drive to stifle irritations and to confine them to just a few anecdotes; in ideal circumstances, these can even be a source of amusement at times. In fact, laughter features quite frequently in relationships with in-laws, in a double-edged humour which conceals all manner of discreet messages (Jonas, 2006). Beneath the superficial tranquillity and good humour, however, all kinds of fine-tuning and adjustments are constantly being made. Alliances and misalliances, proximity and distance, attraction and rejection, all changing on a daily basis, both within the inner circle of the couple and in the wider circles of the two families. Both circles function in a tight interdependence. It takes only a single incident to occur somewhere in this vast interactive network and a whole string of repercussions is potentially set in motion.

Take the case of the Tinsarts.[2] They have recently celebrated their twenty-first wedding anniversary and things are generally positive, even if the impact of routine has to some extent weakened the bond between them, as is the case for many couples (Duret, 2007). She finds herself having to patch up the slightest rifts because the pressure exerted by her mother-in-law threatens to exacerbate them at any moment. The mother-in-law phones them constantly, keeping a close eye on everything the couple does. 'You didn't mention that you were going there. I phoned but there was no reply.' She has even been known to make the 200 kilometre journey from where she lives in order to check on things with her own eyes. 'The fact that we use our free time to see other friends didn't go down very well, because that was time we should have reserved for her. It was something she felt she had a right to.' As a result of these unwelcome intrusions, discussions raged between the two of them, and, on his wife's instigation, the husband finally intervened. 'My husband told her: "It's that or nothing!"' The mother-in-law backed off, but only temporarily. Adopting guerrilla tactics, she prepared a more discreet form of counter-attack, summoning her son to tell him secretly all her negative thoughts about her daughter-in-law. 'I found this mummy's lap-dog attitude very hard to take.' Sharing confidences is a crucial

[2] Comments recorded and quoted by Clotilde Lemarchant (1999, pp. 154–5)

element in the definition of emotional priorities: her husband's reconciliation with his mother was a direct attack on the relationship. Which is why, when the mother-in-law announced her intention of moving to live nearer them, she threatened her husband with divorce if he did not take a firm stance. 'Oh, no! That would have been the end! Just think! It's bad enough with her 200 kilometres away . . . So if she was two blocks away, you can just imagine what it would be like! Oh no! There's no denying it, sometimes I get so stressed over it, I feel as if I'm suffocating. It gets to me, it really does! I keep saying: "She'll drive me mad!" Poor Mr Tinsart, caught in the crossfire, seems finally to have come down on his wife's side, against his mother. So when the latter, during a recent visit, found fault with the way they stored things and started to re-arrange all the kitchen cupboards, Mrs Tinsart, beside herself, demanded that her husband make the seditious creature put everything back. Which is what happened.

Life is not all plain sailing for the Tinsarts. But there are worst cases than theirs, far worse. When the rift forms within the couple itself, for example. Whatever unwelcome intrusions they may have to put up with from their in-laws, the couple can always protect each other, provided they are united. When a serious split exists between them, on the other hand, the slightest little provocation from those around them can aggravate their problems. Especially if the husband deliberately plays on his loyalties in order to attack his wife. Things have improved for Cindy since they moved away from their respective families. She was at the end of her tether. 'It meant I could escape from my clinging, nosy and invasive in-laws, from the six years of sitting through meetings where my husband told them everything that happened in our private lives leaving me feeling humiliated (he still tells his mother everything).' Sadly, he has become even more distant from her, especially since he bought his motorbike. An extreme solitude ('I'm miles from anything, I'm bored, and it's deadly') has taken the place of the tense relationship with the in-laws, whom her husband visits from time to time, usually on his own. As he did soon after buying the infamous motorbike. 'Little mummy's boy needed to show off his new toy. So off he went on Sunday morning to show his motorbike to his mother. Straight after breakfast, he turns round and says: "I'm going to show the motorbike to my mother, straight there and back, do you want to come? I'll be back around 1 o'clock." As I'm not specially keen on my mother-in-law who makes a big fuss over anything new, I didn't go with him and he ended up being away all day and leaving me on my own: morning, lunchtime and afternoon, without a word to say he'd got there safely. My sister-in-law phoned to say she'd invited him to stay for lunch. . . . They must have had a great time! It's incredible how that family manages to make you feel like an intruder!'

'That slut'

It is time to return to more common forms of irritation. Fortunately, such cases where open conflict with in-laws is capable of leading to the break-up of the couple are extremely rare. Much more common are situations where a superficial tranquillity is secretly subject to infinite numbers of tiny frictions and continual readjustments. Discussion between the two parties is fundamental in such circumstances. The deepest secrets must be shared only within the confines of the couple; the (secret) criticism of friends and family is a way of defining the terms of their conjugal unity. The shared universe is built and re-built on a daily basis (Berger, Kellner, 1988). In the presence of others, however, this preferential regime becomes much harder to manage. These people are, after all, close relatives too, they are loved (at least by one of the two). 'What get's on everyone's nerves is when someone in the family attacks and our dear partner acts as if nothing has happened, or even springs to the defence of their clan' (Isabelle). Clearly, extreme caution and diplomacy must be deployed in order to protect the essential (the couple) while at the same time remaining open and attentive to one's family. Often this means being able to spontaneously improvise the constantly changing conditions required to maintain a united front. Yet the two partners do not necessarily see eye to eye in such circumstances, each tending to have a stronger attachment to members of their own family, no matter what strategies may have previously been agreed on in conversations within the couple. Isabelle keeps a watchful eye on her husband, wary of his fine words. Even though he claims (in the privacy of their private conversations) not to think much of his sister and to consider her 'useless' in all sorts of ways, he changes his tune dramatically when Isabelle oversteps the line and pours insults on 'that slut'. A ritual in the form of a verbal jousting match has long been established between them, one which has an element of humour at times, but also the tensions arising from the delicate process of maintaining the balance between proximity and distance in relation to those around us. 'I've got one sister-in-law who I always refer to as "that slut" or something even fruitier, but I know that my darling doesn't have a particularly high

121

opinion of her, and thinks she's pretty useless in many ways. Basically it's become a sort of private joke between us with him pretending to be offended and me laying it on even thicker. But it doesn't stop me going with him to spend New Year with "that slut", complaining the whole way about how much I hate it, how she doesn't even have a job yet still insists everyone brings some food, that it's disgraceful, I've never seen anything like it, and so on blah, blah, blah. . . . In fact I get it all off my chest so that when I come face to face with the slut herself I can be perfectly pleasant and good tempered. By moaning about it beforehand, I manage to preserve some semblance of respectable hypocrisy which is really important. If you said exactly what you thought about everyone, all those family meals would end up in complete punch-ups. So far, I've managed to refrain from giving the slut the slap she seems to be asking for. My dearest turns a deaf ear at times. He knows that if I've barked loudly enough, I won't bite.'

The adjustment is all the more delicate to operate in that it is not simply a straightforward balancing act between two clearly separate worlds: the couple and the two families. Today, family ties are no longer institutionally imposed but are increasingly a matter of choice: close bonds or hostilities between individuals develop freely, close relatives cannot stand each other, genuine affection is felt between in-laws. All of this, although it tends to alleviate head-on tensions, maximizes the potential for the formation of complex and subtle alliances. The result is fewer full-scale pitched battles but more irritations, infinitely variable and constantly changing. Zoé gets really annoyed when her husband licks his knife in front of her, before plunging it back into the butter dish. She could have extended her criticism to her in-laws since their table manners are certainly very different from those she was exposed to during her own childhood. But, surprised by the violence of her own reactions in the face of his uncouth behaviour (in a fit of rage, she puts his socks in his coffee cup), she sometimes finds herself questioning her own upbringing, with an increasingly self-critical eye. 'My father impressed certain principles and good manners on me so deeply that it was as though there was a little omnipresent censor hovering over me, ready to tap me on the head anytime any of the rules were transgressed. I tremble at the thought!' And what if the truth were not after all somewhere between the two, she finds herself wondering, between my excessive rigour and Charles-Henri's laid-back approach (nevertheless still intolerable)? In contrast to what those violent reactions of hers might imply, she is not seeking to form a privileged bond with her father, guilty as he is of having imprinted on her conscience this 'little censor' which makes her so strict. She is undecided. And any such doubt or division, whether about individual, conjugal or family issues, is a potential source of irritation.

The process of regulating the preferences and the interplay between the couple and the family takes place on several levels at once. Each person, individually, works on it in secret. Sometimes with criticisms more virulent than any they would express openly. But sometimes the opposite is true: Zoé keeps her doubts (about herself and her father) to herself, she does not tell Charles-Henri that she is closer to him than he thinks when she puts his socks in his coffee cup. In the broader context of the various family circles, the union of the two partners is also much discussed, often critically (not for the pleasure of criticizing or out of pure unkindness, but because a critical view of those close to one is a fundamental element in constructing a shared world). At the heart of this vast system of mutual evaluation (between the secret thoughts of the individual and the commentary of the wider family), the couple itself defines its own strategy with regard to the degrees of proximity or distance to be observed. Conversation between the two partners is the keystone of this whole architecture of family links, the element that holds everything in place, through the ongoing process of establishing unity. The couple must be vigilant. While giving free rein to the expression of their feelings in making the readjustments needed to establish new and sometimes unexpected relationships, they must guard against the ever-present threat of the formation of opposing family camps, more powerful than the conjugal bond, at the very heart of their daily lives. Clémentine and Félix did not see the danger approaching. But it will be hard for them to forget what has been said loudly and clearly. 'Recently he's really irritated me because I'm not allowed to make any comments about his father and mother. When my mother gets on his nerves, he'll say: "Your mother is a pain." But if I have the misfortune to say his father is "a bore" because he keeps repeating the same things over and over again, Félix will say: "My father may be a bore but your mother is a pain, so you see . . . " And that irritates me because I'm the first to admit it about my mother and I don't see why he can't do the same about his father!!'

It is in the third phase of the conjugal cycle of irritation that the real danger lies. After the frictions of the early stages, quickly forgotten in the excitement of desires and absorbed by the new and rapid changes in their lives, after the stability and calm of the subsequent phase, the obsessive fixation on some seemingly recalcitrant attitudes provokes a resurgence of sporadic irritations capable of causing rifts. At this point, the in-laws can often provide an unending source of material for criticism. Very occasionally this manifests itself in the form of a full-frontal battle like the one between Clémentine and Félix. More often the process is an indirect one, operating by means of hints, discreet harassment, thinly disguised smears. Then a small tragic event occurs which can extend the impact of existing areas of irritation. Without either of them being fully aware of it, the partner has aged, their physical traits have altered. The couple has moved on from the improvisations of the early days and is firmly installed in domestic normality. At this stage it is not uncommon for resemblances between the partner and one of their parents to become apparent, and these are all the more noticeable because they are backed up by memories evoking the parent in their younger days (photos in particular). Families take great pleasure in pointing out such resemblances, which, although sometimes positive, are more often unfavourable. Beyond the purely physical aspects, cultural characteristics, attitudes and habits that have survived from one generation to the next also emerge and open up new avenues of irritation. Clémentine is alarmed by what she discovers. 'I'm convinced he wasn't so irritating at the beginning of our relationship, that he did at least listen to what I said!! But I think he's a bit like his father, he likes to lay it on a bit, just for his own pleasure. I wouldn't go so far as to say that irritation is hereditary, but they do say like father like son!! And god knows, his father can be irritating, almost intolerably so, the way he always has to be in the right. That's so annoying! And Félix, my beloved, sometimes behaves a bit like his father which means he becomes irritating too!! I'm not sure if it's age that accentuates irritation or just the length of time we've been together.' That character trait identified in the other family becomes a kind of obsession, pretext both for all manner of simplifications (everything bad can be imputed to it), and for confusions and unfair generalizations. As Erving Goffman emphasizes (1975) with reference to stigma: a person with the slightest handicap or disfigurement can find himself accused of all manner of evils. And most importantly, uncertainty can then take root, with the result that it is harder to identify who is actually being criticized (the father or the son, the mother or the daughter). Jean is a past master in the art of blaming his mother-in-law as a roundabout way of influencing Agnès. We have already seen that, trapped by his own inconsistencies, he is hardly in a position to openly criticize her over-zealous attitude to housework. But he has noticed that she does not object when the same criticism is targeted at her mother.[3] As a result he seizes every opportunity to exploit the presence of this intermediary to say what he cannot say directly to his wife's face. Which means he can have his say without saying it too overtly, thus gradually strengthening his position. He is unaware that all this is only possible because Agnès has chosen to let him get away with it. Which is probably just as well, in that it has given him an opportunity to build up his seriously weakened self-esteem. He had felt completely undermined by the ridiculous and pointless crises over shirts and buttons. Such humiliations, and the hostile laughter that always accompanied them, had become the hardest thing to take, the very nub of irritation.

Inattentiveness and humiliation

The couple work on the construction of their unity day by day, listening to each other and developing a sense of mutual trust and appreciation. In the aggressively competitive and fragile world in which we live, it is a haven of reassurance, of comfort and of renewed self-esteem. Provided, of course, that the partner is supportive and enthusiastic. At the table, for example, each recounts the little problems of their day, pouring out his or her woes into the sympathetic ear of this unconditional support. The slightest lapse in this duty is perceived as an extremely severe betrayal.

The first level of betrayal takes the form of simple distraction, an insufficiently attentive ear, or the systematic refusal to take the partner's opinion seriously. 'My husband has no sense of direction and yet he refuses to listen to my suggestions when we're going somewhere he hasn't been before. What irritates me most is the way he pretends not to have heard me, and does the opposite to what I tell him.' Lamia is convinced he behaves like this on purpose, with the deliberate intention of disparaging her. This kind of personal attack exacerbates irritation, especially when it results in genuine domestic catastrophes. 'We moved into a house with white tiled floors. After a certain time, with wear and tear, the tiles didn't look quite so pristinely white, pretext for the almost daily insistence that they needed "cleaning with hydrochloric acid", which I firmly resisted. I did, however, plan to clean them properly but without using hydrochloric acid. When I

---

[3] Jean does not know this, but Agnès fantasizes about a different kind of life, where having a tidy house is a thing of the past: her mother is therefore a reminder of her current alienation.

came back from a holiday at my sister's, imagine my astonishment when I found all the metal in the house corroded, and some of the tiles missing. My husband and the acid had done their worst . . .' It is of course difficult to know if the husband in this case was really acting out of a desire to belittle her or if his action was simply a consequence of the usual clash between two conflicting approaches. Similarly, it can be difficult to interpret the behaviour of someone who is fundamentally absent-minded. 'My husband is extremely absent-minded and I find that really irritating.' Gally finds herself wondering about his behaviour. 'He forgets the same things all the time and I sometimes find it difficult to believe that he isn't doing it deliberately. (But why deliberately? Surely not for the pleasure of seeing me fly off the handle. So it must be that he is genuinely absent-minded.) Here's an illustration of what I mean: before going to bed, Akira always goes downstairs to smoke a cigarette in the living room. We've got an arrangement whereby he opens the window while he smokes so that the house doesn't end up smelling of smoke. Four times out of five, he forgets to close the window before coming back upstairs. And the next morning it's freezing cold in the living room. The annoying thing is that if I ask him if he's closed the window, he says he has. The worst of it is that he genuinely believes he has closed it. And that leaves me not knowing where I stand: if I thought he was just saying "yes" for the sake of peace even though he knew perfectly well he hadn't closed it, I'd get angry about it. But the fact is, he really believes he has closed it. The gesture is so routine he can't be sure if it's something he's just done or something he did yesterday. What can you say??? But still, when I find that wretched window open, I feel like giving him a good shaking as though he was a naughty child.' At one level she is inclined to accept that this is simply the way he is, different, an intimate stranger 'who lives in a world of his own', someone who specializes in 'higher things' while she deals with everyday life. 'Akira doesn't get involved in all the little things I call "humdrum reality".' But at another level, this convenient absent-mindedness works in Akira's favour, ensuring him a comfortable position of power from which he can ignore Gally. 'If I dare speak to him, he literally moves away so as not to hear me.' He remains resolutely deaf to her demands. 'I feel rejected on a personal level and also in my role as *alter-ego* within the couple.' She suspects that, in fact, he is not quite as absent-minded as he likes to make out but is exaggerating a facet of himself, for selfish purposes.

Difference is not to be condemned in a relationship. On the contrary, it can play an important part in the construction of a system of complementary roles. Furthermore, the character traits each partner has acquired from their cultural heritage are so deeply rooted that it would be unrealistic to think they could one day be altered. Each therefore endeavours to keep in check the sterile little irritations which inevitably result; the couple is a school of tolerance. If Gally knew for certain that, even with the best will in the world, Akira was incapable of changing, she would probably suppress her irritation. But she remains unconvinced and there is growing evidence to support her doubts. Alice is in the process of carrying out a similar investigation: is Aziz purely and simply absent-minded? Conscious of the fault himself (or else deliberately exaggerating it?), he has got into the habit of relying on her by asking her to remind him about all sorts of things. '. . . . he says in the most serious tone: "Tonight you absolutely must remind me to call my dad, do a virus check on the computer, etc." Which Alice duly does. 'When he asks me to remind him about something that's important to him, I feel as though I've been assigned a special task, that I'm responsible for whether he remembers to do it or not, and that makes me feel important. It's a role I take seriously.' Sadly, Aziz has grown accustomed to being in the agreeable situation of being able to call upon this additional memory as and when he wishes. 'And then when I duly remind him that evening he just says: "Oh, yeah, I'll do it tomorrow." Because unlike me, he systematically forgets everything (I'm a kind of "second memory" for him) and then when he reacts as though it wasn't really that urgent after all, then I must admit I feel like slapping him in the face because it makes me feel stupid for having made the effort of remembering to remind him about something, for thinking I was somehow indispensable because when he asks me to do something he knows I won't forget about it. He relies on me so he can chill out himself because he knows he can count on me for that sort of thing. Then I feel angry and I hate feeling like that, so I end up really resenting him for a while (for me that means a few hours!).' The causes of irritation overlap and accumulate until they end up erupting in an emotional outburst. The absent-mindedness in itself, already irritating enough, is exacerbated by the breakdown in the way the couple's roles function (difference is acceptable when it helps to found such roles); Aziz takes liberties when reminded of what he has to do, despite having explicitly asked to be reminded. His behaviour is contradictory. Yet this internal contradiction does not provoke any sense of personal dissonance (for him these are simply two unrelated episodes), since by switching off mentally, he has transferred the effects of this dissonance onto Alice, who finds these two incompatible versions of Aziz extremely aggravating.

127

But even more aggravating is a final level of irritation. She took his request seriously and was fully committed to it. By turning a blind eye to this romantic self-sacrifice, Aziz ignores her efforts and her very existence. A humiliation which brings an even more painful emotion into play. Trapped into making this unacknowledged sacrifice, Alice swears she will not fall for the same thing next time . . . even though she senses intuitively that this is by no means certain. A new internal scar, a new source of irritation.

Irritation always arises as a result of a dissonance between two conflicting schemas, whether these are about ethical standards, behavioural guidelines or personality structures; the couple multiplies the potential for disagreements (1 + 1 = 4). At first sight, inattentiveness and humiliation do not belong in the same category, their place being more akin to disenchantment and dissatisfaction. However, as our research confirms, the negative feeling experienced also takes the characteristic form of irritation, albeit a particularly painful irritation. For dissonance is indeed present. First of all, because the various forms of humiliation and rejection tend to make people turn in on themselves (André, 2006), a withdrawal which potentially threatens the stability of the couple. Then because the gap between the ideal and the reality continues to widen. Love and dreams are confronted with the unshakeable mediocrity of reality, which sends out shockwaves in the form of all manner of disagreeable internal vibrations. Particularly when it comes to one specific aspect of this ideal: the need for support and recognition of oneself by one's partner, without which true love cannot exist, and the absence of which constitutes a major cause of divorce for women (Francescato, 1992). This is why Gally and Alice are conducting their inquiries: they need to know if there is indeed a dereliction of this intangible principle of the romantic pact. Yet it is not always easy to see clearly. Carla, for example, is not sure where she stands. 'J-P' is attentive and knows how to make her feel appreciated and supported at crucial times. But why these sudden ridiculous humiliations in the supermarket? 'He asks me if I've weighed the fruit and vegetables so I say, "Yes, I have", and then he checks in the trolley to make sure I really have done it. It's exactly the same when it comes to turning off the gas, locking the door, etc. I hate his attitude to me at such times, it's awful. He trusts me when it comes to the big things (like doing well in my exams, or the fact that I was brilliant in an interview), yet when it comes to the little everyday things, he completely undermines me. I don't understand this difference in attitude because in my view if he can't trust me over something trivial, how is he going to do so when it comes to more serious matters? Whenever

128

it happens, I make a point of commenting on it. And I think what gets to me most about it is the fact that he checks things right in front of me! He could at least wait until my back was turned, but no, for him there's nothing at all offensive in behaving like that, whereas for me it's both hurtful and extremely annoying!' The conclusion Carla eventually reaches is clear, a little too clear in fact. She agrees that his actions are indeed purely a result of the conflict between their different attitudes, the confrontation with his absurd obsessiveness giving rise to a new source of irritation (replacing the initial feeling of humiliation). 'It has to be said that he is a total perfectionist and tends to be quite stressed, and he assures me, for example, that, even if he had weighed the vegetables himself, he would still have checked. Which only half consoles me, because I must say this tendency of his to challenge everything, to check every detail, to think of all possible eventualities, even the most unlikely ones, before he does anything at all, irritates me terribly. There are some situations where spontaneity is really important and wanting to plan everything just spoils things.' She is left undecided: what if this trivial little matter in fact revealed a whole new side to his inner thoughts, one in complete opposition to his fine words? What if the scene in the supermarket revealed a hidden truth? One element in particular troubles her: the scene takes place in public, whereas the fine declarations are made in private. Especially since, in another semi-public context (within 'J-P's' family), he spontaneously takes his mother's side and ignores her opinion. Carla's two sources of irritation (his obsessiveness and his tendency to side with his mother) both point to a lack of trust in her. She expresses this with considerable clarity in this Cyrano-like tirade, in response to one of my questions. 'On the subject of feeling irritated by the fact that he defers to his mother, yes, I have told him how I feel. A mixture of feelings. Resentment: "It's crazy that you always have to have your mother's approval!" Anger: "It's terrible that you can't trust me." Cynicism: "You're right. Everyone should always seek their mother's opinion!" Or sometimes I end up just sighing to myself.' Carla is anxious to restore her injured pride and her sense of equilibrium over this notion of trust: 'J-P' needs to learn to trust her, and he needs to start to trust himself, to trust life. 'Returning to the example of the fruit: when he asks me if I've weighed them, I say, "Yes, I have". And when I see him checking, I say, "But why don't you have a bit more confidence in me since I've told you I have weighed them?" I say that in quite a calm tone of voice, perhaps with a kind of despairing smile.' She has decided to take a stand against 'J-P's' anxieties and his obsessive need to check everything, which fuel his lack of trust in her. 'That reminds me of something that happened recently. A week ago, we realized that we'd lost a key-ring with two keys on it: the one to the door leading to all the cellars and the rubbish chute (we live in a flat) plus the one for our own cellar. We tried to remember when we'd last used them and realized that he must have left them in the door which leads to all the cellars. My reaction was: that's OK, I'll go and see the caretaker tomorrow, he's sure to have the keys, whoever found them would have handed them in. His reaction was: "Don't you realize, we're going to have to pay a fortune for a locksmith, our cellar will have been broken into and everything will have been stolen! Our insurance will refuse to pay, because we left the keys in the lock . . ." I said to him: "Trust me, there's no need to worry, we'll be laughing about it tomorrow." He lost sleep over it, and I felt sorry for him because he was so upset but mostly I felt irritated by his tendency to exaggerate everything. The following morning, I found our keys which were still in the door! I said to him: "I hope that will be a lesson for you for the next time." But the only reply I got was a mumbled "Mmm" which wasn't very promising.' The battle is by no means over (though Carla did manage to stop 'J-P' from going down to check in the course of that evening). She now has a course of action which restores both her sense of harmony and her self-esteem.

Refusing to listen or, worse, disparaging or running down the partner, painful enough in private, becomes utterly intolerable in public. How can someone continue to engage wholeheartedly with the complex task of constructing unity when the person they love lets them down in front of other people? Lorenzo feels betrayed. 'When we're having dinner with friends she has this way of just dismissing anything I say with a wave of the hand ("He likes to exaggerate, he does it all the time"). What annoys me is the fact that she belittles what I have to say on the pretext that she knows me "too" well. To give an example, if I complain of having some kind of pain, she stops me in my tracks by saying: "Oh don't listen to Lorenzo, he's a complete hypochondriac." Or, if we're discussing music or films: "Yes, but of course Lorenzo is only interested in stuff which no one else has ever heard of" (in other words, stuff which only he would be interested in and which is therefore uninteresting).' Most disturbing of all is when a particular context of the relationship reveals a new side to the partner, in which he or she begins to resemble a complete stranger, even to the extent of speaking out in an unpleasant way, and giving voice to opinions very different from those expressed in private. In such circumstances, the partner is doubly dissonant: first, by his or her flagrant duality, and also by their failure to conform to the conjugal ideal. But when, in addition, he or she cultivates other bonds to the detriment of the couple, apparently oblivious in doing so to the very person whom love entitles to every consideration, then the internal resentment reaches a peak. 'My beloved is always telling me about some amazing super-cool guy: and he says this, and he thinks that, and he agrees with me on this or that subject. What do I care? Each time it happens I have to put up with several months of euphoria during which time this guy is always right, and always has to be consulted about all sorts of things that are none of his business. And that really irritates me. OK, so he wants to show off in front of the guys he works with, but it's just so annoying!' (Isabelle). The first person who comes along has no right to take the place of the privileged partner. The couple has its rules (mutual support, putting each other first), which should not be lightly broken. Especially of course when the friend who is attracting the loved one's attention turns out to be of the opposite sex. 'The question is: why do I have to put up with the grim early morning face when madam then spends an hour putting on her make-up so she looks nice for what's-his-name in the office? I'm not suggesting anything is going on between them; it's just the contrast between the two different faces that's striking. The miserable face for me, the colours and smiles for the others. It feels a bit as if the world has been stood on its head and I just find it immensely irritating! Especially when it turns out that some handsome bloke happens to be on the scene. From what I've read it's men that are supposed to be like this, seducers through and through and all that. Well, I can tell you now that women can be just as bad, and that it's extremely irritating for the poor husband' (Markus). Extremely irritating too for the poor woman (Zoé, for example) when it's the man doing the strutting: 'as soon as there's a female present he starts to strut around like a cockerel!' Or when the way he looks at other women fails to respect the precedence of the romantic bond between them. 'What irritates me is the way he admires in other people – particularly women – things that he can't stand in me, like dynamism, enthusiasm . . .' (Fidelia).

Dissatisfaction

With inattentiveness and humiliation, we enter the world of conjugal dissatisfaction, often closely linked to irritation and yet clearly distinct from it. Irritation is a precise mechanism, resulting from the unsuppressed dissonances which arise even in close and happy couples.

Caroline withdrew from our research because the relationship had entered a particularly loving and tender period, 'even if occasionally I still feel like strangling him, the usual stuff eh!' The most severe manifestations of irritation often take the form of sudden emotional outbursts. Dissatisfaction on the other hand works in the opposite way: secretly but insistently, by a process of detachment and internal collapse – the private world ceases to have any meaning. It sets in, for example, in the normal wear and tear of life as a couple (Duret, 2007), undermining the bond between the two people and widening the gap between them (Francescato, 1992). As such, dissatisfaction provides an ideal breeding ground for new sources of irritation, in the same way that the tedious repetition of unresolved irritation can gradually lead to dissatisfaction. The two processes merge and feed off each other, dragging the wretched couple down into the depths where repeated crises drive out love. Unresolved irritation can indeed be a dangerous thing.

Malvina is irritated to the extreme. She finds almost everything Richard does irritating and hateful. She delayed living as a couple for a long time, afraid of losing her autonomy and being relegated to a subordinate domestic role. Richard had made her all kinds of marvellous promises, subsequently quickly forgotten. She now finds herself living in exactly the kind of nightmare she had feared. Trapped, with no hope of escape, her sense of dissatisfaction is all the greater in that her situation is not due simply to the wear and tear of everyday life, but because she has been manipulated and betrayed. Yet, in her statements, she speaks more in terms of irritation than of dissatisfaction, and this gives grounds for a little ray of hope. For irritation at least gives off a certain energy, albeit of a negative kind (whereas dissatisfaction tends to be depressive), motivating the individual, driving them to find solutions. Hard as it will be to achieve, Malvina still hopes to see things change.

Irritation is ambivalent in relation to dissatisfaction. True, it generally tends to accentuate it in the long term. But, in the short term, it can also provide a means of expressing negative feelings, liberating some of the accumulated resentment in the process and even occasionally opening the way to positive solutions. On the issue of the TV remote, Caroline makes a distinction between the norm (Marc keeping it in his hand all the time he is watching TV) and the unacceptable excess (when Marc puts it in his pocket while he goes to the WC). The first of these leaves her with 'a constant sense of dissatisfaction'. She wishes their relationship was more balanced. Yet this is not something she thinks about all the time – she has got used to it, that's simply how life is for them now. The unforgiveable excess, however, shakes her abruptly out of her conjugal torpor; irritation revives her expectations. Enough is enough. Marc shows no consideration of her own wishes. The crisis brings out all her hitherto buried thoughts and words. Couples usually sense when a feeling of irritation is linked to an underlying sense of dissatisfaction, and tread carefully in consequence. For, although it may indeed have the power to facilitate free expression, irritation can also aggravate dissatisfaction. Conversely, they also sense when irritation is completely detached from any underlying problems and is purely a way of letting off steam. Not that this makes it any less irritating. For in such a case the two protagonists can wage their minuscule combats with no holds barred. 'I'm particularly irritated by my partner's untidiness. She leaves all sorts of things lying about on the table, whereas I like it to be kept clear, and she leaves her socks lying around in the bathroom for days at a time before she gets round to putting them away. The thing is, I'm quite a tidy person, though not obsessively so, and it's not as if she is completely disorganized herself. I think that's what gets on my nerves, the fact that these are little things which could easily be dealt with: it's not as if it would take a superhuman effort to put the newspapers in the same place each time, or to throw a bit of paper away once she no longer needs it. So why not just do it? That aside, I must point out that these little irritations never get out of hand. We have a really good relationship, and if anything were ever to threaten it, I'm pretty sure it wouldn't be anything to do with that' (Gautier).

Disgust

Irritation can become part of this dangerous evolution which causes it to take root in the critical depths of dissatisfaction. It can also, by a process of crystallization, take the particular and very challenging form of disgust. Nothing could be more damaging to love than this detestable emotion. Yet typically it manifests itself, often in a localized way, in situations involving some kind of physical intimacy, either enforced or unwelcome. In bed, in the bathroom or at mealtimes. Mealtimes, an unexpected conjugal challenge, are incontestably number one in the hit parade of off-putting little habits. A long tradition means that this situation (sitting opposite each other for a relatively extended period of time) has been handed down to us from an era where communication between individuals was not what it is today (Kaufmann, 2005). Today's couple has to be able to sustain this face-to-face encounter. The principal tool for this is conversation, also a means of establishing a common culture. But this is rarely absorbing enough to shield the two individuals from the rigours of this face-to-face observation. Noises and mannerisms, which elsewhere would have simply caused the classic feelings of irritation, in these circumstances provoke the much more disturbing sensations of disgust. Sometimes these incidents occur only infrequently, never- theless provoking strong reactions; witness the little slurping sound Nicole's partner makes with his mouth, which drives her mad. 'He makes too much noise when he's eating. Although he eats slowly, he chews his food carefully, breathing heavily at the same time and making this little slurping sound with his mouth. It's worse when he's tired because then his mouth and eyes start twitching. That really gets me. If I'm eating at the same time, I don't notice so much but if I'm not eating, it really exasperates me and if I start to feel annoyed I have to leave the room because he can see in my face that it's really getting on my nerves.' Sometimes the feelings of disgust are more generalized and ongoing. Since she first experienced the ordeal, Jade has built up a store of detailed observations which enable her to paint this impres- sively clinical picture. 'My boyfriend eats really quickly and hardly even lifts his head between mouthfuls. Sometimes he'll push his food around with his fingers a bit, or hold his fork like children do when they're first learning to use it, or like country people. He often licks his knife and then wipes it on his serviette (which is OK when it's a paper one, but not when it's a proper one!!!): pure elegance! He brings his knife up to his mouth when he's eating a bit of cheese. However, I'm relieved to say, he doesn't eat with his mouth open. Another big thing is that he makes a lot of noise with his cutlery and when he pokes his fork into a piece of food you'd think he was going to make a hole in the plate. He makes a lot of noise when he drinks as well, and blows on hot food even when it's not necessary. It's as though he sucks in his food, rather than eats it properly. I find it hard to enjoy mealtimes because it's as though he's not really there, as though he's physically but not mentally present and I'm on my own. It's supposed to be a convivial time, but I dread it. I've told him how I feel and we've dis- cussed it and he says he's trying to do something about it, that things will improve. But his efforts are short-lived and then he gets angry. Every day I find myself thinking about it, questioning my own reac- tions. Try as I might I just can't get rid of these feelings of irritation. When I watch him eating, it really disgusts me. I feel as if he's about to bring his food up onto the plate with all the belching and hiccuping that goes on. Yet my boyfriend's really good-looking, he dresses well, and he's attractive to women, but there you are.'

The systematic and detailed nature of this description implies that a new level has been reached. As in the link between irritation and dissatisfaction, the problem is not so much the localized manifestation of disgust but the way it gradually spreads, until the entire relationship has been contaminated. Significantly, Jade is still haunted by what she witnesses during mealtimes when she gets to bed: 'Those feelings of irritation caused by disgust affect desire. I need to be seduced by my partner. In those circumstances I find it really difficult to forget how he behaves, that complete lack of refinement. That puts me off and then I need to wait for a while before I can get myself in the right mood. I'm really worried about this relationship; to be honest I just don't know how I'm going to deal with it.' Such an outpouring of disgust is, fortunately, unusual. For, in this area, even more than with classic irritation, feelings can be suppressed, either in the course of everyday conjugal life or in brief magical interludes of loving complicity. Small potential causes of disgust are only observed vaguely, from a distance, and, even more importantly, are quickly forgotten in the course of events. A fundamental aspect of the art of living as a couple is the ability to compartmentalize and isolate negative feelings. Remember the case of Melody, also irritated to the point of disgust during mealtimes when 'HE' wipes his plate with his bread 'like . . . someone with a floor cloth!' 'Yes', she admits, it is indeed a 'put off'. But the negative effects of the incident 'rarely last more than ten minutes'. By the time Melody is ready to cast a loving glance at her man, they have completely disappeared. 'For me the two states are completely separate. It's hot or cold, never warm. I either reject my man, or I'm all over him.' This succession of biographical sequences, each characterized by their frankness, explains why the bed is so rarely cited as being associated with feelings of disgust. It has too many romantic connotations for this to be the case – any such feelings are quickly suppressed. Mealtimes, on the other hand, are ostensibly perfectly banal occasions (though in fact they involve the head-on collision of two private worlds). Which is why those little outbursts of disgust crop up there so freely.

Pathological irritability

Irritation is an extremely precise social mechanism which occurs at the point of contact between two individual cultures. The two protagonists remain unaware of the differences between these cultures despite the fact that it is these that give structure to their most everyday gestures. Nothing could be more normal in the life of a couple, even if the potential link with growing dissatisfaction can occasionally lead to a more dangerous situation. In some cases, moreover, carefully handled minor irritations can provide an opportunity to clear the air, to re-establish psychological equilibrium and to bring into the open matters which are usually kept secret. But it is also true that the emotion released on such occasions can sometimes become uncontrollable, reaching a crescendo with shouts, objects being broken and even, in the worst cases, blows being struck. When it comes to these extreme cases, where straightforward irritation transforms into violence, we are straying slightly outside our subject in its strictest sense. The couple is a complex and delicate mechanism which intrinsically produces the dissonances causing irritation to occur. But the couple and the way it functions does not explain everything. For some people start out on their relationship already riddled with irritation, provoked by all sorts of different reasons: social, psychological, physiological. Here are some examples, though by no means an exhaustive list.

The list would have to include drug addicts who had been forced to give up their habit abruptly, or 'borderline' personalities. Take this short statement from Cali who self-harms. 'I'm twenty and have lived with my boyfriend for two years. I've got a problem: I'm always on edge and some time ago (about a year) I self-harmed whenever things weren't going well (mostly when I felt annoyed about anything). I managed to stop, but the trouble is that now I'm tempted to start again. I'm really struggling to get a grip on myself, I don't know what to do and my boyfriend doesn't know about it.' Or this one from Jennifer. 'I'm on the verge of an emotional crisis with my boyfriend and I don't know how much longer he'll be able to put up with me. I end up shouting so much over the most stupid things that I practically lose my voice! I break things and scratch myself. It's hell!' Mention would also need to be made of all the somatic illnesses which can result in a state of intense and chronic irritation.[4] I will confine myself to those conditions of chronic inflammatory intestinal diseases, and notably chronic ulcerative colitis which is particularly unpleasant. Patients are in such pain that they lose their self-control and are subject to bouts of extreme irritability. Olivia tries to be sympathetic.

[4] It is probably worth pointing out at this point that the term irritation (*agacement*) first appeared in around the sixteenth century, in medical treatises, and was used to describe the state induced by toothache.

'I don't want to upset anyone, but I need your help or some answers to the following question: are all chronic ulcerative colitis sufferers difficult to live with? For the last few years I have lived with my boy-friend who suffers from this condition, and on a number of occasions his bouts of chronic irritability, obsessiveness and intolerance towards me, brought on by his bouts of chronic ulcerative colitis, have led to violent disagreements and even break-ups. . . . And it doesn't get any easier as time goes on. I don't know how to react, what to do when he has one of his "crises". I can sympathize with his illness, but when it reaches a point where he starts throwing crockery around, I must admit I'm not sure if I can continue to cope with the situation.'

Such extreme (and dramatic) cases are not, however, unconnected to the subject we are dealing with. True, the potential for anger is far higher than average and is affected by factors which have nothing to do with the relationship, sometimes with extremely damaging results. But the mechanism itself functions in an identical manner. The triggers in particular, tend to be concentrated on micro-differences, disagreements over how something should be done, objects out of place. 'I fly off the handle every five minutes. But what's happened is that recently I've "finally" noticed and "finally" understood that I'm getting worked up over nothing. . . . and when I say "nothing" I mean something like a single plate left in the sink, or not being able to get through to someone on the phone . . . I'm sick to death of it!' (Alex). In many situations, apart from those genuinely chronic cases, being part of a couple in reality merely draws attention to, or accentuates, an irritability, even sometimes a violent streak, which already existed (Séverac, 2005). It simply exacerbates the risk of explosion.

Aggravating social circumstances

Equality does not exist in the face of irritation. Even though the mechanism which produces it is common to all, individuals vary (depending on their biological make-up, their personal histories and their psychological profile) according to how prone their personalities are to react to irritation. In addition to this bio-psychological diversification, the effects of the context in which each exists must also be taken into account. People use a range of techniques to deal with irritation, many of which are notably improved by the use of various means, both cultural and financial. Elements as diverse as money, living space, degree of comfort, access to good-quality leisure activities, professional motivation, a wide range of interests, etc., can all help to avoid or mitigate the onset of irritation. Conversely, anything which exacerbates fatigue or limits opportunities, forces people into uncomfortably close confrontation or threatens loss of self-esteem, logically tends to make those affected more vulnerable to dissatisfaction and to outbursts of anger. Here, for example, is the sad history of Raf and Dolorès, more eloquent than a long treatise on the subject.

Raf had experienced a divorce and unemployment in quick succession. Just when things seemed to be at their worst, an unexpected fairy tale seemed at last to bring some light into his life. 'I went through a phase of having various short-term relationships (lasting one or two months) and then I quickly realized that this kind of relationship wasn't really what I was looking for. I'd always dreamt of finding a nice, reliable woman to spend my life with. And suddenly there she was, and at last I'd found my soul-mate.' Sadly, the social destiny of those accustomed to hardship dogged the young lovebirds. 'Financial difficulties, or problems relating to her ex, who at one stage threatened to kill himself (to make himself look like a victim in other words). Then she lost her job too, and when she eventually found some work it turned out to be with some really crappy company, with the result that we're now in an absolutely dire financial situation! And I've been struggling to find a job for more than a year and a half now.' Raf feels 'weak, tired and fragile. I was staying positive for both of us, but now I feel at the end of my tether.' Worst of all, things are starting to go badly between them. At first, the struggle against adversity had brought them closer. But now the endless succession of empty and unhappy days has ended up destroying the bond that held them together. 'What's more, our finances are so tight, we can hardly do anything and I feel useless because we can't go out or enjoy ourselves or have any kind of spontaneity in our lives. So we often end up having to stay in and face this grim situation, stuck at home all weekend. I hate that because I'm not at all the stay-at-home type; I like a bit of adventure, surprises, a life lived to the full and all sorts of other things we can't do. Which is why, for the last few months, we've ended up having rows and falling out all the time.' Raf still clings to his dreams, imagining how things could be, of life as a perfect couple. He knows Dolorès has similar dreams. Sadly, dreams aside, as their relationship continues to decline, things are becoming increasingly tense between them with more and more rows breaking out. Both of them wish they could love each other. Instead, everything irritates them. 'I should add that we've both got really fiery tempers which we've tried to keep on top of but during this tricky period, even with the best will in the world, it's pretty difficult to keep all our worries under control. Tempers flare very quickly and we both end up getting carried away, which ends up wearing us down and making us feel really fed up although in fact we love each other very much. Sometimes it really feels as though it's affecting our health, and we're worried about whether our relationship can survive after everything we've had to go through. We don't deserve that.'

Part Three

Small Acts of Revenge and Romantic Tactics

— 6 —

COMMUNICATION DIFFICULTIES

An eye for an eye, a tooth for a tooth

The surge of irritation brings with it an irresistible urge to have things out immediately, to yell and shout in order to give vent to all the negative feelings. 'You mustn't keep quiet over everything otherwise you can end up bottling up all your frustration' (Isabelle). Especially in the case of those, like Rosy, who are particularly quick to react. 'I've got a very efficient alarm system which means I can let something go once but after that all the red lights come on. I don't believe in just letting things get worse while I look on helplessly. I have to have it out at once. I'm not the type to think it over – I just act completely on instinct.' Melody does not really fit into this category. Indeed, we shall see evidence of the extremely cunning romantic strategies she comes up with. She is, however, intransigent when it comes to things she finds really exasperating, notably when 'HE' lets her down with his table manners. 'There's no way I'm going to put up with things that really offend me. So I never suffer in silence. It's just a case of being more or less vehement depending on my mood (the worse that is, the less tolerant I am). Afterwards it's up to my husband to make the first step towards making amends, since he is the cause of my disgust! Then it will depend on how deep the rift between us is and how much effort he is prepared to put in to win me over and patch things up between us, as to whether our relationship gets back onto an even keel or not.' Unfortunately, 'he refuses to take things lying down and puts up quite a fight', defending his right to be himself and to be able to relax at home, and trying all sorts of different tactics. 'More often than not, he pretends not to have heard my comments, avoids the question, changes the subject, leaves the room, waits for it to blow over. If I'm

143

in the right mood, I'm not going to let him get away with it as easily as that so I repeat my comments. If the wall of silence continues, then I go for cold war tactics and I opt for the same silence. Without making a scene. We carry on in an atmosphere of pure politeness which doesn't suit him at all. So then, either he comes up with some utterly hypocritical excuse ("Sorry, I forgot! Oh, do you think so? How come?"), or else he counter-attacks ("Well, what about you?"), at his own risk since open conflict can turn very nasty, or else, more often, he goes for some kind of distraction (a compliment, a witty remark) which defuses my irritation, or at least counterbalances the negative effects, even if it doesn't completely get rid of it. If the kids are around, they watch with amusement, waiting to see who gets the upper hand. If the atmosphere is right, they'll join in and tease their father. Otherwise they keep out of it.' They keep out of it because Melody has decided to raise the stakes, giving free rein to her anger in order to wear down 'HIS' resistance and provoke some kind of result. 'When things have just built up to the point of explosion, I'm certainly not going to try and stop it. It takes a huge amount of energy and total conviction to argue with him and persuade him to change his behaviour (the insincerity he's capable of at times makes me lose my temper very quickly). So it's in my interests to let anger get the upper hand. It's the quickest way of getting him to change his ways.'

Not necessarily, or at least not in all circumstances. Anger, deliciously liberating as it can be, is, however, seldom effective. Firstly, because emotional outbursts rarely help to clarify the arguments, given the difficulty in any circumstances of explaining the fundamental reasons for discord. 'The more annoyed we get, the less open we are' (Marie).[1] Such outbursts can even end up making people say things they would not normally have said. 'Every door in the flat bears the scars, there are holes in the walls, we've said the most awful things to each other without meaning to at all, it's a question of who shouts the loudest' (Mimie). And secondly, because anger begets anger, drowning out ideas in the surge of violent emotions. It sweeps the fragile crew into the dangerous world of cruel attacks. 'He threatens to hit me (which has never happened) and says he's going to go out on the same days as me. Voices are raised and things end up being said which are not easily forgotten.' Cassiopée gives as good as she gets. 'I lose my temper and hit him, I scream, I threaten to jump out of the window and count how many more years I've got to put up with it all. I find it really hard not to explode.' The shouting does little to

---

[1] Comments recorded and quoted by Céline Bouchat (2005, p. 80).

clarify matters and even less to bring about any kind of mutual under-standing. Yannis is all too aware of this. Tempted as he is to tell her all the things that he finds irritating about her, he refrains from doing so when he sees 'from the look in her eyes that I'd better not look for trouble'. He only raises his voice, briefly, once the enemy appears to have calmed down somewhat. Lamia too steers away from discus-sions which get out of hand and which 'always lead to arguments' without any concrete results. Irritation comes from the depths of the inexpressible, arising from conflicts between schema which are for the most part subconscious. Which is why it is difficult to discuss them with any degree of clarity, especially when anger clouds the issues. Emotional outbursts do have some advantages. They bring a feeling of liberation to the irritated person: they can even make it possible to discuss hitherto unspoken matters thereby improving communica-tion in the future. But they rarely lead to genuine and lasting results in terms of what caused the irritation in the first place. The follow-ing example from Melody is therefore somewhat exceptional. It is true that her reaction, so sudden and dramatic she did not even have time to feel irritated, was crowned with success. A minuscule success, however, over one very specific gesture, which 'HE' himself probably regretted as soon as he had done it. Melody had prepared a different meal for herself. 'Just as I was starting to eat my salad, HE had the nerve to poke his fork onto my plate like some sort of vulture and snatch some, just like that, before he'd even sat down. I didn't feel the slightest irritation, just a straightforward and spontaneous reaction: if he'd wanted the same as me, he need only have asked, especially as the meal was really delicious. I just came out with it like that and he was forced to apologize. After that everything returned back to normal very quickly.' A Pyrrhic victory in fact. The epic tone and the hagiographical style are in all probability a compensation for all the defeats she has had to swallow over table manners.

Hot and cold

Something or other provokes irritation. Which then ends up being irritating in itself, leading to an internal split within the individual and producing a chain reaction of dissonances: did I over-react in the cir-cumstances? Should I try to be more reasonable or was I right to react as I did? Should I strive for an ideal or just accept things as they are? How is it that the other person, for all their promises, seems so little inclined to change? Thousands of such questions keep cropping up and are destined to remain unanswered. The issue must be discussed. Since shouting, liberating as it can sometimes be, does little to clarify matters, couples try the alternative tactic of discussing the subject in a cooler, calmer way. Eline has been perfecting the alternative technique for some time, having tried the hot-tempered approach to little effect. 'I tend to be quick to react when there's a conflict, and when that happens I'm incapable of any kind of detachment. In the heat of the moment I lump everything together and go for a combined attack, challenging everything, in a dramatic but completely pointless way.' As an alternative, she has developed a tightly controlled strategy of intervention. 'I try not to discuss the issue in the heat of the moment because that would only lead to angry and pointless discussions. Later, I try to find some way of making sure that Jack understands my problem whilst at the same time making it possible for us to discuss things openly so that I can see his point of view too. Of course I'm not saying it works every time! In fact he sometimes accuses me of coming up with a "ready prepared" subject, already carefully analysed and practically resolved. . . . But it does mean that we can often come to a compromise or find a way of solving problems together.' Unfortunately, such rational discussions rarely work in the very specific field of irritation, where the feelings involved are so difficult to discuss that the process of cooling down tends instead to make both parties (and especially the one causing irritation) withdraw into their shells and only half-listen. 'On the other hand, watch out for discreet or apparently restrained comments – they are often the most treacherous. When things are reasonably civilized, it is possible to calmly inform the other person that this or that attitude, habit, way of doing things bothers us ever so slightly. "Please darling, would you mind not putting your phone down on my lacquered furniture because it scratches it. Thank you my sweetheart." And the sweetheart listens with only half an ear. Which is a mistake, because one of these days, he's going to find his phone has been calmly but firmly flushed down the toilet because that's the 2,347th time he's been told the same thing and enough is enough. Make no mistake, patience is not a bottomless pit, and if you're not careful it can dry up altogether, which is often extremely painful because it can seem to happen quite out of the blue' (Isabelle).

Eline manages to get some results by adopting a cooler approach because their couple (in the early stages of establishing their domestic arrangements) is particularly open to discussion. On closer examination, however, it becomes clear that the method is only effective on one side. Jack, less organized (or less Machiavellian) is taken by surprise every time and never manages to come up with any kind of counter-attack. A situation he finds mildly irritating. Although generally fairly placid by nature, he finds he can only get his point across when things reach a critical point. 'Much calmer by nature, Jack tends to put things into perspective more. He won't mention the things that he finds irritating about me unless I blow my top. Take the housework for example. He waits until I start going on about something before expressing his own opinion and explaining how irritating my approach is to him. Then it's up to me to calm down so we can have a more constructive discussion.' Eline, much quicker to react, now tries to steel herself towards a more detached approach which will enable her to put her point of view more clearly, while Jack, more placid (or simply more laid-back), fans the flames a bit in order to be able to have his say. Each in their own way, they manage to juggle hot and cold in such a way that they generally reach an agreement. The most common scenario is summed up by Eline: 'I get angry, Jack gets angry, we calm down, we talk it over.' She gets most irritated and is usually the first to express her feelings, which means that Jack, in turn, is able to get things off his chest. Eline cools down immediately afterwards and sets out the terms for negotiation. 'Naturally at first we both stick to our guns. But since the object is to find some kind of solution, we each end up giving in a bit in order to reach a satisfactory outcome. Not that there ever is a truly satisfactory one: either one or the other of us is frustrated, or we end up with a situation which is vaguely satisfactory for both of us. It all depends on the extent of the irritation and the scale of the outburst. If it's about trivial matters, we usually resolve things fairly quickly. If it's about more important things, it can take several days and all manner of discussions before we come up with some kind of solution.' Even in their particularly open situation, cold-blooded discussion alone is not enough; it needs to be sparked off by an emotional outburst. Yet, since such outbursts cannot be controlled, the outcome is not always the one intended. 'I'm fairly hot-tempered, so we either have a discussion, even if it's not very pleasant and rather heated, or we end up having a full-scale argument with all sorts of bitter and unkind words which generally do more harm than good.' Discussion about the things that irritate us is inevitably a dance around the rim of a volcano.

The language of gestures

Which is why indirect techniques of communication tend to be generally favoured, those that enable (little) things to be said without

147

saying anything too overtly. In particular, by the carefully controlled release of emotions in the form of little comments expressed as
a kind of explosive parenthesis (Kaufmann, 1992). Although the
content of such remarks can be violent, their effect is mitigated by
two characteristics which throw the other party off the scent. The
first of these is the fact that the comments are not addressed to anyone
in particular, but are uttered indiscriminately for the speaker's own
benefit (in a therapeutic sense) and for the attention of the guilty
party, and by extension therefore for the world at large (which, of
course, remains impervious). The partner can choose whether to
respond or not, to hear or not hear, or to half respond or hear. The
second characteristic, even more striking, is that the critical comment,
always extremely brief, has only a short-term impact. No sooner has
it passed the speaker's lips than it is forgotten, to the extent that, even
when pressed to do so, the speaker may refuse further explanation.
Such circumstances allow the adversary no time to adopt an appropriate stance in the face of this minute and unexpected aggression.
A situation which is often mutually beneficial. Nothing need change
and things can quickly return to normal. All that remains is a discreet
trace left in the memory of the person responsible for the irritation,
provided of course they were ready to listen.

Such manipulation of the spoken word requires a certain experience on both sides. For words, once spoken, can at any moment lead
on to a more general confrontation. Even when muttered in a barely
audible fashion. Marc grumbles every time he puts the dustbins out,
because the fact that he is obliged to do this job irritates him enormously.[2] But Marie-Agnès cannot bear to hear this grumbling, which
she in turn finds irritating (since Marc does little else around the
home). Her ears are pricked to pick up the slightest murmur. Many
people prefer to say something without actually saying it in a still
more radical way, avoiding even the few words muttered through
pursed lips. Instead, they express themselves through mime, behaviour or gestures. Later, we shall explore the precious mysteries of
sulking, which in its passive form can be seen as a temporary refusal
to communicate. Our intention here is to deal with the more explicit
manifestations of this form of expression, notably body language and
the manipulation of objects. The paradox is that this method of communication by default, perceived by its protagonists as less risky, is
in reality subject to so much imprecision and misinterpretation that
it can end up producing quite the opposite of the (moderating) one

---

[2] Comments recorded and quoted by Johanne Mons (1998, p. 102)

desired. Yannis, for example, gets very irritated when his partner 'dumps her screwed-up towel on the edge of the bath'. He has told her about this time and time again, not always in the calmest of tones. And her reaction to this exasperation? She sticks her tongue out at him! Realizing that this made Yannis even angrier, she went on to express herself more openly, declaring: 'It won't be the last time – let's hope it doesn't kill me!' (Yannis). A perfectly reasonable comment, all things considered, though a step up from sticking out the tongue, which therefore probably had far less aggressive connotations (no more than gently mocking) than Yannis supposed. The interpretation of the language of gestures varies considerably, depending on whether one is on the side of the irritated or the irritator. The irritated person often thinks they are being less overtly critical by not saying anything. Yet their gesture, extremely irritating in itself, can be taken as an even more violent provocation. Aurore is very irritated by the hair Sonia leaves in the shower and which blocks the plug.[3] She makes no comment, simply leaving the hair in a little pile on the side, a sort of unspoken message whose meaning she feels is extremely explicit. Sadly, Sonia is left feeling unrepentant by the sight of that little pile of hair. 'It just seems stupid to me. People should finish what they've started' – in other words, the hair, once collected, should have been put in the bin. So, next time she has a shower, poor Aurore finds her little pile waiting for her. A thousand times more irritating!

After breakfast, which he has on his own, Pedro puts his coffee cup in the sink rather than putting it in the dishwasher, thus breaking with the family rule Fidelia has established. 'I'm sure he does it 90 per cent on purpose.' As far as she is concerned, the message is clear. 'Generally speaking, the fact that the cup is not in the proper place spells out the message: "I don't do my share of the household tasks. That's a woman's role."' Which irritates her acutely. She even suspects that he exaggerates the gesture intentionally in order to irritate her more. 'It makes me angry because I feel I'm turning into the martyr of the household even though we both work and often I know Pedro's done it on purpose to annoy me – which is precisely what happens!' The gesture, in all probability perfectly anodyne at first, has gradually crystallized into being a powerful message with far-reaching consequences. Sometimes 'a source of amusement when the atmosphere is calm' turns into 'a source of confrontation when the atmosphere is more tense; even the kids know that'. The ritual is always the same; the interpretation is contradictory and changeable.

[3] Comments recorded and quoted by Céline Bouchat (2005, p. 82).

Communication through gestures and through objects, simple and obvious for the person doing the communicating, is not only difficult to interpret (more likely to cause new irritations than to resolve old ones) but also in some cases extremely obscure. Caroline is very irritated by the sight of 'those clothes left lying everywhere' by Marc who has a habit of leaving a trail of items of clothing, both clean and dirty, wherever he goes. She gets her own back in a way she finds highly satisfying because it seems appropriately violent. 'I pick everything up, even if it's clean, and put it all in the washing basket.' Marc cannot find his clean clothes; no matter, he gets out some fresh ones. And Caroline finds herself with huge quantities of washing. Irritation and how we deal with it do not operate within the realm of pure reason.

The use of laughter

The language of gestures, like the little comment, is therefore of limited use. Its effect is marginal at best and it tends to be more about individual therapy than about improving either the relationship or communication. Subtler or less overt forms of speech are more efficient, particularly those referred to by specialists as having 'double meaning' – in other words, those open to two different interpretations. The little comment is already close to this category. The speaker says something, which he or she then immediately glosses over, allowing two possible interpretations. A considerable number and range of variations on this technique are available for couples to use. I have already mentioned the use of indirect criticism, ostensibly directed at the in-laws but actually meant for the conjugal partner. If that person senses they are being targeted, the accuser can quickly beat a retreat, claiming vigorously that their remarks referred exclusively to the in-laws. This is the decisive tactical advantage of using wording which potentially carries a double meaning. A common manifestation of this is to resort to thinly disguised and allusive attacks. A little like the language of gestures, these say something without actually spelling it out directly, and can operate on a number of different levels, even allowing the user to progress gradually to more explicit remarks.

One technique remains, however, more effective than any others, and that is the use of laughter, of humour and ridicule. 'It's really the only way to get something said without causing offence and without World War Three breaking out. But you've got to know how to use it and that's not always easy' (Markus). It is indeed extremely difficult

150

to establish a humorous distance once irritation is in full swing and one or the other party is carried away by negative emotions. The process is more effective for minor irritations (where the successful use of humour can allow other, more major issues to be diffused), or, after a certain lapse of time, when a suitable occasion presents itself. 'When she turns up with all her shopping bags, I don't find it at all funny. On the contrary, I'm beside myself and ready to explode, it's an impossible situation. But at some other time, when we're on holiday or having a drink, the subject will come up by chance and I'll make a joke about it, which gets us in the right mood and makes us both laugh. For example, I might say something about the hundredth dress, which she can't even fit into the wardrobe, and which she will never even wear (that makes her laugh!!). And it ends up with me acting out the scene and saying "Yeah – it's not bad", with an exasperated and helpless expression (which makes us both laugh!!). It's quite surreal really when I think about it!' (Markus). Surreal indeed. For the scene is superimposed onto reality, as though taking place in some other, unreal world, yet where the events and the gestures and even the actors are the same. In this case, not satisfied with simply having a double meaning, the humour parallels real-life existence, presenting an alternative vision of the conjugal relationship. In the same way that certain causes of irritation end up crystallizing into pretexts for letting off steam, this technique of conjugal self-mockery works by turning the spotlight onto certain incidents from everyday life which are then gradually transformed into rituals. Children are often expected to play their part in this little show, where the family takes pleasure in distancing itself from things that irritate them (and which at other times they would end up getting angry over). Children or a wider public. Martine and her husband often pretend to argue. 'Our friends find it funny; they are fascinated when they see us like that. If we've had a few drinks it can get a bit out of hand and then they find it harder to keep up.'

Such a method has multiple advantages. It allows people to talk about things that make them angry yet without saying too much. It shows them how to approach the brink of the abyss without toppling over the edge and gives them the opportunity to practise techniques of self-control and to distance themselves from the sources of irritation. Markus starts telling his stories in order to criticize his wife in a light-hearted way (since he cannot do so directly and in a more serious manner). But, as he does so, he gradually turns the self-mockery onto himself, gently ridiculing the person who says 'Yeah – it's not bad.' In the somewhat fictional world of laughter, they construct a conjugal

151

unity which is proof against irritation and which can be re-used, provided they can keep it in reserve in some corner of their memory.

Unfortunately, laughter is short-lived, and the protagonists are disinclined to remember the instruments of peace when, seized with irritation, they suddenly find themselves at war. Unfortunately too, laughter is not unequivocal. Pleasant and beneficial as it generally is, it can often have the opposite effect and end up provoking irritation instead of alleviating it. It is therefore something to be used with considerable caution. Take the case of Pedro, who, Fidelia suspects, is 90 per cent guilty of acting deliberately over that cup in the sink. Something else irritates her too: he keeps making the same grammatical mistake, confusing the future and the conditional tense, 'even though he knows perfectly well that it really grates on my ear when I hear it'. For Pedro deliberately exaggerates this; of that she is 100 per cent sure. From his point of view, her irritation is ridiculous, especially when he also has the excuse of not being French. So he sets out instead to transform irritation into mockery by accentuating his mistakes in a comical way. But this is lost on Fidelia; she is not amused, not even slightly; these jokes end up irritating her even more. A mistake easily made in what is a tricky domain. Initially, Pedro could easily have made the error of thinking he could transform a private joke into a conjugal one. By persevering, however, he is sending out a signal to say that he is no longer using laughter in the same way: what was an instrument of peace has now become a weapon of war. Laughter shifts imperceptibly from one to the other. Estelle and Julien have taken on complementary roles within their relationship: she is completely laid-back, to the extent that she regularly forgets to lock the doors; he is alert to every possible risk. She has taken to gently teasing him about this, seeing this as part of her role in fact. Up to a point he was happy to go along with this, laughing half-heartedly while she laughed her head off. Until they were burgled, and Estelle continued to make fun of his obsessive precautions. Julien no longer finds it at all funny.

Laughter unquestionably becomes a weapon of war in situations where the irritator appropriates it to exacerbate irritation even further. In the least serious cases, the perpetrator hides behind the mask of conjugal self-mockery, regretting (with varying degrees of sincerity) that their sense of humour is not shared by the partner. But, abandoning all reserves and tricks, he or she can act purely with a view to provoking irritation. Like a small act of revenge, all the harder to combat in that laughter is generally seen in such a positive light. Alice likes to be in plenty of time for the train, but when Aziz is travelling with her he always gets there at the very last minute. Not only does he go deliberately slowly, but he also teases her about her fear of missing the train, mimicking what she says and does. Humour can be very difficult to live with. Jean was intensely irritated by his unironed shirts and the buttons which kept coming unstitched. All of which Agnès found highly amusing. The more annoyed he became, the more she laughed and, even though they now have someone to come in and do the ironing, she still finds it funny. Nothing could be more cruel and irritating to Jean than this laughter, which to him was inscrutable, incomprehensible and gratuitous. Laughter can indeed conceal all sorts of mysteries.

Inside the mind of the irritator

It is indeed a weapon of choice for the irritator (particularly male) seeking to defuse the reaction, coming as it does somewhere between consensual laughter (conjugal self-mockery) and aggressive laughter: the joke as a distraction. The technique is not dissimilar to the little comment made by the irritated person, except that the atmosphere is very different (humour replacing irritability). In both cases the principle consists in introducing some kind of disruption, thus making room for a series of contrasting biographical episodes. The little room voices criticism and then immediately forgets it, returning to a state of conjugal normality. The humorous distraction sets out to achieve the same goal (bringing the episode to a close) but in a different way. The major difference being that, since in this case the initiator of the tactic is not the person experiencing the emotion, they cannot therefore predict if their attempt will meet with success. They try their luck, often muttering their joke under their breath, uncertain whether to commit themselves, even afraid that their humour might be interpreted as an attack. The opponent is tested in order to ascertain whether it is worth attempting to bring the episode to a close by using humour more overtly.

Whether humour is used or not, the irritator rapidly becomes a master of the art of distraction and evasion. Sometimes by choice, but more often simply as a result of the position they occupy within the couple. They are conscious of causing irritation, they sense it, they know it (though not always quite to what extent). They are aware of causing irritation but struggle to identify the reasons for it and, even more, to understand them. Secretly, they disagree fundamentally about the causes of the irritation. Even when an attempt at a change of behaviour is made, under pressure, either to please the partner or to restore peace between them, it is never more than partially successful. Because the implicit memory of the individual is often stronger than their conscious thoughts when it comes to everyday facts and gestures. Between the enemy's protests and his or her own underlying reality, the irritator senses a glaring difference. Sensing intuitively that there is in reality no concrete solution, the irritator thinks, not without a certain logic, that the easiest thing to do is to pretend not to have heard. Or, where that is not possible, to concede (false) promises or to try some kind of distraction. A gamble which sometimes pays off. 'More often than not . . . he tries a bit of distraction (a compliment, a joke) which stops me feeling irritated, without really resolving anything of course, but at least it offsets the negative effects a bit' (Melody). But a gamble which fails when the silence, the evasion, the distraction, the unsuccessful attempt at humour or the false promises repeated for the thousandth time end up provoking even more irritation than the original incident. 'When I reproach him about something, he doesn't even attempt to stick up for himself, he just says, literally: "Yes, it's true, you're right." AAHHGGRR! I never want to hear that phrase again! It would be nice to be wrong occasionally' (Viràg).

Most of the time, the irritator irritates in spite of themselves and is (more or less) genuinely sorry for the irritation they cause. But eventually, this irritation (which they see as being without foundation) can begin to irritate them too. We have seen examples of this where laughter shifts in tone, imperceptibly becoming more conflictual, where the irritator ends up imposing their rhythms and their particular way of doing things. When this happens, the interaction of contrasting roles on which the couple is based can prove explosive as the practical complementarity is transformed instead into so many causes of confrontation. Particularly when the irritator admits to acting deliberately and clearly has no intention of trying to alleviate the irritation. Back to Alice and Aziz catching their train. 'I can't stand being late; I'd rather be early in fact. He's more laid-back. As far as he's concerned, there's always plenty of time, no need to get stressed and rush around, so not surprisingly it's a nightmare when we have to catch a train together. He knows perfectly well that I get stressed on those occasions so he exaggerates by being deliberately slow and saying "I think we're going to miss it." In other words he does his best to make me even more on edge; he pushes me to the limit and thinks that's entertaining. And I must admit I'm an extremely gratifying and easy target in that respect, because I don't just walk into the trap, I run headlong into it. We both know that's the case, but I still can't help falling for it. The worst thing about all this is that we've never actually missed a train. Of course I never have time to buy myself a magazine or something to eat and sometimes we don't end up with very good seats, but we never actually miss it, which is all that matters for him. None of my little "material" and "superficial" preoccupations and demands really count. On the way to the station, up until the moment we are actually on the train, I'm a complete nervous wreck and he just finds it funny because I've got myself into a state over what he thinks is nothing. Once we're on the train, then I feel a sense of relief and I tell him what I think of him, that sometimes I could almost kill him, that he's childish (I should say that he takes these comments as a compliment!). But he's so sweet and he always ends up being so charming (without making the slightest effort) that I end up quickly forgetting all about it. Each time it happens, I vow that next time we'll travel to the station separately, that we'll arrange to meet on the train, but of course it never happens like that.' Aziz opts for conjugal self-mockery (obviously extremely biased in his favour) which Alice partially goes along with. Although following his own preferred approach (rather than seeking any kind of compromise solution), he never intends any real harm and is not trying to be hostile or to get his own back in any way. The playful dimension is very much to the fore; Aziz loves playing games. 'As far as he's concerned it's just a game and I'm the perfect victim because the slightest thing sets me off, I'm just incapable of making allowances, of working out if he's serious or not and, on top of that, my reactions are not too unpleasant as far as he's concerned. I don't lose my temper and I don't stay annoyed for long or make a huge scene about it. So he makes the most of it, especially as he's a great one for a bit of teasing. He loves it.' An additional factor has helped establish the episode as a ritual: Alice is no longer convinced she is in the right. The dissonance, initially between the two of them, is gradually becoming more of an internal conflict, especially in view of her own irritated reactions. 'In fact I don't think Aziz's little intrigues are really worth losing my temper over and sometimes I even find myself wondering if I'm not more irritated by my reaction to events than by the events themselves [. . .] I'm cross with myself for falling into the trap, for not managing to stay calm in the face of what's going on, and that of course is what irritates me most about all this.' For Aziz, Alice's doubts and her increasing tendency to turn her irritation onto herself constitute an open invitation for him to carry on amusing himself in exactly the same way. And if by any chance their relationship ever became more strained (which, of course, I hope will not be the case), he would find himself in possession of a very powerful weapon.

The irritator who acts in full knowledge of what they are doing will not necessarily stop at a little gentle teasing of their prey. They may be tempted to use all sorts of cruel and sadistic tactics as a way of getting revenge for their own irritations and frustrations within the relationship, and even for things that happen outside it. The limit is crossed as soon as he or she starts to take pleasure in the suffering caused, even over the smallest details. Isabelle had exposed the inner lout in her husband and knew that he knew it. 'It was his favourite game: to aggravate and push the other person into a corner.' She would go into the 'blackest rages', and her outbursts ended up paying off. 'He admitted he had a slightly sadistic streak: whenever he sensed a weakness, he couldn't resist putting the knife in.' Clémentine is about to expose Félix in a similar way. 'As he's a terrible actor, I can tell immediately when he's exaggerating' – in other words, when he irritates deliberately, simply for the wicked pleasure of irritating. At this level of non-communication and hostility, the two protagonists start to perfect a whole arsenal of cunning tricks. Beneath life's tranquil surface, in the inmost depths of secret thoughts, many little acts of revenge are brewing.

Secret acts of revenge

Living as a couple does not imply a state of war. Conflicts are the exception rather than the rule, or spread only in extreme circumstances. If I have sometimes used military terminology, or described the partner as an adversary, this vocabulary generally applied to isolated situations, quickly forgotten. For, in ordinary circumstances, conjugal life is dominated by the peaceful quest for unity and harmony. Such harmony, however, although sincere and genuine, does not prevent the two partners from experiencing, with varying degrees of clarity, all kinds of minuscule irritations and small passing moments of dissatisfaction. All of which is perfectly normal. Some people are scarcely or never even aware of these, perhaps because they are so deeply in love they are transported beyond reality, more probably because they choose to suppress any potential source of dissonance. Generally speaking, the situation is as follows: the couple is formed around an infinite number of differences, many of which are accentuated by the dynamics of their lives together (complementary roles). Dissonances are inevitable; it is how we deal with them that varies. We have seen examples of angry outbursts, which rarely lead to solutions being found; we have seen attempts at calmer, more level-headed conversations and the limits of these; we have looked at the language of gestures with all its ambiguities; we have looked at the use of laughter, sometimes effective but also capable of being transformed into aggression. All of these represent attempts to communicate, mostly in an indirect and roundabout manner. We shall now focus on some more implicit and personal methods. One of these featured in an earlier book (Kaufmann, 1992), in connection with ways of dealing with dissatisfaction (which on this point are very similar to those used to deal with irritation). I highlighted the technique of 'secret defection', in reference to Albert Hirschman's classic thesis (1972), in which he identifies three possible responses to annoyance: being openly critical, remaining loyal, and resorting to defection or silent flight. The partner who feels annoyed, irritated or dissatisfied can either say so (at the risk of opening hostilities), or they can suppress their feelings in the belief that their reactions are inappropriate (at the risk of being upset by exactly the same thing at a later stage), or they can seek some kind of secret compensation for their feelings, in order to re-establish their psychological equilibrium. This is the secret defection, which operates on two different levels. At a first level, the irritated party simply notes a number of negative points about their partner, storing them into a very flexible buffer memory capable of being affected by subsequent events (it has the advantage of fading relatively quickly, particularly if the partner then behaves in a more agreeable way: positive wipes out negative and negative wipes itself out provided it has not taken too strong a hold). It is only when the cause of irritation or dissatisfaction is constantly repeated, when there is an accumulation of unpleasant incidents, of deliberate hostility on the part of the adversary, that this very specific memory can no longer be erased. The secret defection then enters a second stage, with the elaboration of specific compensations, devised in secret. The irritated party considers some selfish attitudes, focusing on his or her own desires and interests to the detriment of the couple. The little vexations they have been subjected to are paid for at the expense of the relationship, as they distance themselves and behave less generously to the partner. For everything has its cost within the couple, where so many different currents converge (money, work, feelings, words, offences and caresses, etc.). A cost fixed intuitively, on the basis of a momentary and overriding sense of satisfaction/ dissatisfaction. Often very little is needed to restore equilibrium, the most trivial thing being capable of re-establishing inner calm and bringing the irritated or dissatisfied partner back into the conjugal fold. The secret defection, even at the second level, is not a declaration of war against the couple.

The treatment of irritation differs a little from the treatment of dissatisfaction. The latter, deeper and recurrent, imperceptibly widens the rift between the couple, leading in the worst case to break-up. Irritation, on the contrary, does not automatically jeopardize the bond; acknowledging feelings of irritation and being able to express them can even be a proof of healthy communication between the couple. The manifestations of irritation are, on the other hand, often more brusque and more intense than those associated with dissatisfaction, for irritation expresses itself very quickly in the form of an emotional release. The little acts of revenge provoked by dissatisfaction accumulate inexorably and take root over a long period of time. Those associated with irritation are so impulsive that they are sometimes difficult to keep secret, often manifesting themselves by an action designed to release tension or through body language. Like when Zoé puts Charles-Henri's socks in his coffee cup. Or when Rosy stuffs into Charly's mail-box the clothes he carelessly left behind after a snatched night together (was he secretly hoping Rosy would wash and iron his shirt?). In certain circumstances the irritated person hesitates between a secret act of revenge and a more explicit gesture, since the same behaviour is capable of triggering either of these tactics, so different in the way they are expressed. Pat is extremely irritated that Anaïs refuses to do the washing at 60°. On some days, however, when he is particularly exasperated, he nevertheless manages to keep his feelings in check by plotting his revenge. He says nothing and lets her get on with it; waiting until Anaïs has dried, ironed and put away his clothes. Then he takes them out discreetly, crumples them up a little and puts them back in the washing machine. Depending on the number of items and the chosen method (thoroughly crumpled up and put right inside the machine, or still quite neatly folded and conspicuously placed on top of it), Pat is opting either for a private act of revenge or for a telling gesture. The latter, undeniably aggressive, brings him immediate satisfaction, but at the same time it potentially leads to a dangerous and tiresome series of confrontations. The more subtle act of revenge on the other hand, although less satisfying at the time, allows him to calm down more gradually.

By being cloaked in absolute secrecy, the little act of revenge becomes a strange instrument indeed. All the techniques we have looked at so far have involved a confrontation between two people balancing the preservation of individual distance with their conjugal commitments. Even the worst confrontations involved some sort of communication. Here, on the other hand, a single individual controls the proceedings. Yet without knowing exactly what use will be made of them. Secret revenge is in fact structurally ambivalent. The irritated person uses it as a way of avoiding a confrontation, with a view to restoring an inner equilibrium which will allow them to re-engage with conjugal normality. In other words, although the technique does not appear in a very favourable light, the outcome (consensual and peaceful) justifies the means. Unfortunately, these means, because they procure an unhealthy satisfaction, can at any moment become an end in themselves. The irritated party experiences a certain pleasure without necessarily reflecting too deeply on the consequences of their actions. Alone with their secret, without the constraints (but also the security) of the conjugal rules, it is easy to get carried away. The little acts of revenge turn into gratuitous acts which no longer contribute to the process of conjugal unification. Indeed, they have the opposite effect. In some cases individuals can even derive positive pleasure from manipulating their partner in this way (Picard, Marc, 2006). Remember the scissors, bone of contention between Bernard and Géraldine. In the course of our research it emerged that this was in fact a deliberate gesture, dreamed up by Bernard as an unhealthy revenge for the intense irritation generated by Géraldine's sloppy approach to the laundry. The couple have since separated. Remember Agnès and her curious habit of only ironing the shirts at the last minute in spite of Jean's irritation. In her case, too, our research reveals that this was an act of revenge for a deep sense of dissatisfaction. Out of love, and because he expected her to, Agnès gave up her professional ambitions when she met Jean, taking on instead the role of housewife and mother. A role which brought its joys, but which also deprived her of what had begun to haunt her dreams: the other life she had never experienced. She had not premeditated her actions. On the first occasion, it had happened purely by chance. Nevertheless, she had been quick to observe this ridiculous irritation and had laughed about it. Laughter which, for reasons not altogether clear to her, made her feel much better. More or less consciously, she found herself setting in place the conditions which would allow this ritual to happen again. She had discovered a private vengeance which enabled her to re-establish her equilibrium. For Jean, however, the enigma of his wife's laughter, of the shirts and the buttons was far from soothing! Tempers would undoubtedly have frayed even further had they not hit upon a solution (that of having someone come in to do the ironing).

159

A frequent characteristic of the secret act of revenge is that it takes place in a completely unconnected context (the scissors in response to the laundry, an enigmatic laugh for the sensation of being trapped). The goal is not after all to retaliate (an eye for an eye, a tooth for a tooth) or to resolve the issue, but rather to compensate on some internal level. Malvina resorts to self-mockery as a way of calming herself down. She does not use it when the couple are together, or in her secret thoughts: instead she saves it for when she is in public, recounting the details of their private life in epic-comedy style. Richard's worst misdemeanours are given a new context and are stylishly re-worked in order to bring out their most ridiculous side. Her girl friends are soon in fits of laughter, encouraging her to go a step further, to paint an even cruder picture (to Richard's detriment, of course) and to expose yet more details of their private life. She has taken to addressing an even wider audience. 'I tend to be very open about my feelings outside the immediate family circle, much to the delight of my colleagues. As soon as I walk into the smokers' staff-room (that's where the nicest people are!!), I'm off, recounting my adventures in lurid detail. The fact that they know I exaggerate makes them laugh all the more and for me it's a way of letting off steam when I've had to keep quiet and just let things blow over, because when all's said and done, even if I use all the strategies I've mentioned, sometimes it's still hard not to say anything.' Since she cannot discuss the issues with her partner, she does so elsewhere, and in a manner so lurid and so unflattering to Richard (who probably deserves it) that later, when she has calmed down and is back in her tedious home life again, she is not immune to feeling a few twinges of remorse. This helps her to accept her painful day-to-day existence. In this example, there is at least a link between what happens in private and what is recounted in public – both are based on the same set of facts. But secret revenge can also occur in a radically different terrain, completely unconnected to the original source of irritation. A classic scenario is that of 'sexual self-sabotage', analysed with reference to numerous cases by Helen Kaplan (1995). The need to compensate in one way or another can sometimes result in the partner's demands being met with a less than encouraging response (various pretexts, fatigue, deliberately making oneself unattractive, unresponsiveness), particularly when personal physical desire is somewhat lacking. 'I can't possibly make love to someone who has behaved as though I'd committed a crime against humanity just because I didn't season the salad properly and who regularly forgets to put the dustbin out', exclaims Nathalie.[4] The difference in terms of sexual demand between men and women – with men in general tending to retain a keener interest than women within established relationships (Bozon, 2002) – gives more weight to this kind of secret revenge as far as women are concerned. Coldness in bed can compensate for all manner of disillusionment and disappointment.

The hapless husband is often completely in the dark as to why his advances are rejected, unaware that he is the victim of deliberate retaliation. He can only register his dissatisfaction in secret, perhaps even plotting a compensatory act of revenge himself. Once this stage of sly attack and counter-attack is reached, it is often preferable for a couple to find a way of discussing things openly even at the risk of raised voices and arguments. For the secret act of revenge, a harmless enough therapy in the early stages, causes havoc once things start to escalate. Isabelle remembers those extreme situations where 'we both ended up looking for ways of getting on each other's nerves'. And Sarah is 'afraid of being horrible to Peter, just because he irritates me'. Even though such discussions may not be an easy matter, it is generally preferable to make the effort. It is a process which requires enormous tolerance and a readiness to be open to the other person's view of things. Yannis, for example, is still a long way from accepting that he is not the only one in the right. 'The thing that irritates me most about my partner is the fact that she "forgets" to turn off the lights – or the heating – whenever she leaves a room. So I let slip a little comment along the lines of:"Hey, this isn't the Palace of Versailles!" Or: "When we get the next electricity bill, you can pay all of it!" To which she replies: "And what about you, you leave your shoes all over the place!" And that leaves me speechless, because, as I point out to her, that has nothing whatsoever to do with turning off the lights, and me not putting my shoes away won't have any effect on the bills.'

Looking back over this chapter, I have to admit that the vision I paint of the couple may indeed seem a dark one, given that conflicts, however small, are by no means the norm and violence even less so. Nevertheless this aspect of the subject needed to be dealt with in detail in order to demonstrate just how complex communication can be where irritation is concerned. Now, however, it is time to leave such gloom behind and enjoy the altogether more agreeable spectacle of more constructive attitudes. Such attitudes may arise from the humdrum and repetitive social interaction which the two partners

---

[4] Comments recorded and quoted by Pascal Duret (2007).

willingly embrace, as a way of minimizing emotional friction. Or they may result from interludes of a more magical and romantic nature. But there is evidence too of some more remarkable techniques, these also favouring (for the better, however) secret and very personal thoughts, and it is these which will be analysed in the following pages. Love sometimes grows in strange and clandestine ways.

— 7 —

LOVE'S SECRET WAYS

Minuscule victories

When calm is restored to conjugal life and things return to what is fortunately the usual pattern, the two partners forget about their irritations. They do not therefore profit from this emotional cooling-down period and the opportunity it brings for reflection and analysis to devise useful tactics for the future or to assess and compare different approaches. If they do manage to do so, they generally reach the conclusion that outbursts and confrontations produce little in the way of concrete results. Not that this prevents them from getting carried away all over again the next time angry irritation erupts. 'Because it makes me feel better' (Fidelia). As Melody finds it more and more irritating when 'HE' wipes his plate with a piece of bread 'like . . . someone with a floor cloth', she has made a deliberate decision to be more verbally aggressive in her response. 'I comment on it all the time. For a long time I restricted myself to a discreet little comment, something along the lines of: "That's just not done." But with age (and looks being not what they were) I've gone up a gear, insisting for example on a more healthy diet. So now, as soon as he starts his little game, I say at the top of my voice: "Oh no, not that!" Then I sigh: "Couldn't you at least try to make yourself attractive for me?" HE complies immediately (after many years of experience): "Oh, sorry". But I know he'll start again all too soon, that his greed will get the better of him!' Compared to the cost to the relationship which such open confrontation always entails, any gains can seem extremely derisory (and short-lived). If, however, the irritated party is aware of how resistant and intransigent their partner's behaviour is, they may indeed feel that such gains are in fact less negligible after all. And if, in addition, their efforts have even the slightest effect on their partner, minuscule victories may well serve to diminish their irritation. Many irritated people succeed in calming themselves down in this way, through a process of self-persuasion based on the microscopic gains won in the fight. Take the flowers Melody received on her birthday. 'It took years of reminding him when my birthday was and how much I loved to get flowers. Now HE remembers, which I find particularly satisfying because I know just how hard it was for him to change his ways.' Or, in Isabelle's case, the tube of mayonnaise (as a substitute for toothpaste). 'I'm in the process of converting my favourite squidger to the pleasure of seeing the mayo emerge in a beautifully smooth, regular flow, the moment a little pressure is applied to the tube. Personally I couldn't care less, I hate mayonnaise. He just didn't get it with the toothpaste but at least he seems to be getting the message with the mayonnaise. You've got to be flexible.'

Gally is on the point of obtaining a minuscule victory without even trying. She finds it irritating that Akira refuses to make the slightest effort to participate in any household tasks. Recently, however, now that he has started teaching young children, he has taken to watching closely whenever she bakes cakes, attracted purely by the educational aspect of this activity. But for Gally, this change of attitude is promising. 'It has to be a good sign.' Considering the number of years she has battled over this issue, she is forced to admit the sorry truth that her outbursts have failed to produce any significant result and that she has effectively been hitting her head against a brick wall. Consequently she is now experimenting with some different tactics along more peaceful and secretive lines. 'As far as controlling my irritation goes, I've found the easiest thing is not to pay too much attention to it. I've tried raging and getting angry, to no avail. He's embarrassed, wants to put things right, but never makes any attempt to explain his behaviour. Nor does he promise to be more attentive (at least he's honest). I try and preserve a sense of humour and keep things in perspective (of course it's absolutely normal not to know how to mix the vinaigrette dressing when I've explained how at least twice a week). And the fact that he doesn't react violently means that we can also defuse confrontations: shouting your head off all on your own, as though at a brick wall, doesn't do much good, except maybe to get rid of a bit of your annoyance. So I quickly give up on that. Sometimes I think if I was really on his back all the time and didn't let the slightest thing slip, he would end up changing. But think of the huge amount of time and energy that would take when there are so many more constructive things to be doing. And I hate the idea of having to behave like a proper shrew. So I try not to let myself get in such a state over little things.' She is determined to keep her feelings in check and to put things in perspective, and is developing a self-critical approach to her outbursts, resorting to humour and making the most of Akira's calm attitude. Or else she is trying to convince herself that he is not acting deliberately. 'Especially as his absent-mindedness doesn't just affect me – he's affected by it himself. This morning he was particularly annoyed because he'd poured orange juice instead of milk onto his cereal. And I must admit that when that sort of thing happens, he doesn't try to blame anyone else – it wouldn't occur to him to accuse me of putting the bottle in the wrong place or anything like that.'

The various tactics Gally refers to all have one thing in common, something they share with what we shall now focus on: they reject open confrontation with the adversary, turning it instead against themselves, or at least against that particular version of the self affected by the irritation, a self consumed with anger and locked into the self-centred little world of its own convictions. Such a struggle against oneself is necessary to bring about a change in attitude, and, even more significantly, a change in fundamental identity. Even if the tactics involved seem relatively passive and straightforward, this is no small change but instead a radical about-turn.

The about-turn

Irritation transports the individual into a narrow realm of certainties which construct a clear vision of the conjugal universe: the other person is wrong, irremediably wrong. 'It's also a way of getting back my independence, of distancing myself from the other person so that I can recapture the sheer pleasure of being' (Melody). Once the initial shock is over, the reassuring and stabilizing nature of these sudden flashes of truth can even procure a curious pleasure, especially as the feelings they evoke are comfortingly familiar. The individual becomes his or her old self again, reviving old patterns of behaviour which had been partially forgotten. The purely individual identity is more contained and simpler than the complex and changing role which must be played out within the couple. Most of the tactics we are about to examine, therefore, are aimed at finding ways of escaping from this individual isolation, attractive as it is; the individual must initiate this turn-around themselves (with the help of the various pretexts provided by their partner).

The most visible aspect of the identification process consists in unifying and making more malleable the representation of the self: life unfolds like a story which we can narrate to ourselves. Beneath this smooth surface, however, temporary identifications (immediate, contextualized and operational) function in contrast through constant and abrupt shifts, causing images of self to alternate with contrasting biographical sequences (Kaufmann, 2004). The individual successively adopts multiple courses of action (Thévenot, 2006) and displays varied facets of identity. And it is this sequential pattern which makes it possible for the irritated person to find a way out of the autistic impasse. Whereas they had hitherto clung to those rediscovered certainties which seemed so unshakeable, they now return to a conjugal normality as though nothing had happened. The process follows the same path for the irritator (thus triggering a virtuous circle). Carried along by their established behaviour patterns, they often irritate without meaning to, and are intuitively aware that they have caused upset in the opposing camp. Feeling vaguely guilty as a result, they seek to make up (a little) for their wrongdoing by trying to mend their ways. Repetition of this experience moreover leads them to the realization that this is in fact a very efficient method of drawing back from conflict and avoiding any reprisals. Some even become expert at 'making a conciliatory gesture' (Melody). Like Charly for example. 'When he calls me back, everything is forgotten' (Rosy). Or Marc. 'I'm so lucky. I've got a man who has such an expressive face, he can apologize with just a look when he's gone a bit too far. And then, when he says: "You're right, I'm going to make a real effort", I just melt' (Caroline). Or even Richard, the cause of such acute irritation. 'He's ready to admit his mistakes and generally speaking he's the one to make the first gesture towards reconciliation (I'm sure that's why we're still together). Then suddenly all my irritation just melts away' (Malvina).

Once the worst of the crisis has blown over, the two partners observe each other surreptitiously, seeking a pretext that will help them justify their conversion. In the absence of a spectacular about-turn on the part of the irritator, like that of Charly, Marc or Richard, the most trivial detail may be enough to induce the irritated partner to initiate some almost imperceptible change in their own behaviour, leading in turn to a softening on the other's part, and so on. The return to normal after the crisis is made more manageable by this kind of subtle interaction, where each encourages the other to emerge from their individualistic seclusion. Sadly, in some cases one partner resists or else adopts an impenetrably stubborn air (which is almost as bad). When that happens, the irritated person is condemned to act alone.

When irritation melts away

The simplest tactic is to let the (internal) storm blow over and wait until feelings calm down of their own accord. It is very difficult to define to what extent this perception of a purely natural physical movement corresponds to reality. Certainly, feelings reach a peak at the moment of the initial shock, and therefore logically diminish again afterwards. Melody is not aware of having to put in any particular effort. 'I don't feel as though I'm having to control my feelings. It's more a question of letting things subside naturally, of allowing the disagreeable moment to "melt away".' In that second stage, however, the change in emotional content very much depends on the context of self-perception. A highly critical view of the partner will keep irritation levels high. Any weaknesses in what one autistically regards as self-evident, or simply a less clear-cut or more distanced view of the situation, can, on the other hand, reduce irritation. This is undoubtedly the reason why irritation can sometimes seem to melt away of its own accord, since the irritated person acts without even being aware of it. In a passive and not particularly creative way, he or she simply takes a more distanced view of the facts. Although still conscious of what has irritated them, they are able to distance themselves from it in a way that attenuates their emotional reactions. Yet this is by no means a natural process; the distancing effect is achieved as a result of how the incident is perceived. Witness the fact that this perception can vary if, for example, the irritated person maintains a fiercely critical vision of their partner, in which circumstances the irritation remains very much present. It should not be concluded, by a process of simplification which would be the inverse of the naturalistic concept, that individual perception is responsible for everything and controls emotions in particular. The two overlap and link together closely. The starting point is undoubtedly emotional. It is the irritation in itself that suddenly jolts the individual from his or her normally peaceful and consensual way of seeing things. Emotion and critical vision then unite to forge an alternative identity which is individual, even to the point of being autistic. Then, once the worst of the storm has blown over, the 'melting away' can take place gradually, step by step, in a sequence combining a diminution of emotional intensity and a more distanced and less harsh perception of events. The irritated person is therefore scarcely conscious of making an effort, even less of developing a strategy: instead they are content to allow the turn-around in identity to take place gradually, step by step. Such scarcely perceptible steps nevertheless enable them to completely reverse their position.

Take this sorry tale of the shoes underneath a radiator.[1] Daniel and Christine's kitchen is on the first floor, and both of them keep their outdoor shoes on when they go upstairs, eager to get back to their cosy little home. The shoes are then put under the radiator (where else could they go?) and they can relax in their slippers. As a result, shoes have a habit of piling up in this odd place, much to their irritation. By way of a solution to this, they agreed on an official strategy: they would each take their shoes off in the garage, on the ground floor, where there was a suitable storage place for them. Unfortunately, they continue to go up just as they used to, which means that the sight of that pile of shoes under the radiator is even more irritating, especially to Daniel, who ends up losing his temper at the end of each week. 'We keep piling shoes up under the radiator in the kitchen. And every Saturday I end up shouting about it because that's not where shoes should be kept. I insist on all the shoes being taken down to the garage.' Christine, although just as irritated as Daniel (and probably even more so given that his request for the shoes be taken down to the garage is clearly addressed to her), has opted for a different tactic: she prefers to keep her feelings to herself and say nothing. This is the result of experience. She has observed that nothing is to be achieved by shouting (the shoes still end up under the radiator) and that therefore it is best avoided. Indeed, she even takes her sacrifice one step further by taking the shoes down to the garage without a word of protest. The interviewer asks her if shouting a little might not do her good. She accepts the possibility but goes on to say: 'I'm saving that for a more important occasion.' Since the irritation provoked by the shoes does not reach maximum intensity for her, she prefers to deal with it as quickly as possible by self-sacrifice and silence, in order to conserve her strengths for other verbal confrontations with Daniel. By doing so, she even gets rid of the more personal irritation provoked by her own shoes. The loving self-sacrifice is, in a sense, rewarded.

The irritated person develops tactics without realizing it. Particularly as a way of distancing themselves from the facts. For example, by physically moving further away from anything likely to remind them of the original source of irritation. 'If things start to get on my nerves, I'll quite often leave the room, otherwise he'll be able to see from my face that

[1] Comments recorded and quoted by Johanne Mons (1998, p. 105)

I'm getting more and more irritated' (Nicole). As well as removing the sight of whatever caused the irritation in the first place, moving away has another advantage. It enables the irritated individual to switch identity briefly, taking refuge for a short period in a kind of bubble of personal autonomy. Several of those interviewed spoke in terms of the "breathing space" that they associated with such occasions, often enabling them quickly to forget the facts a little and to calm their irritation. 'I get myself together first', as Melody so clearly puts it. This is also the method used by Fidelia, who describes it in more detail. 'I need time just to stop and take a breather.' For example, a trip (without Pedro) with her girlfriends, 'enough to make a new woman of you'. It is also favoured by Yannis, who has officially instituted a policy of personal breathing space as part of the conjugal set-up with a view to keeping irritation levels down. 'As a general rule, we allow each other our own free "time-slots": I might go to a concert or to a football match with friends, she goes out to eat or shop with her girlfriends; she goes away for two or three days on a work trip, I stay at home with our daughter, and vice versa, when I have to go away for work myself. It works very well and we love getting back together after these little breaks. We both feel this freedom to come and go is an indispensable part of our relationship and helps to keep it strong and positive.' Whether the sequence is short and improvised or longer and more structured, the mechanism is the same; these short individualistic interludes prompt (doubly) a return to conjugal normality. First, by distracting attention from the facts and so making it possible for irritation to 'melt away'. Then, especially where the interlude lasts for a while (which is where a discreet and restrained little act of revenge can have a positive effect), it can incite feelings of guilt, with the recently irritated individual anxious to re-discover the familiar touchstones of their conjugal identification and to re-immerse themselves in it. This moment of transition between two identities is also conducive to more detached reasoning – a strong identification and the ability to think critically being scarcely compatible (Kaufmann, 2004) – generally resulting in a cessation of hostilities. Three elements combine to subdue irritation: physical distance, reduction of emotional intensity, a tendency to a more analytical approach. Irritation does not melt away of its own accord.

Physical therapy

'The way I switch from one feeling to another: I think that, having made my comment which can be more or less discreet depending on

169

the circumstances, I look away and get on with some activity of my own, and that "calms me down" and can make him change his behaviour (in the case in point, I clear the table).' Melody combines three techniques. A brief critical comment (muttered beneath her breath); looking away, which signals the end of the critical phase; and finally, concentrating her attention on a mechanical activity in order to calm herself down. The latter (using a physical activity as a way of dealing with an emotional upheaval) is not confined to irritation. It is widely used in other contexts (for example to deal with anxiety, shame, etc.) and is also a way of dealing with cognitive problems such as mental overload. In my research on cooking, for example (Kaufmann, 2005), many people I spoke to mentioned this idea of manual therapy. Whether the activity in question is a complex one, requiring intense concentration, or whether it is a familiar and routine one, the result is the same: it 'empties your mind' (Candy) of all negative moods and thoughts. 'I don't think of anything in particular, just about the cooking. I think about the taste – I really don't think about anything else, that's why it's so relaxing; because I'm so focused' (Tony). Not thinking about anything and being completely focused (two incompatible modes from a strictly cognitive point of view) are the same thing as far as he is concerned. Because both free him from other existential thoughts which are troubling and tiring. 'Cooking is my anti-stress. It's the only thing I've found that de-stresses me. When I get home from work, it's my way of taking a breather' (Tony).

Cooking, however, is rarely used as a strategy for dealing with irritation. It is too regular an activity, something that takes place at set times (whereas irritation strikes when least expected and must be dealt with at once), and its complexity requires too much intellectual mobilization. As a way of soothing nerves frayed by irritation, the ideal therapeutic gesture is, on the contrary, the most simple and automatic one, using whatever objects happen to be at hand. It is important to act for the sake of acting, to do something which is both purely physical and very simple. The extremely pared-down nature of the activity in question suggests (in the same way as for the sudden melting away of irritation) that the mechanism is a purely natural one in which physical gestures drive out any negative thoughts. Yet, here too, it is the gradual interplay between the diminution of emotional intensity and the changes in the way the incident is perceived which is crucial. Irritation melts away with a more distanced view of the events. The physical activity is also about distancing, but in a different way. In this case the distancing applies not to the facts but to the image of the self. Each individual's image of themselves at any

170

one time takes shape from and depends on a range of very different elements. Sometimes it may be the result of an analytical thought process, sometimes a more narrative account or a vivid visualization: all of these developing an image of the self, now generally referred to as reflexivity (Giddens, 1991). Yet this view of the self can disappear and be replaced by a simple sense of existing, for example through powerful emotions (Le Breton, 2002), or, in a more diffuse way, by becoming absorbed in physical movements (Laplantine, 2005; Sauvageot, 2003). Indeed, physical therapy combines the two kinds of distancing, for the dilution of the self-image also serves to obliterate the perception of the facts since it is the reflexive superstructure as a whole which becomes less distinct. Furthermore, this double movement wrenches the individual from their conjugal socialization, by confining them within the limits of their own bodies. Many people described coordinated techniques enabling them simultaneously to withdraw from the context of irritation and to refocus on themselves through some kind of activity. Like Melody, for example, describing the immediate aftermath of an outburst of anger. 'So I looked away, I got up to go and wash up a saucepan, without saying anything, so as to discreetly withdraw from the conversation. HE saw what was going on, and didn't push the matter, instead just saying "I'll see you in the bedroom for the afternoon nap" (he has one almost every day). I replied "I don't know", and then he went off into the bedroom. So, with all my irritation gone, and the washing-up done, I went and joined him (because for him, whether we get up to anything or not, the afternoon nap is really sacred!).' A radical reversal of the situation, a speedy resolution, and with one thing leading to another, the two of them engaging in a very different sort of physical therapy.

Calming oneself down through some kind of physical activity is, however, not always an easy matter. For action of any kind potentially sends a message to the irritator, and therefore risks being confused with the language of gestures and interpreted in an altogether different way. Therapeutic activity is intended as a way of cutting all ties, both with the events leading to irritation and with the partner, of erecting an impenetrable barrier to the external world so that the irritated person can retreat back into themselves. The slightest sign given by the physical action can, however, have the exact opposite effect of inviting communication. Yet the irritated person is also torn with the desire to confront the issue, and finds it extremely hard to act purely in their own interests. Melody, for example, clears the table immediately as a way of calming herself down when HE dips his bread in the sauce. She does so briskly, the plates clatter together, making a considerable amount of noise. Is it all purely for her own benefit? Or is she also sending HIM a message? In all probability she is steering a course somewhere between the two. With the complication that, since the two are completely at odds, the slightest signal is capable of wiping out the effects of her therapeutic action. Fortunately, since a favourite tactic of the irritator is to pretend to have seen and heard nothing, such small slip-ups pass largely unnoticed. And Melody can continue to clatter her plates. Yet things are not entirely resolved for all that. The ideal is to have some small gesture, often ritualized in some way, and designed purely as a way of clearing the air. Using an ordinary action with all its implications, a domestic task for example, can raise other issues, and may even end up provoking further irritation. When Pedro puts his bowl in the sink instead of in the dishwasher, Fidelia sometimes reacts with immediate anger. On other occasions, she hesitates between a whole range of different reactions. Her favourite: 'Smile to myself', put the bowl in the dishwasher, 'and get on with other things'. She does not, however, manage such internal detachment very often. Instead, she leaves the bowl ostentatiously in the sink, and embarks on some intense and vigorous household activity as a way of relieving her feelings. Once her irritation has died down, a feeling of doubt creeps in as to whether she has acted for the best: she has after all ended up doing the very thing her irritating husband wanted, the very thing she finds so annoying, and her hyperactivity has meant the result is even more thorough. And all the time, the bowl is sitting in the sink mocking her until she puts it away. On other occasions, she goes for a completely different tactic: she leaves the bowl where it is and does not do any tidying, instead embarking on a sort of silent domestic strike. But with irritation still gnawing at her, and without the distraction of intense activity to make her feel better. The confusion of conflicting tactics ends up driving her into such a state that her irritation becomes even worse. Further proof, if any were needed, that activity (in common with the melting away of irritation) is not a purely physical and natural mechanism.

Judicious use of sulking

Looking away or concentrating on gestures which make you feel better are ways of isolating yourself from the scene that causes irritation, of seeking refuge in a personal identity quite separate from the conjugal world, and especially of refusing any communication with

172

the adversary. Many of those interviewed spoke of the need to display a momentary 'coolness' for that very reason. 'My coolness is a result of irritation (I'm not in love anymore); it's a spontaneous reaction which reflects the way I feel at that moment.' Melody displays such coolness even when communication between her and her partner has not broken down. 'It might mean changing the subject, talking about something else, but still with the same coolness.' Like most elements connected with irritation, this 'coolness' is ambivalent, and can give rise to conflicting interpretations. The first of these is that this is a critical message aimed at the adversary, a logical consequence following the emotional crisis. 'Talking to him warmly straight after my bitter little comments would involve feigning feelings I just don't have at that moment; after all that irritation and what I've thought and said about him, I don't feel much like reaching out to him' (Melody). The message is sometimes heeded, and can even prove effective. 'If he realizes what's going on, HE uses it as a signal, and if he's in a good mood (or in the wrong), HE will make some effort of reconciliation (a little joke, an offer of help, a kind gesture).' Explaining further, Melody shifts almost imperceptibly into the second interpretation: the coolness is no longer a message, but instead a way of indicating a temporary neutrality and blocking communication. 'It would be like turning the other cheek, and that would be going too far! I'm not going to run the risk of getting irritated again immediately. I need time to get myself together. I don't see it as some kind of sign or punishment meant for him, because: (1) HE doesn't always notice! (2) Don't forget that I have some doubts about the cause of this irritation (is it HIM? Is it me?).' Coolness is a deliberately inexpressive attitude, marking a pause in communication. As Fidelia puts it: 'I distance myself without getting involved in arguments about it.' Echoed by Lamia, who resorts to 'tight-lipped silences' while waiting for the crisis to 'blow over'.

For many irritated people, however, coolness alone is not enough. These people feel the need to move on to the next level: sulking. This too can be ambivalent, taking different forms depending on the methods used. Some sulkiness is aggressive and obstinately impenetrable, sending out messages which are difficult to understand but very powerful. We are not concerned with these here. Where the intention is to find a solution to a crisis, a moderate sulk can in fact be a way of breaking with the biographical sequence of events which has provoked irritation. If this is to happen, emotional neutrality is essential. Such a result can only be attained if the irritated person is prepared to put aside the inner convictions they had focused on at the height of the crisis. The resulting blank expression is then an indication that the individual is working on re-establishing their internal equilibrium. An invisible and secret task, which cannot and must not be discussed. 'Some people don't say what it is that's annoying them, but you can see from their faces that something is not right. But of course, you don't know what it is, because you can't read their thoughts. So you ask the person who's sulking, but they are only interested in sulking and not in answering questions' (Isabelle). To the outside observer, sulking appears incomprehensible and sometimes even ridiculous. In reality, the sulker is often forced to resort to this strange tactic, which, in its moderate form, paradoxically attempts to create the conditions suitable for a reconciliation to occur, though without being able to admit it, and all the while keeping up a sullen expression. It is a tactic favoured by children, similarly often trapped by their inability to express their feelings of dissatisfaction and their little problems. (For different reasons: the irritated half of the couple cannot say anything without rekindling the source of the irritation; the child is silent because he or she lacks an adequate vocabulary and has an inferior status). Faced with the cruel world which does not understand him or her and to which he or she can say nothing, the child retreats into a private world by sulking. It is, for example, in the attic, so Gaston Bachelard tells us (1948), that the ultimate sulk takes place, the sulk to which there are no witnesses. Within the couple, the irritated partner also isolates themselves by sulking (in the same way as when they look away or engage in some kind of frenzied activity). They refuse to display any vindictiveness but nor are they prepared to give any indication that they are ready to return to a state of normality within the relationship. They are in a curious no-man's-land, as though suspended between two possible identities. As a result, all forms of expression, whether linguistic or physical, are neutralized. 'I sulk a bit, I'm not as smiling, cheerful, playful, talkative, interested in him as usual. And the worst of it is that he doesn't even notice and so it doesn't bother him in the slightest: I'm the only one who ends up suffering!' (Alice). Aziz does not notice anything is wrong, or rather he chooses not to notice, experience having no doubt taught him that the glacial reception he is getting is of no great consequence and will not last long. Clearly, much depends on the type of sulking, for there is sulking and sulking. When he insists on getting on the train at the last minute, he knows that Alice's sulk will be short-lived, almost a game, and that he will easily win her round again. Yet on those occasions when she feels he shows a total lack of consideration (when he asks her to remind him about various things, and then, when she does so, says he'll do them later), Alice is unable to restrict herself to the kind of sulking which simply indicates a state of neutrality. 'When that happens it's true that I sometimes express my anger in my own way, in other words by sulking. I feel entitled to show that I'm not happy so I allow myself to sulk. I want him to understand what I feel like on those occasions. But at the same time I don't really enjoy sulking, it's not really in my nature. I don't feel right when I'm angry and I hate that feeling. I find it really hard to hold things against someone I love for very long, at least when it's not about anything particularly serious.' Even when she has no alternative but to go into a more eloquent sulk, Alice is anxious to get out of it as quickly as possible. For her it is not the distancing and the neutrality indicated by the discreet sulk which enables her irritation to subside, but the interplay of conflicting feelings and thoughts. Her resolve is undermined by remorse and doubt. Like those secret little acts of revenge, the little lapse, brief and restrained, allows equilibrium to be restored.

Moving out of the realm of radical neutrality, the aggressive sulk involves playing on the dialectics of opposing emotions in order to restore conjugal normality. This is achieved through a counterbalancing effect: the more unpleasant the sulk, the more the irritated sulker feels guilty and wants to return to normality. Other strategies for dealing with irritation work in a similar way, using the dialectics of opposing emotions but simultaneously rather than successively. Like humour, they are open to a double interpretation, although in a manner much less agreeable and at times even painful. These include all manner of grumblings, mutterings and groanings, making it possible for the irritated person to feign a counter-attack which is in reality strictly imaginary. 'I'm lucky enough to have a charming man (otherwise I would have swapped him long ago) who takes me where I want, helps with the housework, and has lots of good qualities. And then, sometimes, he has to have a little moan. Like the time when he grumbled all the way from Marseilles to Andorra, about how he was fed up with the road and this awful weather, and that he had a good mind to turn round and go back. One of my friends was with us at the time and we begged him not to do so, assuring him there wasn't much further to go, and that there was no point coming all this way and not getting to our destination. It was in the early days,[2] and as I was used to a much more difficult temperament,[3] I was convinced the

---

[2] Of their relationship.
[3] With her previous husband, the deliberate tube-squeezer.

stupid man would do it. In fact, he had no intention of doing so, as he knew perfectly well, even if I didn't. It was just that he was feeling irritated and he needed to let us know. We finally got to Andorra, with everyone in a terrible state, especially the other woman and I who had spent the entire journey with our fingers crossed. When that happens now, I let him have a good old moan to himself; I know he'll get over it' (Isabelle). Such moaning and groaning, although it can ease the situation at the time, turns out to be a deplorable method in terms of the benefits it brings. Especially when the adversary, with the benefit of experience, knows perfectly well that the mutterings have no real significance. Isabelle even manages to turn the performance to her own advantage. 'Once we've arrived, I just point out that he has been really rather odious, which usually wins me a little compensation from a contrite husband, in the form of a cake or a little detour to see something I'm interested in. I am quite Machiavellian.'

Seeing reason

By looking away, engaging in some kind of frenzied activity, or putting on an impenetrable sulky front, the irritated person is rewarded by a doubly advantageous result: the burden of negative emotions is lightened leaving them free to analyse the situation in a more cold and distanced way. True this capacity for reflection is not without a certain amount of effort. Caroline refers to a process of patiently 'chipping away', gradually allowing 'the bomb to be defused'. Nor is the resulting analysis necessarily easy either. The advantages and drawbacks of the two alternative identities (individualistic resistance or conjugal capitulation) are assessed and compared. Even though she always ends up reaching the same conclusion, Alice has her doubts each time, and there is every chance that one day she might reach another decision. 'About the train, it's true that the irritation I feel before I get on disappears pretty quickly once the train gets going and I think that's partly because I'm relieved we didn't miss it after all but also because I can't really say with any great force of conviction that he really did annoy me. He doesn't take me seriously and jokes in a nice way about my stressed attitude and he ends up making me feel more relaxed because of the stupid things he says (he's really funny and very entertaining). I'm just too weak and I can't stick to my guns, I forgive very quickly, too quickly probably even by my own standards. I'd like to have the force of character to really make him understand that I genuinely do hold it against him, that he

176

does really annoy me at those times, but I can't do it and in the end I'm quite glad it's like that, even if in a way I could kick myself. It all gets so complicated! I avoid confrontation because I really don't like it and because it's easier like that and also because I don't want to be one of those "annoying bitches" who kick up a fuss over the slightest little thing.'

In spite of frequent hesitations, reflection in the cold light of day generally favours conjugal capitulation for a number of reasons. First of all, there is the realization that a continued individualistic revolt will have serious repercussions, both material and social. This is what makes Nicole think she has allowed herself to get 'unreasonably annoyed'. Once the dreams fuelled by violent emotions have disappeared, reality comes back with a vengeance. Mountains would need to be moved. But the justification needed to do so – strong as it seemed in the heat of the crisis – rapidly disintegrates on reflection, shrinking to the faintest trace (to be preserved in secret in some corner of the memory and kept in reserve for some future crisis). Then there is quite simply a need for some calm after the storm, when the effort of prolonging the conflict would be just too stressful. But the most interesting reason undoubtedly lies elsewhere, in the abrupt overturning of the vision of self. As emotion subsides, doubts rapidly set in; where everything seemed perfectly clear only moments before, the picture is now more confused. Was he or she guilty of acting deliberately to irritate even more? Or were they quite unaware of causing irritation and sometimes even anxious to try and change their ways? The victim is not quite so sure any more, and the more he or she hesitates, the more a new vision of themselves begins to emerge, similarly riddled with doubts. Is their own attitude not open to the same criticisms? Were they not extremely unpleasant, even violent, in what they said, or pathetically stubborn in the way they sulked? At this critical moment in the thought process, the excesses committed in the heat of the moment are recalled in a new light, in such a way that they can even begin to fuel the dialectic of opposites. This is where, for example, the little act of revenge, even if carried out slyly, and precisely because of that (provided the perpetrator was aware that it was so), can become a useful tool for re-establishing conjugal harmony. After shouting and crashing the plates around in a way that forced HIM to remove his bread from the sauce, Melody starts to sees herself in the unflattering guise of the kind of woman who is 'uptight, cantankerous, authoritarian'. 'You feel you've really been horrible', says Élise.[4] And Rosy,

---

[4] Comments recorded and quoted by Céline Bouchat (2005, p. 71).

troubled in retrospect by the idea that her exaltation was disproportionate, is forced to this sad conclusion: 'I feel I've been ridiculous.' We have already observed that crystallization can focus on the most trifling incidents. Even in the heat of the moment, the irritated person senses intuitively that there are all sorts of other things below the surface. But when the time comes for more rational analysis, they are ashamed to discover that what seemed to be a huge hurricane was in reality a storm in a tea cup. This sorry revelation often plays no small part in the sudden urge to make a fresh start.

Reframing the scene

Once emotions have subsided, the partner is viewed in a less critical light and, in some cases, an element of self-criticism may even creep in. At this point, it takes only a small gesture or a signal from the partner for the couple to be ready to embark together on an upward spiral. Unfortunately, this does not always happen. The irritator persists stubbornly in his or her course of action, unmoved by the sulking or frantic activity and deaf to all protests. The victim is then forced to be creative, coming up with every imaginable kind of trick. One of the simplest of these is to try another take of the scene which sparked off the irritation in the first place. It should be remembered that irritation is the result of the intimate confrontation between two cultures, both unaware of the differences between them. The establishment of complementary roles within the couple is one way of resolving the situation, since the difference then serves to structure the conjugal entity. Another way is to avoid confrontation by creating additional individual space, usually by extending the spheres of personal activities acknowledged and accepted by the partner and the rest of the family. Frédéric Hardy (2005) cites the case of an extremely irritated music-loving father. 'He gets really angry. He's fed up with seeing his CDs left lying around all over the place; it's a proper little battle.' So, for the sake of peace, he decided to build a small personal auditorium in the attic. As for Rosy and Charly, the fact that they live apart means Rosy can 'storm out' as soon as something irritates her (and justify her actions later by e-mail). 'We have lots of safety valves to help us avoid confrontation.' But most of the time the definition of what can be considered personal or conjugal, and the acknowledgement of the legitimacy of personal space, remain very much a grey area.

Every situation is at the centre of a set of forces which help to frame its definition (Goffman, 1991). We are not in control of the experiences in which we become involved. This is clearly illustrated by looking at spheres of autonomy: the person who believes their personal space is safely recognized often quickly finds it challenged. The experience of conjugal irritation does, however, have the particular characteristic of being played out at times between two people (in the course of heated exchanges), at other times internalized in solitude. The irritated person who withdraws into themselves is essentially engaged, in a virtual mode, in trying various takes on the situations he has just lived through. He, or she, experiments with different angles to investigate how they affect his perception, in particular by shifting the boundaries separating the individual from the collective. Many scenes which have caused irritation in the past have ended up in this sorry situation because of a confrontation between private worlds which would have been better kept separate. Reliving the scene *a posteriori*, once it has been edited, is a way of completely overturning the feelings it provokes. And the repeated use of such a process ends up taking on a certain educational value and can change the way facts are perceived even at the height of the storm. Take the case of Lamia, infuriated as long as she can remember by all the little objects which regularly fall out of her husband's shirt pockets. 'Another thing that irritates me on a regular basis and which I fail to understand is the way he insists on using his shirt pocket for his money, his mobile phone or his credit card. He only has to bend over slightly and everything falls out (and he's lost all the things I've mentioned on more than one occasion), yet he persists in doing it. For years, whenever I've seen him doing it, I've repeatedly suggested he put them somewhere else.' But to no avail; he continues to do exactly the same. What Lamia finds most irritating is the thundering 'Shit!!!' he utters on each occasion, further proof that she is perfectly justified in her attempts to get him to change, since he would be the first person to benefit. After persisting in vain for so long (and being even more irritated because of the dissonance with this unobtainable yet so obvious ideal), Lamia has changed tactics. 'Now, in the morning when I hear that sound of things falling out of his pocket and the "shit" that invariably accompanies them, I still feel really irritated, but I also smile to myself as well.' Although the shift is still not perfect, she has succeeded in reducing the irritation enough to be able to step back and see the funny side of the situation. She has convinced herself that, since it is after all his things that keep falling out, she need not pay any attention to what is happening and can ignore his behaviour completely. Or, better still, she can see the funny side of this rather absurd ritual.

179

It is interesting to observe that what irritates most in situations where there is a forced mingling of dissonant private worlds can be transformed into a source of amusement when the scene is viewed as though from an external context. The previously irritated person metamorphoses into a calm, smiling and indulgent spectator. The difference which caused the problem in the first place has been transformed into an object of curiosity and amusement – something agreeably exotic. Isabelle was astonished when she first discovered her new husband's obsession with keeping the car immaculate. She quickly learned to restrain herself so as to avoid provoking pointless rows. 'I know now that the car is sacrosanct and must be kept absolutely immaculate: nobody eats in the car; check shoes are clean before getting in.' At the same time she observes that 'taking the trouble to think about it' can also be a source of personal pleasure, part of being in love. A gratifying effort therefore, and, more importantly, one which avoids endless rows. 'The day I tread mud into my dear one's car and not only fail to do anything about it but also tell him to get lost if he says anything, that will be the beginning of the end for our relationship.' Since then, to her intense satisfaction, she has even learned to see the funny side of the situation. 'And you know it's quite touching to see him shaking out the car mats – it's just so much him, and it even makes my mother laugh too.' By the magic process of reframing the scene, the most irritating characters can be re-drawn in the guise of someone with an immature personality, someone clumsy and comical, who inspires laughter, tenderness or pity. It is not uncommon in such circumstances for women to see their husbands as almost childlike. When she is really in a good mood, Fidelia thinks that Pedro's refusal to put his bowl into the dishwasher is 'childish'. 'And it makes me smile.' This man–child association (which in other circumstances, as we have seen, can be extremely irritating) enables Lamia to put even more calming distance between herself and her partner. 'On the subject of what I feel about the fact that my husband is always losing things out of his shirt pockets, what makes me smile is that it's as though I'm dealing with a little boy who keeps doing the same silly thing over and over again and it's a feeling not dissimilar to the sort of tenderness I feel about the silly little things my son keeps doing.'

The little private cinema and voice off

Dreams are much more than mere dreams; they also help to prepare the ground for future reality. Between dreaming for its own sake and dreaming of what ultimately turns into a plan of action, various stages can be identified. Hazel Markus (Markus, 1977) emphasized, for example, the intermediate stage of 'possible self', which remains a virtual identity, while at the same time combining all the elements necessary for it to become reality. She also refers to 'working schemata': the day dreaming individual blends the virtual with fragments of reality in order to generate credible scenarios. The framing and re-framing of images is not, therefore, an anomaly. It is an essential part of the much wider process by means of which reality (past, present and future) is passed through the filter of subjectivity which gives it its full meaning (Kaufmann, 2004). The individual who daydreams purely for his own pleasure and the one who fine-tunes the details of a 'working schemata' that he is going to attempt to turn into reality may seem poles apart. Yet they have one thing in common: they set a great deal of store by their images, including the most virtual, and by the craziest scenarios. Furthermore, this principle underlies personal identification, which is now based on the meaning given by the indi-vidual themselves, regardless of the reality of the situation. A reality which, of course, will quickly descend with its full force to crush any misguided fantasies. We can only believe in dreams for the time it takes to dream them; but during that time we truly believe in them.

These few lines seemed useful to me, for this imaginary paral-lel world we are now going to explore is a favoured weapon in the armoury of the irritated person seeking to reinstate more positive feel-ings. Certain forms are extremely inventive and playful (Caroline sees Marc as an alien), and might indicate that this kind of daydream is simply a means of compensation. However, even at this initial stage, the process is only effective precisely because genuine identification occurs. Of course, Caroline does not truly, rationally and in any lasting fashion believe that Marc might be a Martian. But as long as the thought lasts, she is able to lose herself in these characters, as though absorbed in a novel. When she finds herself feeling irritated by the sight of her man in the morning, 'bleary-eyed, hair sticking up all over the place, no trace of a smile, no manners either', she takes refuge in a consoling little personal cinema. 'So, a bit like when chil-dren who have been scolded tell themselves that someone else has taken their parents' place overnight, I tell myself that Marc, in the morning, is not Marc at all but an alien who has taken his place. The real Mark will come back during the course of the day. Just creating this science-fiction scenario in my head cheers me up.' The efficacy of the technique can sometimes take even her by surprise. 'And then, at the sight of my cheerful face, it's Mark's turn to be irritated.' The

181

principle is always the same: you need to be able to believe more in the little internal cinema than in the reality in front of your eyes, regardless of whether the little cinema reinterprets the same scene (Marc turning into a Martian) or ventures into a completely different universe. Alice, for all her gentleness, imagines (for the space of two seconds) slapping Aziz (or even killing him!). Something she would never do in reality. Yet it is because she believes it (for a split second) that this image calms her down.

In this field of imaginary parallel worlds, there are some real experts. Malvina is one of them. I should reiterate that the sheer volume of irritation provoked by the insufferable Richard is significant. The fact that she is nevertheless able to deal with it must be largely attributed to the excellence of her imaginative efforts. Very vocal, she talks less in terms of images than of her 'voice off' technique. 'We were spending one weekend in three at his parents' place. On his own "territory" he's completely different: only the opinions of his mother and his friends count. That irritates me because it means I have to be so careful about everything I say and that's just not me. To help me cope with this, I've invented a voice off. When he's holding forth about something or other or when he believes the stupid things they come out with, I make up my own little commentaries or I think up replies which I'll probably never actually voice (sometimes I get so absorbed by this little game that mealtimes are over before I even know it!!!).'

To cope with the everyday reality of their lives together, Malvina has an even more impressive technique. Her parallel world goes beyond mere fictional creation because, regularly and with the utmost seriousness, she makes notes in a secret diary. 'In fact I use two other methods. The first one is something I've "patented" with my girl-friends: it involves writing down in a notebook anything that's upset me, such as his cutting remarks or some of his attitudes for example, so that I can confront him with them at some later stage, as evidence in an argument over something similar. But, as I don't always have my notebook on me when things blow up, I end up jotting them down later, when I've calmed down a bit. That has the advantage of allowing me to put things into perspective a bit more: when I come to write things down, some of them seem pretty trivial. Sometimes I don't even remember to note them down at all but it doesn't matter because at the time it still helped me to think I was going to.' It is in the heat of the action, at the moment when she thinks about what she is going to write in her notebook, that she believes in it most. When it comes to actually doing the writing, she is already someone else, someone more reasonable. These two stages, linked as they are, each fulfil a different role. Imagining what she will write in the notebook and imagining that what she writes will become reality (in the form of some kind of powerful revenge) calms her down. Then, being able to reflect more calmly on the incident helps her put things into perspective and prepares her for a return to normality. A return which is always painful and difficult, and for which she needs to have other weapons to hand, still based on scenes conjured up in her imagination. 'The last method is something I'm not particularly proud of: I imagine leaving him. Then I visualize the flat I'll live in (an untidy one since that's one of the main stumbling blocks between us: I'm really untidy) and the way I'll dress (he's jealous and I find it irritating that I have to dress in a way that suits him). Yet I never imagine the scene in which I tell him it's over, because usually the two preceding stages are enough to calm me down sufficiently.' Even when she dreams about leaving him, Malvina is paradoxically working towards bringing the couple back together. It is an intense and secret process. 'As you see, all these are "internal" strategies. On the "external" front my expression is sulky and quite sullen (which irritates him because he prefers things to be out in the open).'

Accentuating the positive

Sunk in the misery of negative emotions, the irritated partner anxiously awaits a sign inviting them to resume the conjugal identity. When none comes, they are condemned to work towards reunification on their own, with all the skill and creativity they can muster. They must deploy their treasures in secret, often without saying anything, by remaining distant or adopting an icy manner. Such appearances should not, however, be misinterpreted, for the individual in question is in fact working towards a renewal of the romantic bond, beginning with a return to conjugal normality, the conditions for which need to be prepared. Even though still a little irritated, still inclined to mutter or sulk, they are already secretly at work looking for ways forward, using their bodies, objects around them, their critical thoughts, their dreams. Situated somewhere between thoughts and dreams, the last technique we will examine is one of the most interesting. We have seen how astonishingly powerful the imagined parallel world can be when it is used well. But to do so requires skills which are not always easy to put into practice. Even Malvina sometimes fails. 'If I'm at a low ebb, my method very quickly comes up against its limits because I just can't manage to think up a dream I can lose myself in sufficiently.' When this happens, there is no other alternative but to fall back on the reality of the relationship as it appears to be. Yet still without giving in. Reality can be framed differently, for example by cutting out one area of autonomy where confrontation was particularly aggravating. It can also be confronted directly by manipulating categories of perception. The partner is not, after all, a fixed and unchanging entity. This is particularly evident with irritation, where just a few small elements can cause exasperation. In the heat of the emotion, these irritating details block out everything else; the partner can no longer see the wood for the trees. As emotions cool down and a more distanced and reflective approach is possible, a more balanced view can emerge. At that stage, things improve still further, when the irritated person not only gets things into perspective but also starts to focus again on the positive aspects which he or she had temporarily lost sight of. A process which can feel like rediscovering the partner all over again, with reassuring clarity. Discreet joys and forgotten charms are recalled to mind, gently dispelling any lingering bitterness. If the about-turn happens at this moment, all sorts of little enchantments can suddenly take the place of the negative feelings. Because an excess of emotion in one direction leads to a similar excess in the other. But also because the terrain had already been prepared by this scrupulous analysis focusing on the best in the other (an analysis which is often scarcely more objective than the hotchpotch of criticism at the heart of the irritation). After the worst, comes the best.

What happens is a detailed selection process, which, in its initial stages, can still retain a coldly technical character. 'You have to make allowances. I remind myself that he's got other qualities, that the flawless pearl doesn't exist', says Jade, with a certain degree of reserve. No such reticence for Melody. 'I like being in love, I stay at home for HIM, for the children. If I'm no longer driven by love, I don't see the point.' After HE has made her shout and crash the plates about, she is in a hurry to escape from this painful sequence of events as soon as the negative feelings have started to abate. In order to do this, she selects the best things, focusing on his more loving and endearing qualities. She looks for ways of encouraging him to emphasize these and to present himself in a new and better light. The selection is by no means confined simply to perception, individual and secret: it helps set in motion a new interaction, based on what is best about both of them. 'I think that I try instinctively to neutralize what's happened, and then set out to create a more positive situation in which HE will want to please me and show me again all the things I love about him. I suppose I'm giving him another chance in a way.' Melody is also

184

selective with regard to the more immediate physical aspects of what she sees in front of her, in an attempt to capture those elements (especially his gaze) which she knows will work their electrifying magic on her, just as when they first met. 'Then, when I look at him, I seek his eyes, looking for that old spark. It's as though that wipes the slate clean. And "I forget", until the next time.'

Some readers may reproach me for not having kept the promises contained in the title of this third part, and feel they have been cheated, that love has scarcely featured here at all. Instead a litany of all manner of tactics and subterfuges, whereas Love is reputed to be something radically different, a phenomenon, pure, clear, divine, coming from some indefinable beyond, a far cry from the mean and petty preoccupations of ordinary human existence. Sometimes it does indeed have these sublime qualities, when a bubble of enchantment (temporarily) allows the lovers to soar above reality. But alas, for the most part the two partners find themselves battling instead with reality as they encounter it. Starting with the rawest of reality, they toil away at it, with energy and intelligence, day after day. Love is a living sentiment, continuously evolving minute by minute: it is absolutely essential to keep working at it in all circumstances. This task is often secret and hidden, at times even downright painful when one or the other of the partners has to go through the agony of abandoning their egoistic certainties. The apparent mediocrity of these techniques obscures the fact that they are part of the vast task of transforming identity. They create the foundations for a different self, once again ready to re-engage in the conjugal relationship. From then on, the way is open for all manner of more demonstrative expressions of love along the traditional lines. Without that earlier secret fine-tuning, these could never have seen the light of day. And this is why, after all the bitterness and rage, the tricks and hypocrisies we have observed in the course of this book, our story nevertheless has a truly happy ending.

CONCLUSION

Any new research subject has its own particular atmosphere. So the researcher discovers as he or she immerses themselves in the subject, for good or ill. From the outset it was clear that irritation was a highly charged subject which provoked strong reactions almost as soon as it was mentioned. Clearly, this little emotion touched a sensitive chord and had much to tell us about our times. Should this lead us to the conclusion that previous generations were less subject to irritation? It would be reasonable to suspect not. Might not Héloise and Abélard themselves have experienced discreet but trying feelings of irritation in their domestic lives: We shall never know, for, since the archives remain silent on the subject, we have no basis for comparison or judgement. We can only speculate.

I should like to advance the following theory: if irritation has indeed always existed, the mechanism which produces it is nevertheless in the throes of a profound historical transformation characterized by an increase in terms both of the causes of irritation and, simultaneously, of our capacity to deal with it. This second aspect explains why life has not become more intolerable for all that. Nevertheless, the fact remains that the potential for irritation is constantly increasing.

A number of factors are responsible. Most significant is the dramatic change that has taken place in the relationship between man and his social environment. In traditional society, the individual was carried along and supported by a structural framework which defined both the roles to be filled and the meaning of existence. The route through life was mapped out in advance and the different social levels fitted neatly together, each echoing the same message, which led to complete integration. Often relating even to the smallest details of existence. Kate Gavron (1996) describes, for example, the extent to

186

which attitudes to cooking continue to be strictly codified amongst the Bengali community in London, and how respect for the traditional codes is handed down, so that fish, for instance, can only be prepared in certain ways. She quotes the case of a young girl wishing to be more innovative in her cooking methods but afraid of being criticized by her mother-in-law: 'Didn't your caste ever prepare meals then? Don't you know how to cook?' With life so closely regulated within each social group, there was little room for irritation. Of course, frictions did often occur and all sorts of day-to-day problems and disagreements forced a certain degree of flexibility to be introduced. But such frictions were resolved by adjustments within the existing frames of reference which themselves remained largely unchallenged. However, irritation increases as new possibilities begin to emerge, blurring existing guidelines. It is, along with mental fatigue, part of the price to be paid for individual freedom, a price whose true cost we are only now discovering.

The huge scale of contemporary uncertainty is a product of history, a recent phenomenon. This is because the first wave of modernity did not fundamentally alter the social position of individuals in their daily lives. Instead, tradition was replaced by large-scale republican pro-grammes (such as education, for example) which continued to confine individuals to imposed roles and collective truths (Dubet, 2002). It was not until the much more recent breakdown of the second wave of modernity, around the sixties, that cracks started to appear in this perfect holistic structure. Cracks caused by the hammer blows of indi-viduals discovering this new sense of autonomy and the intoxicating freedom of choice that now existed in every possible domain.

The institution of the couple was the first to be affected. Gone was the 'off-the-peg' approach with its clearly defined complemen-tary roles for men and women. In its place the new era of 'made to measure' allowed space for improvisation and experimentation, the chance to do things your own way. Not a single aspect of private life remains immune from this quest for autonomy and freedom. Education, vacations, eating habits, health: all are called into ques-tion and everyone fashions their own response, with the conjugal compromise, the new hard labour, proving complex and delicate to establish. With the additional complication that the conflicts about what should be considered true or fair within the relationship are not the only fault line exposed by the abandonment of traditional roles. We have seen examples of several others through the course of this book, notably the issue of sharing household tasks, or agreeing areas of autonomy. We should note also many other areas of increased possibility, for example with regard to the variety of patterns of behaviour. In the course of my recent research on the preparation of meals (Kaufmann, 2005), I demonstrated that, whereas in former times the cook worked to a timetable and a set of habitual gestures which followed a fairly regular pattern, today's woman (or indeed man, who might now be in charge of doing the cooking: yet another area of uncertainty!) is constantly forced to choose between fast food and food prepared with enthusiasm and passion. A choice which brings with it latent irritations, magnified still further by the possible reaction of the partner, complaining for example about yet another pizza, or, worse still, about the special dish which (even though slaved over lovingly for hours) turned out not to be to their liking.

Essentially, the situation can be summed up as follows: the assertion of individual independence creates ever more scope for improvisation and free interpretation, which conversely involves couples in an immense task of harmonization and unification. This is by no means an abstract task, based simply on the good will of the two partners. On the contrary it is a work of great precision, requiring a high degree of skill and a meticulous attention to detail at all times. Take the simple example of ordinary consumer goods. Families make every effort to limit the number of products they buy in order to avoid too much mental fatigue and chaos. Yet they are not immune to the charms of advertising and the various temptations put in their way. As industrial innovation continues to multiply, the number of products to choose from – even the simplest cleaning product – can suddenly become a source of irritation, on both a personal and a conjugal level. Witness Isabelle's comments: 'When you see the way they keep churning out new products, all sorts of useless bits and pieces, changing the packaging, coming up with twenty-three different makes of coffee, it's clear that manufacturers are not exactly there to bring peace to the household. I remember a row we had over some polishing cloths which my beloved claimed were completely useless. I'd already had to do the shopping on my own for some reason I can't recall now, plus I'd bought him his stupid cleaning cloths which anyway don't clean anywhere near as well as the good old duster and from time to time a bit of good old-fashioned wax polish which smells wonderful into the bargain whereas those wipes just make everything wet and mucky. But still – anything to get him to do a bit of dusting. Anyway I was convinced that I'd bought the right cloths. So we both studied the packaging, which admittedly looked a bit different; dark brown instead of light brown and white wipes rather than orange ones. But in small letters in one corner it said "new formula with something or other . . . I can't remember what", and then the stupid things start shedding fluff all over the place, where-upon my beloved starts complaining about how it's bad enough that he's been lumbered with the ghastly job of doing the dusting so for god's sake at least have the decency to provide him with the proper products because it's not as if he hasn't got loads of other stuff to do! And he hasn't got all day either!'

Irritation is further exacerbated here because the disappointment over the purchase is part of two different visions about who does what and how. Here we touch on a paradox which is undoubtedly one of the little dramas of contemporary society. The plan, a magnifi-cent one, was about individual emancipation, in a spirit of openness and attention to the other person. *Libres ensemble* (de Singly, 2000). In this context, nothing could be more sacrilegious than being con-strained to behave in a prescribed way, especially one which puts men and women on two completely separate planets. Today's couples are consequently keen to avoid over-formalizing certain areas and are experimenting with shared activities. Yet nothing could be worse from the point of view of potential sources of irritation, which find countless pretexts to insinuate themselves. Couples have just two ways in which to prevent shared activities degenerating into detestable irritations. The first and most delightful is where love takes hold, ena-bling the couple to break free of daily routines and banish individual frontiers. Unfortunately, this cannot be forced. And the new regime centred on individual choice sometimes prevents it happening. Take, for example, the very symbol of conjugal togetherness: sexuality. The rise in expectations has led to discrepancies between the ideal and the reality, creating a source of much incomprehension and conflict (Bozon, 2004). Trying too hard opens the door to irritations, even where least expected. However, when it comes to activities requir-ing less emotional exchange, such as the household tasks, another method – in some ways the exact opposite – becomes possible: avoid areas of friction or lack of clarity and define clearly the place and function of each partner. In the kitchen, for example, there is usually either a single chef in sole command, or a chef and a sous-chef, who may swap roles depending on the dish being prepared.

Roles are the real issue here. We thought we were rid of them, or almost, especially those which have divided men and women through the ages. Nothing seemed more detestable or more out-of-date. We had convinced ourselves that only vestiges remained, a deep-seated historical memory which remained resistant to new ideas. Yet this research on irritation undermines this optimistic vision. What is the message of this book? First: that dissonances, products of modernity, generate irritation on a more and more massive scale. Secondly: that individuals are capable of developing the capacity to deal with these. All of which would be simple enough if that were the end of the story. Unfortunately, there is also a third point: one of the major techniques for avoiding irritation involves building on each person's strengths and allocating complementary roles. Indeed, we have seen to what extent this has been a central element in the way today's couples are structured. It is this powerful mechanism which reactivates the sexually differentiated historical memory, and gives it its full power of resistance. It is no longer enough therefore to analyse the opposing positions of men and women within the couple as simply an inheritance from the past (and even less, of course, as a purely biological factor): account must now be taken of the conjugal mechanism itself, in the light of its most recent developments.

I have used the term "little drama", for, although irritation (especially other people's) often makes us laugh, it may also give us cause for tears. We find ourselves trapped by a contradictory injunction, setting our need for peace and tranquillity against the liberating effects of modernity. The first injunction is that which drives us to seek personal well-being and conjugal peace. Who could not, or would not, want to do so? In today's increasingly aggressive and stressful society, the answer must surely be nobody. It is therefore the opposing injunction which is at risk of being quietly jeopardized, the very one which was the driving force behind the two-pronged programme of emancipation of the last half-century: perfect equality between men and women, and individual creativity, a far cry from the unacceptable imposition of assigned roles.

The frictions between the dream and the reality of this noble project will, I fear, continue to be a rich source of irritation for a very long time to come.

METHODOLOGICAL APPENDIX

A new research technique

For the first time I have conducted my research without the help of my little tape-recorder, instead communicating with those taking part via e-mail. Initially, requests for participants were issued on flyers, handed out at my various public appearances, and distributed in the press (newspapers and magazines) in France, Belgium and Switzerland. My warmest thanks to those journalists who helped in this way to put me into contact with my correspondents, notably Ariane Bois, Danièle Laufer, Natalie Levisalles, Isabelle Maury, Sylviane Pittet and Elisabeth Weissman.

I could have opted for a different electronic medium, something more open and interactive (such as a blog or a chat room). But I was afraid of being overwhelmed and wanted to be able to retain control of the process so e-mail exchanges seemed a better solution. Even if other fascinating technological options no doubt remain to be explored, I have no regrets over my choice: research conducted by e-mail proved to be an extremely efficient and flexible method, easy to work with. Once those interested in taking part in the project had contacted me, I suggested they express themselves as freely as they wished. The following is the standard text, adapted where necessary, sent to them in reply.

Thank you very much for your response and for being prepared to participate in this project. The principle is simple: we will communicate by
e-mail, as frequently as you wish, and you are of course free to withdraw from the research at any point, or not to respond to any questions
you feel are too difficult or too specific.

191

Irritations are numerous but often minuscule, quickly forgotten and sometimes scarcely even noticed. As a result, it is not always an easy matter to remember them or to discuss them. This is why I have chosen the more 'intimate' medium of e-mail for this research project, giving maximum flexibility in terms of time. Once you have sent me your initial comments, I shall reply and we will then exchange further e-mails to explore the subject in more depth. This first contribution can be extremely brief and may refer to the most trivial irritations. It is simply a starting point. You could list one or two examples of things you find irritating and attempt to describe your feelings in this situation, the way you go about re-establishing your psychological equilibrium, etc. But it is really up to you to decide what you want to include in that first statement.

Our e-mail exchanges can also be a way of 'getting things off your chest' should there be an occasion when you feel particularly irritated and want to express your feelings 'on-the-spot'. It is entirely up to you to decide what is appropriate. We are in this together and we shall see where it leads.

Irritation can be provoked by all sorts of different things. By a gesture, for example, a different way of tidying or not tidying things, of eating, watching the TV, pursuing personal interests, having different rhythms, etc. Or by a slight feeling of dissatisfaction, barely acknowledged even to oneself. Thousands of these crop up in the life of every couple, and nothing could be more normal. The successful couple is not one that never experiences irritation, but rather one that knows how to deal with it.

Each contribution prompted certain questions on my part – both about the facts themselves and of a more conceptual nature. I then sent back these queries (or my own interpretations of the material, with the request that these be confirmed), and the lines of communication were opened. A communication so rich that it quickly became apparent I could not possibly keep up with all my correspondents. This meant I was forced to select some of them on which to focus, and for this I must apologize to all the others, who would no doubt have liked to have gone further. But the sheer weight of material I received, combined with the necessity of a prompt and continuous follow-up (rather than simply accumulating the material initially), imposed a certain degree of selectivity. In compensation, the scientific benefits of such a technique are considerable, based as it is on permanent conceptualization, ongoing and immediate. Whereas traditional research separates the evidence-gathering phase from the processing one, here the two happen simultaneously and fuel each other. Up until now, I have rarely experienced to this extent the satisfaction of being able to test hypotheses on the spot, by formulating my questions to suit my correspondents. The second advantage of e-mail-based research is the extraordinary density of the material submitted. Admittedly, one loses the tell-tale hesitations and the impulsive spontaneity of face-to-face interviews, along with the poetry of the spoken word. But one gains in terms of the sheer density of information, with so much packed in that at times it can be difficult to select which parts to include.

The question remains to be asked as to the degree of sincerity of this type of communication, compared to face-to-face interviews. In my view it is extremely difficult to come to any clear general conclusion. Even in face-to-face interviews the degree of sincerity already varies considerably, depending on the nature of the subject matter and on the attitude of the researcher (Kaufmann, 2006). The same applies when it comes to the use of e-mail as a research tool. I can only observe that this method enabled some of the participants, guided by the researcher, to be so deeply involved that they reached a state approaching that of self-analysis. Such people were genuinely trying to gain a deeper understanding of themselves, of their partners and their relationship. And in such circumstances there is little scope for dishonesty (or for omissions). While it is difficult to prove that this method is more effective in revealing the truth than face-to-face interviews, it is undoubtedly the case that the effort in terms of analysis and argumentation required to obtain such truth is clearly greater.

It would be easy to be misled about the sincerity of most of the contributions because of their written form, generally felt to be less authentic than the spoken one. The style of writing varies considerably from one person to another, some adopting the rapid and direct style, close to speech, which prevails on the internet, others opting for a much more classical style; some emotional, others coldly analytical, some funny, some serious, etc. The style itself generally gives little real indication of the degree of involvement and sincerity. With the exception perhaps of the delightful Isabelle, whose colourful and fluid style, as it gathers momentum, hovers between writing for the sheer pleasure of it and genuine self-analysis (I have therefore had to edit her contribution, thus depriving myself, alas, of the greater part of it). Very often, a cumbersome style (a far cry from the more 'spontaneous' spoken form) is by no means a sign that the comments are any less sincere. It may even imply an attempt at self-analysis. A research project conducted by e-mail will not necessarily produce the same result as one using interviews. The interviewer is more distant, with the result that the interviewee tends to speak more to themselves.

My direct correspondents

Most of my sources began by introducing themselves, recounting their life-stories, both private and professional, in great detail. I made the decision, however, not to publish all of this information. For, given what was after all the intimate nature of the subject, the lack of any guarantee of anonymity could have had unforeseeable repercussions for the couples involved. I have therefore limited myself to a few main elements in each case, often in the form of an extract from a longer account, in their own words.

As the time approached for me to submit my manuscript, it occurred to me that it would be interesting to add a little update on the latest developments in each of their stories. Between three and six months had gone by since we had been in touch, during which time I had heard nothing further from them. I was in truth rather curious to find out myself, although I was aware that I could not incorporate this new material in my text (with all research projects, one must know when to stop). The flexibility of the e-mail-based research meant I could indeed put the cherry on the cake in this way. I have chosen a selection of the replies and include them below, exactly as I received them. Not everyone chose to reply (a little over two-thirds). Partly this was due to technical reasons, with several addresses no longer valid (things move quickly on the net). Partly it was because of other reasons, some no doubt preferring not to be involved any further.

These 'Stop press' extracts make fascinating reading (it was indeed hard simply to reproduce them without being able to analyse them!). As evidence of the passage of time, a considerable number of changes had taken place in the various households (pregnancies, births, house purchases and, sadly, separations too in the case of Maya and Igor, and Zoé and Charles-Henri and possibly soon for Jade). Such changes have had very different effects: sometimes the situation has got worse; sometimes, fortunately, things have improved. Perhaps the project played some small therapeutic role. Melody emphasizes this aspect: 'Looking at feelings of irritation under the microscope changes their character. The secret entomologist I have become takes the sting out of my irritation as a wife. What's more, HE doesn't read the e-mails but he knows what I put in them, what examples I use, and the presence of a third party makes him much more careful about what might upset me!' In other cases, nothing has apparently changed, and it is striking to find that the same annoying little details are still the focus of irritation and remain at the heart of conjugal life. The minuscule crystallizations have scarcely altered, and continue to dominate the lives in question: a fact which is a mine of information in itself.

Here is the text of this final appeal for information.

> After several months of silence, here is the latest news. My research on irritation has progressed well and has proved fascinating. It will be published in book form next February. I am currently working on the final draft of the manuscript, with a September deadline. It occurred to me that it might be fun to add a little paragraph as a 'stop press' item for each of you. Could you tell me in just a few lines (it could be just two lines if there is nothing much to tell, or 5–10, or more, though no more than 30 or 40) if there have been any developments regarding those little conjugal irritations since we were last in touch? Feel free to write about anything which comes to mind, whether about how the general atmosphere has evolved or about a specific event which has happened during these last few months.

The names used in the text and below are, of course, fictitious. Normally I choose them myself. In this case, the interviewees chose their own pseudonyms. Again I gave them total freedom. Here then is my cast list, to whom I can never fully express my gratitude for their close cooperation (as we know, the distance afforded by the internet helps bring people together).

Alice and Aziz

Alice: 'I'm fairly easy going but I have certain principles and values which are very important to me such as openness, loyalty, respect, trust, honesty, and if these are not taken seriously and respected I get incredibly upset. I am in fact a willing "victim" and I know it.' A victim for Aziz, who thoroughly enjoys upsetting her.

Aphrodite and Francis

Aphrodite: 'When we first met, ten years ago, we must have been quite modest and shy with each other because neither of us ever let ourselves go in front of the other. When I think about it, I reckon it was probably about five years before these little habits set in, at about the same time as routine took over . . .'

Stop press

'The summer has arrived but in terms of irritation nothing has changed and I don't thing anything ever will now. Sir is in the habit of picking his nose and chewing his nails . . . and he loves it!!!! Why stop just because I'm there? No that doesn't bother him in the slightest! As for me, it gets on my nerves as much as ever. I try not to pay attention but after a while I can't help it, I shout or I hit him (on the hands!!). I keep threatening to take a photo of him with his finger stuck up his nose, just so he can see what he looks like!'

Carla and 'J-P'

Carla: 'Luckily, this tendency to consult his mother about certain things, or to ask his parents for their advice, seems to be wearing off as time goes on. After all we've only been together for six months and before that he had never lived with anyone. So I think he sometimes just needs a bit of reassurance from the person who's been beside him all his life: his mum.'

Caroline and Marc

Caroline: 'In fact even at the age of 36, a man is still an adolescent. On the other hand, when I'm tired out, when I come in from a bad day at work, when our daughter is exhausting (as children of two and a half so often are) or my hormones are playing up, then I fly off the handle and it all comes out. In fact I deliberately look for ways of provoking an argument in order to be able to let off steam a bit. But I'm so lucky. I've got a man who has such an expressive face, he can apologize with just a look when he's gone a bit too far. And then, when he says: "You're right, I'm going to make a real effort", I just melt.'

Stop press

'What's the latest on the irritation front? Nothing much in fact because our lives have been pretty much turned upside down by the arrival of our second child, now two and a half months old. And we are so thrilled with our gorgeous family. . . . Although that reminds me of the supreme IRRITATION, the one which happens in the middle of giving birth when we women, bent double with the contractions (I had a rather "intense" and very, very quick birth with an epidural which worked perfectly once everything was all over! . . .), hear our men folk declare: "No, no, it doesn't hurt, it's all in the mind! . . . " I think I crushed Marc's hand hard at that point and he was lucky I didn't bite one of his fingers clean off. . . . His laid-back attitude just infuriated me!! However this irritation relating to childbirth fades very quickly when you see the way the new father looks at his child, a look which expresses so many things and so much love. What an adventure birth is. For everyone concerned! And since then, not a single irritation. Maybe it's just because I'm too exhausted because of the sleepless nights . . . haven't even got the strength to pick a fight. . . .'

196

Cassiopée

'I work very hard and often have to work in the evenings. My partner finds this difficult to accept and if I get back later than 1.30 a.m., he goes into a jealous rage just as if I was 14 years old – I'm actually 44.' Her husband is 63.

Stop press

'As a result of taking part in the project, I'm making progress and I think he is too:
– I've learned not to pay too much attention to things which don't matter (little mannerisms). And my children (11 and 4) are always ready to comment on things themselves, which sometimes makes a difference: they have more influence than I do;
– I'm more willing to let him tidy the kitchen and do something with the children rather than me doing everything as soon as I get in;
– I try to praise him more for the things he does do: various repairs around the house, the jewellery he repairs;
– I try not to make everybody do things at my speed – though it's very hard;
– because of my current state of mind, the everyday little vexations seem ridiculous and I try not to focus on them too much;
– I'm fully aware that he's not going to change but as his chief fault has always been to see the glass as half-empty – whereas with me it's the other way round – I'd like him to realize how lucky he is and to enjoy what he's got rather than focusing on all those negative little details which can poison your life.'

Clémentine and Félix

Clémentine: 'My husband is kind, charming . . . His one fault is that he doesn't listen to what you say to him!! It's not that he's deaf, he can hear perfectly well – it's just that he hears what you say to him but doesn't actually listen!! It's so irritating!!! Sometimes, he enjoys irritating me, and as he's a pretty useless actor, I can spot straight away that he's putting it on!!'

Stop press

'Since we were last in contact there's been some news: a new baby!! So here I am with two children . . . no, three children, aged 2 months, 3 and 33!!! My husband irritates me because he behaves like a child and that's just so irritating!! Recently he bought himself a new high-tech phone with amazing ring-tones, a big screen . . . Since then all he thinks about is his mobile!! On the rare occasions when we get to spend time together as a family, he just fiddles with his mobile phone or reads the handbook!!! Even before he got it he spent evening after evening on the internet comparing . . . mobile phones of course!! He's like a child with a new toy, except that he's 33!!! It was exactly the same with the new tractor we bought for the farm, and the new lorry. He's the same when we go away for the weekend; I have to do the packing for everyone. At 33, I just wish he'd start acting his age!!'

Eline and Jack

Eline: 'I'm currently working in public relations, and my partner and husband-to-be (we are getting married in May) is an engineer. We've known each other and have been living together for two years. We are 32 and 35 respectively. Both of us had had other relationships before we met, we've lived with other people, with whom we had a different kind of life; we've lived on our own, been single . . . So, when we got together we each had our own lives, we both knew what we needed and what we were looking for. In terms of character, we complement each other. Jack tends to be calm, discreet, sociable, introverted, reassuring, materialistic, very adaptable and ready to go along with things. I tend to be dynamic, extrovert, spontaneous, hyper, stressed, sociable, an organizer and initiator of various projects, a dreamer and not at all in touch with practical realities.'

Eliza and Robert

Eliza: 'I met my boyfriend 10 years ago (we are both 26). We met when we were at school, in the sixth form; we were in the same class. We "grew up" together: school, university, work experience, first jobs, first apartment, first holidays . . . the lot really. We finished studying three years ago and that's when we really began living together. So things started to get properly serious and we took the plunge. I think it was the fact of having a job and therefore a salary (which meant we could be independent from our parents) that made us realize our lives were really changing. In fact we're still aware of it now with the everyday things: doing the accounts, the shopping, the cleaning, the ironing: and that's where it starts to get complicated!!!'

Stop press
'As far as I'm concerned, lots of upheaval, because, after being off sick for quite a long period, I'm back at work and we've moved into a new flat. You're probably thinking that's irrelevant. But in fact it isn't at all. Because the change of flat, the end of my health problems . . . has breathed new life into things and given us fresh routines (and therefore a new way of organizing things as a couple), helped, in my opinion, by

198

the absence of internet and by the desire for a new start (but especially the internet). The new start shows itself by a more equal division of the domestic tasks, with my boyfriend taking charge of the ironing for example. We do more things together and our vision of the future has changed. We try to make the most of the present now, going away on holiday or for weekends. Which means he's a lot less "stay at home". And at last we're starting to plan things together, like moving, having a house built . . . I'm worried about having internet back again, because that could be the end of all these changes but I'm determined to keep our relationship fresh just like it is now.'

Fidelia and Pedro

Fidelia: 'My second son had problems with his girlfriend and was really shaken up by it: which was a big worry because this son is very fragile even though he's 24. Afterwards I met Pedro and it's he who's helped me bring him up, as well as his older brother. Then Pedro and I had another son together – he's now 18. We've always supported each other with the children and for me that's always been the priority. For a year now we've had "an empty nest" because the children are only there occasionally. To my surprise it's not as hard as I thought it would be.'

Stop press

'What's the latest on the little things that irritate us as a couple? . . . It's a bit like the weather, changeable and a bit unpredictable. I think the "little" irritations actually reflect the "big" ones, the frustrated expectations, the differences in our upbringing and culture, life's routines. Things like: "He should have realized that I wanted him to remember my birthday. I did remind him about it but he's too busy with his work and I don't count" – that's the latest irritation!'

Francky

'We've been married for 21 years. I'm 45 and my wife is 2 years younger. We've got two boys, aged 18 and 15. Nothing unusual about any of that. Things started to change in our relationship four years ago when I sold my company. One day an opportunity to sell came along – it was a good one and I couldn't afford to ignore it. The financial conditions were frankly exceptional and meant I could become . . . "A man of independent means".

The big problem in all this came because of the increased amount of time I was spending at home.'

Stop press

'The irritations are still there but they haven't got any worse. I'd even go as far as to suggest that they may be starting to get less. It so happens that we, my wife and I, have just spent two weeks without the children. Which seems to have meant that there have been fewer causes for irritation. Looking at my home life as if it were a company, a reduction in "personnel" means fewer conflicts with the assistant manager (my wife) with the result that the management of everyday life is considerably easier. Conclusion: take the two grumpy teenage boys out of the home and you will find things quickly calm down which means there are less things to get irritated about.'

Gally and Akira

Gally: 'We are both 30, we've been married for 6 years and have known each other for 9 years. My husband is extremely absent-minded and that really gets on my nerves. Our biggest problem for us is not having children: for a long time we weren't in any hurry (studies, first jobs . . .). Now the need is more pressing (especially for me) and I know that I could persuade him quite easily (it's not as if he was against the idea). The only thing is, I'm worried I'd end up looking after the child more or less on my own. Not that Akira would want to end the relationship but I'm concerned he'll just carry on behaving the way he does now. I can just imagine the result! Which is what makes me think twice about taking on another child in addition to the one I already share my life with.'

Stop press

'As an update, I can treat you to the latest example of my husband's "absent-mindedness" (he shows no sign of changing). Last week we went out to a bar for a drink with some friends. A young woman he didn't know had joined our usual group. She was sitting on a high stool and was wearing a rather clinging dress. Anyway it was immediately obvious, as soon as you looked at her, that she was at least 6 months pregnant. She quickly started talking to my husband because someone had told her he was a head-teacher and she wanted to know if he knew any way she could get a place in the crèche. It was urgent she said. My husband put her right by explaining that crèches and primary schools were completely separate which meant he was unable to help her. Later the young woman left, getting up from her chair slowly and making a point of supporting her belly with both hands. One of our friends made the comment that it must be awful being pregnant in this heat. Whereupon my husband exclaims: "Why, is she pregnant?" Of course, everyone burst out laughing. But he was absolutely serious, he hadn't noticed a thing (one might

200

well ask why she would have been talking to him about crèches, but that hadn't occurred to him either). Our friends found his absent-mindedness (as usual) extraordinary and very funny. I did not. I just found it exasperating to be reminded once again that he just doesn't pay the slightest attention to things. It's true (as a girlfriend said) that he doesn't look at other women, which ought to be reassuring for me. Except that he doesn't look at his own wife either. I wonder how long it would take him to notice, if I ever took the decision, that I was pregnant myself???'

Gautier

'The thing is, I'm quite a tidy person, though not obsessively so, and it's not as if she is completely disorganized herself. I think that's what gets on my nerves, the fact that these are little things which could easily be dealt with: it's not as if it would take a superhuman effort to put the newspapers in the same place each time, or to throw a bit of paper away once she no longer needs it. So why not just do it? That aside, I must point out that these little irritations never get out of hand. We have a really good relationship, and if anything were ever to threaten it, I'm pretty sure it wouldn't be anything to do with that.'

Isabelle

'If on certain days my darling other half squeezes the middle of the tube, or if he puts his mobile phone down on my pretty lacquered table which is so easily scratched (but for God's sake how many times do you have to be told not to dump it there!) I will happily forgive him because he has always managed to find his own way to the laundry basket and he changes the toilet rolls, praise be to him. At other times no, I've done my bit, and frankly it was a thousand times worse, what with the cigarette ends floating in the coffee dregs – you should try it, it's a great way of annoying the idiot who's going to be washing the cup.'

Stop press
Over the last few months Isabelle and her boyfriend have been looking at properties, with a view to buying a (first) home. New differences, hitherto undetected, have come to light as a result. 'The combination of someone who loves old buildings and who goes into raptures over anything that's a bit dusty, dilapidated but with "fantastic potential", and an obsessive who can't stand dust, badly made things and cupboards which don't close, promises to be an interesting one. And indeed it has been. The evening *debriefing* is an excuse for the two of us to call each other every name under the sun. One can't stand galley kitchens and the other says "but darling, when you've got friends round it's so much

nicer to be able to chat while you're preparing the food", "er yes, so you do the cooking now do you? – that's a first, and I suppose that means I have to try and do the washing-up surreptitiously, do I?". The same with the separate toilet and bathroom issue, a major issue for us. One goes round tapping all the pipes for some obscure reason, the other spends their time scrupulously checking the tiles on the work surfaces to check they're perfectly straight. We turn our noses up at certain wall-papers, but not at the same ones. He makes a fuss about frilly curtains, but what's the point, they're not going to leave them anyway! Yes, but they're so ugly and they can completely ruin a living room and make it look utterly kitsch. And that's that. I picture the magnificent bar we could have in pride of place there, he can only think about how you'd have to break up this and re-plaster that and rip out all the tiling, and he's already getting into a sweat about it while his other half is rushing excitedly from room to room planning what it's going to be like. Just the thought of it all gives him backache.'

Jade

'I'm always on the warpath, fighting on several fronts at once. My emo-tional experiences all seem to follow the same pattern. The older I get, the more choosey I become. I'm almost 47, divorced, with a little girl of 11, I'm extremely independent. When I try to turn a blind eye to the things that irritate me, it's because I'm trying to force myself to be less rigid, attempting each time, or as often as possible (depending on my mood) to question my own reactions. I console myself with the thought that there's no such thing as perfection.'

Stop press

'My relationship with my boyfriend, if I can call him that, has got worse by the day – you can't teach an old dog new tricks. He continues to speak and behave in ways which verge on the unacceptable. I've tried everything, kindness, diplomacy, he's made an effort over some things but I sense that it's a real struggle. Seriously irritated by his behaviour these last few months the gloves are off and I don't hold back from letting him know when he's being disrespectful. He doesn't seem to have any self-respect, any pride. As a result I am quite hard on him and don't mince my words. In spite of that, he takes no notice and is still very clinging; he gets suspicious, jealous, a bit possessive, nosey and extremely indiscreet. Take the example of the chrysanthemums he bought me. I'd already told him I hated those flowers but he did the same thing again recently. This time he bought me two bunches (the second bunch was free, as he had the cheek to inform me!). I asked him who had died (secretly I was thinking it was our relationship . . .). I'm sure he didn't do it on purpose but I'm not going to keep making excuses for him any more when we've been going out together for three years. I haven't had a physical relationship with him for eight months, I just can't help it, he's let me down, he doesn't thrill me any more, I'm ashamed of him in public, he's "slow". I'm not making plans any more; I'm just letting things go downhill.'

Kasiu

After a long list of complaints, Kasiu ends with these words: 'Whew!!!! Apart from that everything is fine, he has lots of great qualities and I adore him. We met when we were both 19 and we're 33 now. I have my faults too and you have to be able to make concessions if you're going to succeed as a couple.'

Stop press

'The really big issue isn't an irritation any more, it's a PROBLEM: my mother. Nothing new about it but it's on my mind because I almost killed her yesterday. She would like to have her children all to herself and can't bear any of their partners. The worst possible way of creating tensions within the couple!!!!

And then a husband who adores children and wants me to have a second child, which irritates me hugely. In one sense I'd really like to, but on the other hand I don't think it's a good idea because of the crazy way we live what with the bus or tube, stress at work and being broke at the end of each month because of ridiculous property prices and the taxes they hit us with.

As far as the little things go, nothing's changed: with him it's the elbow on the table when we're eating and for me the eternal dilemma of how to have my hair done (should I let it grow or have it cut short?) and those endless diets which upset my system so much that the scales have leapt up 20 kilos!!!!'

Lamia

'On the subject of what I feel about the fact that my husband is always losing things out of his shirt pockets, what makes me smile is that it's as though I'm dealing with a little boy who keeps doing the same silly thing over and over again and it's a feeling not dissimilar to the sort of tenderness I feel about the silly little things my son keeps doing.'

Stop press

'I can give you a whole list of things which irritate me at the moment and it's just as well that you've got in touch again because right now things really are coming to a bit of a head. . . . The irritations stem from the fact that the kids are on holiday (and our parents aren't yet) and that we've both got demanding jobs. His worship gets home in the evening feeling tired and irritated and incapable of seeing beyond the end of his nose, not realizing that madam, between the three phone lines in the office (plus her mobile), the fifteen-strong team she manages who are constantly in and out of her office, the files piling up on her desk, also has to organize:

– the dinner;
– the running of the house and the jobs which have to be done in the summer (washing the carpets etc. . . .);
– the children's timetable (who they are going to have round to play, what they're going to eat, the Disney comic to buy);
– phoning the kids at regular intervals to make sure that they're wearing their hats and have got plenty of sun block on;
– ordering the school books (yes, here in Morocco you have to do it in plenty of time because the books are imported and they always run out of stock);
– preparing the list of what to pack for the holiday, far too much according to his worship, who as it turns out, finds himself rather grateful for the after-sun cream (having not worn the tee-shirt I'd carefully packed for him), and the antiseptic cream (having not worn the beach shoes I'd bought for him and managing to step on sea urchins).

And then what does his worship do? He turns up at the breakfast table, dressed, neatly shaved, and that's when he says (every morning): "Oh, I feel so guilty when I see the kids stuck mindlessly in front of the TV all day long. Send them to my sister's." When he knows that yours truly can't stand his sister and he **doesn't know** that his dear sister calls *him* to suggest sending the kids and then calls *me* to ask me to send along a meal for them. And when I have the misfortune to say: "They've had enough sun these last few days at your sister's. Let them just relax at home for a bit now", it's the scandal of the century. That REALLY gets on my nerves!!'

Lorenzo

'When she drives I get really irritated. She drives too slowly, is too cautious, doesn't take her right of way, etc. When it comes to the kids, she worries about the slightest little thing (in my opinion). Accuses me of dressing them any old way when it's me getting them dressed.'

Stop press

'Nothing new really, except . . . Well yes, actually, two little anecdotes. 1. Our two daughters (5-year-old twins) are going away on holiday with their grandparents for two weeks, and my wife announces: "Oh,

I've got to pack their cases because it's no use waiting for you to do it and it's always me who ends up doing it!" To which I reply: "I can do it if you like." "No, no, no. Certainly not. You'd forget half the things they need." Which is fairly typical isn't it? She wants people to feel sorry for her, rather than letting someone else do the job. 2. the other day, I pointed out to her that the tidiness and discipline she imposes on the whole household goes out of the window when it comes to her own paperwork. She grumbled but didn't say anything.'

Malvina and Richard

Malvina: 'I was single for thirty years. That year I went off to India with a copy of *La femme seule et le Prince charmant* in my luggage . . . and a lot of things started to make sense. For a long time, while I was still militantly single, there were things about some of the couples I saw around me, including my own parents, that I found unacceptable. For example, the way roles were allocated according to gender (along the lines of men go out hunting and women do everything else), in other words the failure to share tasks. Anyway, I was on a bit of a high horse over all that, then once I got into my thirties, the hormones kicked in and I wanted to settle down. Which suited him too. By the laws of homogamy we met through one of his work colleagues, we had the same level of qualifications, his parents were craftspeople, from an agricultural background, mine were agricultural labourers. In his eyes I was the perfect woman to bring up his children – I'm a teacher. I liked him because he didn't run a mile when I talked about commitment – I wanted a child quickly – and his views were very much in line with my own principles: "I don't see why you should iron my shirts. You're not my maid." Four and a half years later, our little girl is three and a half and . . . he drives me CRAZY!'

Stop press

'When I got your message my first reaction was one of surprise: "That's true, he hasn't really got on your nerves for quite a while!!" But on reflection there have been quite a few sources of irritation. In fact I think it's a sort of desensitizing process, something you gradually get used to. Since I last wrote to you we've acquired some land of our own and have started to construct a wooden house. There was the occasion when the architect was trying to impose his views on me and my darling (in front of the architect) said that if I wasn't satisfied then I'd better build my own house! Then there were the dealings with the bank: after wasting hours of time in meetings with the different banks, he short-circuited me and insisted on using his own!! In general, what gets on my nerves is the way he systematically either gets in ahead of me or corrects what I've done as soon as I've finished doing it. For example: at 8 o'clock in the morning we agree that I need to call a supplier and at 9 he rings me to say he's done it . . . and at the slightest disagreement, he throws in my face the fact that I haven't done a thing towards the house. Then there are the money worries: we've both got good jobs, but he wants every-thing immediately, so we spend. As I don't have any savings, he lends me certain sums, saying we'll sort it out later; then, as soon as I buy some little thing he announces that I've got to pay him back immedi-ately. As you see, the sources of irritation haven't gone away but it's true that they only really affect me at the time now because I know that he's got a very impulsive temperament and is always ready to apologize.

Anyway, today is one of the best days of my life because we've just discovered we're going to have a baby and his joy wipes out all the irri-tation he's caused!!! However I know there'll be more to come because he wants a boy (he'll be "damned" if we have another girl) because he doesn't want all his inheritance to go to some no-good or other (as though the riff-raff were only ever boys and girls were too stupid to get rid of them!!) There's no end to it!!'

Markus

'My first wife irritated me because she was really extremely lethargic, in every way. With the second one, it's the opposite, she wears me out, she's a permanent tornado. Perhaps that's why, for fear of provoking the tornado, I don't say anything when she irritates me, for example when she comes back from the shops with useless gadgets she's spent a fortune on.'

Stop press

'Your research has had a curious effect. By writing what I wrote, it reo-pened the wound and made me feel even more irritated than usual. There were two or three little outbursts, whereas normally I just switch off. And then afterwards it had the opposite effect. I found myself think-ing that all this was ridiculous and pointless. This summer there's a real calm in the house. Whew! I just switch off even more, I've become quite a specialist.'

Max

'Other little irritations: the bedroom window left open at night: letting in noise, sometimes rain in the middle of the night, but above all the cold . . . Especially when someone can't stop tossing about all over the place. There are fights over the cover or the duvet in the heat of the "battle". It also lets in all sorts of wildlife . . . spiders, mosquitoes . . . That's certainly the worst. . . . The sight of the bed in such a mess at the start of the day . . . the sheets all over the place, the cover half off the bed, the duvet rolled into a ball, when the other person likes things to be neat and tidy and wants to be able to slip into a crisply made bed in the evening!'

Maya and Igor

Maya: 'At first I didn't take much notice of the fact that he never knew where anything was and when we were just sharing the same place rather than really living as a couple, I thought perhaps he just didn't want to rummage around and wasn't quite sure where things were kept. But gradually, this habit of his has become more and more irritating to the extent that I no longer answer the question!'

Stop press

'I'm really sorry not to have been able to provide you with anything more substantial. In fact, as I am separating from my boyfriend it is not easy to be very objective about the things that irritated me about him.'

Melody and "HE"

Melody: 'I appreciate grace, elegance. My husband is a handsome man who could have tremendous presence, but he couldn't care less about all that. With this little gesture of his, in the space of thirty seconds, HE takes me back to the working classes and physical slovenliness (I'm talking beer, sausage, beer-bellies and a good post-beer belch). Seduction score minus 40! The fact that my own children don't irritate me in this kind of situation seems like further confirmation, they are not yet fully independent, "finished"; I can, and must, still guide them; plus they don't need to seduce me sexually. The last thing I want is to be a mother to my husband.'

Stop press

'Here we are, just back from our holiday, and it's exactly as I thought: "It's all a matter of sex-appeal!". My husband, handsome as a god when he's dressed up (for a wedding), can walk in the ONE dog mess on the Croisette at Cannes, to the amusement of the tourists sat on a nearby bench, and I smile and say proudly: "That's my man, and I've been in love with him for 25 years". Mind you, lolling around, on holiday, difficult to prise off his sun lounger, I was more than just irritated – more like completely exasperated. All the more so because we were staying in a place full of old couples, and the sight of those beaches heaving with plump old dears and their saggy looking husbands, flabby but so sweet and docile, didn't exactly make me look forward to my old age! My usual reactions: looking away, then feeling irritated, some sharp remarks, when "enough is enough". Or rather not enough. And of course the usual dishonest rubbish from our hero who claims: "If it wasn't for you and the kids, I'd be off on a rally in a four-wheel drive." I just shrug my shoulders faced with this armchair adventurer, I explain for the hundredth time that it's all about seduction. Cue more dishonest rubbish: "I can't do seduction!" Another shrug of the shoulders from me. So how come I've stayed with him so long then? I distanced myself, barely even responding to him, sometimes I thought about walking away, about living on my own, rather than with this dead weight at my side draining my energy.

He managed (one wonders how) to revive his sex-appeal, as easily as changing gear in the car; so I went straight from being a shrew to being tender, won over, playful, and off we go again . . .'

Mimie and Michaël

Mimie: 'Let me introduce myself: Mimie, 22 years old, a student. I've been living for ten months with my boyfriend Mickaël whom I've known for three years. I'll quickly tell you how it all started; we met at school in the lower sixth and it was strange at first because Mickaël, who is five years older than me, was reluctant to get involved because of a difficult past. Our biggest problem is that we're finding it more and more difficult to talk to each other, things quickly escalate with me going too far, which I get from my mother, and him becoming aggressive because he can't stand what he calls my childishness or whims . . . it makes him furious.'

Stop press

'At the moment we're going through a calmer period, because with everything that was going on, we've tried to react in the most intelligent way possible, in other words we're both working on doing our own thing and leaving each other in peace, which has meant that, given the fears each of us had, we've been able to discuss things more calmly and move things on a bit. It's strange but I feel that the difficulties we've had in living together might be largely the result of the fact that we've both found it hard to break away from our own family ties, something much more deeply rooted than I ever thought. I realized that I was unconsciously reproducing my mother's gestures as though they were indisputably the right ones, the only possible ones. And those "violent" outbursts that we had (I speak about them in the past as though they will never happen again . . .) have really made us realize we had to do something about the situation. Michaël had imagined himself with someone rather like his mother, and horror, it turned out to be his mother-in-law! And as for me, I'd hoped to find in him the ideal father, whereas in fact he behaves exactly like his own father.'

Mireille

'He got on my nerves to such an extent that I've thrown him out, after 6 years of living together. . . . He was, is, and always will be STINGY!!! That's hard, very hard, especially when it's the man you love, and who, what's more, was my second husband.'

Nicole

'There are irritations and there are the unbearable things which are more difficult to cope with. There are so many of these that it feels as if we must be incompatible. For a starter, let me tell you about one little thing. He makes too much noise when he eats. [. . .] I'm what you might call hyper and my husband is slow, to the point of being bone idle. The fact that my husband needs more sleep than I do really gets on my nerves, especially when he gets up late after staying up until all hours.'

Rosy and Charly

Rosy: 'Married for ten years to a crazy German, lived on my own for fifteen years, now with a hopelessly disorganized Italian lover' – in other words, Charly, who adores mayonnaise and lives in his own place.

Stop press

'Any news. . . ? It's crazy how some things can change so much in the space of a year . . . My "crises" seem so far behind me now. My Italian and I each still live in our own places . . . but I don't get irritated about that anymore . . . could that be down to the blood pressure medication we're both taking . . . ? Or because my mother is so pleased I've found someone that I don't want to let her down? Perhaps because I'm in "energy saving" mode at the moment. And I think even more importantly, he's basically so kind, that he just doesn't deserve having to put up with someone difficult . . . so I make an effort! And he senses when things aren't going well and puts things right by saying "something's bothering you isn't it?" which calms me down. This month we're celebrating three years together: are those irritations just something that

209

happens in the early stages? I think so because after that either they become real obstacles or they just disappear.'

Sarah and Peter

Sarah: 'I'm nearly 51, I've been living for three years with a man I met three and a half years ago. He's a man who is exceptionally kind to me, always doing little things for me, attentive . . . TOO MUCH SO! I was married for 25 years to a very cold, unaffectionate man, cruel even towards the end of our relationship. And here I am with the exact opposite.'

Stop press

'Since we were last in touch, the situation hasn't changed, I still haven't got used to that laugh of my partner's, but I try not to mention it any more, because I don't think that he'll change. When we're on our own I can ignore it, but when we're with other people, family or friends it really embarrasses me. I could carry on asking him why he keeps on laughing like that at the end of each sentence, but I know it won't change anything. "I can't help it, accept me as I am" There we are – what more can I do? I must have my little faults too . . .'

Virag

'The thing that irritates me most about him, is his immaturity and I really think that is the source of all our problems [. . .] We've got three children, and I honestly feel I've got a fourth one all to myself. When I talk to my friends about it, I feel guilty, because there are much worse things than that, but at the same time I can't help feeling irritated on a daily basis.'

Stop press

'As far as irritations are concerned, my man realizes now that what he thought was a "cool" character trait could be really irritating in everyday life. I think he's always known it, but didn't think it mattered. It's true that when someone's got a major fault that's really obvious it's easier to put up with than when there are just little insidious irritations. It wasn't so much his faults that I minded, but the fact that he didn't do anything about them and didn't change them to fit in with family life. Anyway we reached a point a few months ago where I told him in no uncertain terms that I didn't love him enough to put up with him. That really shook him. He made an effort and I'm pleased to say that things are a lot better but I know he'll have to be reminded on a regular basis. I'm trying to be more patient too, to put things into perspective more, but sometimes it's very difficult to argue with the way I feel.'

210

Yannis

'My girlfriend is 31 and I'm 34. We've been together for 7 years and we've got a little girl who's three and a half. We don't really have many major rows. Mostly that's for two main reasons: we discuss things a lot, we understand each other pretty well, and we give each other – where possible – a certain amount of freedom. The other reason is that we noticed that often any rows we had were to do with things outside our little family: a stressful situation to do with her job or mine, a relative, a friend, colleague who had upset one of us.'

Stop press

'Well, in the space of a few months, quite a few "little things" have happened. In October, our second daughter will be born, which will mean a reorganization of our living space and all sorts of things that will or won't need to be changed: decorating (or not) new curtains (or not), etc. Not to mention the usual pregnant woman stuff: "Do I look fat? Do you think these clothes still look OK? Do you think I'll be as "good" a mother as for the eldest?" Etc., etc. + mood swings, tears, fatigue, ("I'm exhausted, I'm going up to bed"). The answer to all this? There isn't one. In my case, keep things in perspective (never offer a definite opinion or take a radical and definitive position on anything, because whether it's "black or white", you'll be wrong and she will blame you!) So I prevaricate, I go along with whatever she wants, and I tell myself this won't last for ever.'

Zoé and Charles-Henri

Zoé: 'I'm 39 and have two children aged 9 and 7. Their father is dead. My boyfriend has lived with us for four years now [. . .] The tension between us mostly comes from the fact that he behaves in a way that's completely the opposite to the way I'm trying to bring my children up (good table manners, putting things away, language).'

Stop press

'There are big changes on the horizon: we've decided to separate. He's leaving, to give me room to breathe and enjoy life fully with my children. In fact, the little irritations sometimes got really out of hand. I could only see the things that weren't working. In the end I couldn't cope with our relationship. We know what's gone wrong but there's no going back. At least he would like to, but I just can't anymore. I don't have either the strength or the energy. I need to be on my own, at breakfast time, on my sofa, in my bed, in my bathroom, in my head, with my children. I realize now that the passion we felt at the beginning of the relationship stopped

211

me noticing lots of little things which I didn't think mattered but which actually set the "tone" of our life together. It was only by letting myself be nonchalant and carefree that I was able to survive.

Certain aspects of daily life became unbearable. In fact, in the important matters, there was a gulf between us because we were much too different in terms of who we were and how we lived. It was as though I was suddenly given a jolt, I came back to earth again. I realize that emotionally I haven't got my balance back yet and this episode in my life has affected me both physically and psychologically. It's time for me to repair the foundations which have been badly shaken, so I can give my children the support they'll need. I just don't want to have anyone around while I'm doing that.'

A research project cannot be emptied out like a bag

A false image prevails concerning the techniques for the analysis of contents: that of a bag that simply needs to be emptied out for the results to be known. Nothing could be further from the truth in terms of scientific methods, since it is the work carried out on the material and that alone which leads to new knowledge (Kaufmann, 2006). This kind of work could go on endlessly, on any given research project. No bag will ever be completely empty.

Without going quite to the extreme of constantly going back over the same research, I now increasingly try to look at past material from a fresh perspective (my tapes are securely stored as though they were a priceless treasure), hoping to re-engage with it in a longer and, I hope, fruitful dialogue. I genuinely think that one should never completely lose touch with the people one has interviewed at one time or another. Readers of my previous books, *La Trame conjugale* (*Dirty Linen*), *Le Cœur à l'ouvrage*, *Premier matin* and *Casseroles, amour et crises* will perhaps be surprised, and I hope pleased, to reacquaint themselves in the course of these pages with Agnès, Léon, Colombine or Ninette, in the throes of some new adventures. Anyone wishing for further biographical details about any of these need simply consult the appendix sections of the relevant book.

I also increasingly try to consult the work of other researchers on related subjects, and to quote their subjects. It seems to me that this introduces a small but sympathetic nod in the direction of a collaborative spirit. A few details about the individuals concerned, along with references to the relevant works, are provided in the following list. The list also includes a third group of participants, chosen from chat rooms I came across in the course of surfing the net, an inexhaustible source of introspection and confessions of all descriptions.

My other sources

Agnès and **Jean,** *La Trame conjugale*
Alex, chat room source
Alphonsine, material obtained by letter
Anaïs and **Pat,** *La Trame conjugale* (in which Anaïs was called Anne. Her name has been changed to avoid confusion)
Anita and **Luc,** both bakers, both 38, married for 15 years (Bartiaux, 2002)
Anne and **Louis,** Anne is a journalist and Louis a decorator. They have lived together for six months (Alhinc-Lorenzi, 1997)
Annette and **Alex** (Maschino, 1995)
Artemiss, 17, chat room source
Aurélie, 24, temp (Garabuau-Moussaoui, 2002)
Béatrice, 28, part-time executive, married to **Alain,** 32, technician (Eleb, 2002)
Cali, 20, in a relationship for two years, chat room source
Candy, *Casseroles, amour et crises*
Christine, 53, nurse, married to **Daniel,** 56, manual worker (Mons, 1998)
Cindy, material obtained by letter, married for 30 years
Claudie, 37, teacher, and **Pierre,** 36, journalist, married for eleven years, three children (Gacem, 1996)
Colombine and **Franck,** *Premier matin*
Dorothée, 41, housewife married to **Roberto,** 39, one child (Kaufmann, 1988)
Estelle, 29, engineer, married to **Julien,** 31, pharmacist (Kaufmann, 1988)
Eve, 54, nursing auxiliary, step-family (Martuccelli, 2006)
Géraldine and **Bernard,** *La Trame conjugale*
Jennifer, chat room source
Juliette, *Premier matin*
Léon, *Le Cœur à l'ouvrage*
Lola, *Le Cœur à l'ouvrage*
Mrs Blanc, 56, housewife, husband 60, retired senior executive (Caradec, 1996)
Mrs Louis, 53, housewife, husband 65, retired senior executive (Caradec, 1996)

Mrs Tinsart, 51, married for twenty-one years (Lemarchant, 1999)

Mrs Vannier, 50, housewife, husband teacher (Caradec, 1996)

Madeleine, *Casseroles, amour et crises*

Marie-Agnès, 36, office worker married to **Marc,** 39, teacher (Mons, 1998)

Marie-Anne, 55, housewife, husband sales rep., married for 30 years (thesis in progress by Sofian Beldjerd)

Marie-Lyse (Duret, 2007)

Martine (Flahault, 1987)

Mr Berg, 59, middle manager, in the process of a divorce after 37 years of marriage (Caradec, 1996)

Nathalie (Duret, 2007)

Olivia, chat room source

Pascal and **Ninette,** *La Trame conjugale*

Pénélope, 34, her boyfriend is 31, chat room source

Raf and **Dolorès,** chat room source

Sabine and **Romain,** *La Trame conjugale*

Suzette, *Casseroles, amour et crises*

Tony, *Casseroles, amour et crises*

Thomas, student (Bouchat, 2005)

Vincent, *Premier matin*

BIBLIOGRAPHY

Alberoni, F. (1993), first French edition 1981), *Le choc amoureux?* Paris: Pocket.

Alhinc-Lorenzi, M.-P. (1997), *Étude de cas d'une cohabitation juvénile. Le rôle des objets comme marqueurs de l'intégration conjugale,* post-graduate diploma in Social Science, under the supervision of P. Gaboriau, René Descartes University.

André, C. (2006), *Imparfaits, libres et heureux. Pratiques de l'estime de soi,* Paris: Odile Jacob.

Bachelard, G. (1948), *La terre et les rêveries du repos. Essai sur les images de l'intimité,* Paris: José Corti.

Bartiaux, F. (2002), 'Relégation et identité: les déchets domestiques et la sphère privé', in M. Pierre, *Les déchets ménagers, entre privé et public. Approches sociologiques,* Paris: L'Harmattan.

Beck, U. and Beck-Gernsheim, E. (1995), *The Normal Chaos of Love,* Cambridge: Polity Press.

Berger, P. and Kellner, H. (1988), 'Le mariage et la construction de la réalité', *Dialogue,* 102.

Bouchat, C. (2005), *'Ici c'est chez moi, chez eux, chez nous . . . et chez personne à la fois.' Une approche ethnologique du cohabiter en 'kot',* Sociology and Anthropology dissertation, under the supervision of Olivier Gosselain, Université Libre, Brussels.

Bozon, M. (2002), *Sociologie de la sexualité,* Paris: Nathan; Armand Colin, 2005.

— (2004), 'La nouvelle normativité des conduites sexuelles, ou la difficulté de mettre en cohérence les expériences intimes', in J. Marquet, *Normes et conduites sexuelles. Approches sociologiques et ouvertures pluridisciplinaires,* Louvain-la-Neuve: Academia-Bruylant.

Brenot, P. (2001), *Inventer le couple,* Paris: Odile Jacob.

Bromberger, C. (1998), *Passions ordinaires: du match de football au concours de dictée,* Paris: Bayard.

Brown, E. and Jaspard, M. (2004), 'La place de l'enfant dans les conflits et les violences conjugales', *Recherches et Prévisions,* 78.

Buser, P. (2005), *L'inconscient aux milles visages,* Paris: Odile Jacob.

215

Caradec, V. (1996), *Le couple à l'heure de la retraite*, Rennes: Presses Universitaires de Rennes.

Castelain-Meunier, C. (2005), *Les métamorphoses du masculin*, Paris: PUF.

Cosson, M.-E. (1990), *Représentation et évaluation du mariage des enfants par les mères*, Masters Sociology thesis, under the supervision of François de Singly, University of Rennes 2.

Damasio, A. (1995), *L'erreur de Descartes. La raison des émotions*, Paris: Odile Jacob.

Desjeux, D., Monjaret, A. and Taponier, S. (1998), *Quand les français déménagent*, Paris: PUF.

Douglas, M. (1992), *De la souillure, Essai sur les notions de pollution et de tabou*, Paris: La Découverte.

Dubet, F. (1994), *Sociologie de l'expérience*, Paris: Seuil.

— (2002), *Le déclin de l'institution*, Paris: Seuil.

Duret, P. (2007), *Le couple face au temps*, Paris: Armand Colin.

Eleb, M. (2002), *À deux chez soi. Des couples s'installent et racontent leur maison*, Paris: La Martinière.

Flahault, F. (1987), *La scène de ménage*, Paris: Denoël.

Festinger, L. (1957), *A Theory of Cognitive Dissonance*, Evanston: Row, Peterson & Co.

Francescato, D. (1992), *Quando l'amore finisce*, Bologna: Il Molino.

Gacem, K. (1996), *Les propriétés individuelles dans la chambre conjugale*, Masters Sociology thesis, under the supervision of François de Singly, University of Paris 5.

Garabuau-Mussaoui, I. (2002), *Cuisine et indépendances. Jeunesse et alimentation*, Paris: L'Harmattan.

Gavron, K. (1996), 'Du mariage arrangé au mariage d'amour', *Terrain*, 27.

Geberowicz B. and Barroux, C. (2005), *Le Baby-Clash. Le couple à l'épreuve de l'enfant*, Paris: Albin Michel.

Giddens, A. (1991), *Modernity and Self-Identity. Self and Society in the Late Modern Age*, Cambridge: Polity Press.

Glaude M. and Singly, F. de (1986), 'L'organization domestique: pouvoir et négociation', *Économie et Statistique*, 187.

Goffman, E. (1975), *Stigmates. Les usages sociaux des handicaps*, Paris: Minuit.

— (1991), *Les cadres de l'expérience*, Paris: Minuit.

Hardy, F. (2005), *Portes qui claquent, mots qui blessent. Analyse compréhensive des habitudes liées à la territorialité familiale*, Sociology dissertation, supervised by Jean Pierre Pourtois, Mons-Hainaut University.

Hefez, S. and Laufer, D. (2002), *La danse du couple*, Paris: Hachette Littératures.

Hirschman, A. (1972, first edition 1970), *Face au déclin des entreprises et des institutions*, Paris: Les éditions ouvrières – Économie et Humanisme.

Hoyau, P.-A. and Le Pape, M.-C. (2006), 'Femmes au volant; une analyse sexuée de la conduite automobile', 2nd Congress of the Association française de Sociologie, Bordeaux, 5–8 September.

Jonas, N. (2006), 'Beaux-frères, belles-sœurs. Les relations entre germains affins', *Terrains et Travaux*, 10, *Dynamiques du genre* issue, edited by Anne Revillard and Laure de Verdalle.

Kaplan, H. (1995), *The Sexual Desire Disorders. Dysfunctional Regulation of Sexual Motivation*, Levittown: Brunner/Mazel.

Kaufmann, J.-C. (1988), *La peur de la porte,* research undertaken in the context of le Plan-Construction for the Ministry of Housing and Public Works.
— (1992), *La Trame conjugale. Analyse du couple par son linge,* Paris: Nathan. (1998), *Dirty Linen: Couples and their Laundry,* London: Middlesex University Press.)
— (1997), *Le Cœur à l'ouvrage. Théorie de l'action ménagère,* Paris: Nathan.
— (1999), *La femme seule et le Prince charmant. Enquête sur la vie en solo,* Paris: Nathan; 2nd edition, Armand Colin, 2006 (2008, *The Single Woman and the Fairytale Prince,* Cambridge: Polity Press.)
— (2001), *Ego. Pour une sociologie de l'individu,* Paris: Nathan.
— (2002), *Premier matin. Comment naît une histoire d'amour,* Paris: Armand Colin.
— (2004), *L'invention de soi. Une théorie de l'identité,* Paris: Armand Colin.
— (2005), *Casseroles, amour et crises. Ce que cuisiner veut dire,* Paris: Armand Colin.
— (2006), *L'enquête et ses méthodes. L'entretien compréhensif,* Paris: Armand Colin.
Kiley, D. (1996, first edition 1983), *Le Syndrome de Peter Pan. Ces hommes qui ont refusé de grandir,* 'Opus' collection, Paris: Odile Jacob.
Knibielher, Y. and Fouquet, C. (1982), *Histoire des mères, du Moyen Âge à nos jours,* Paris: Hachette-Pluriel.
Laplantine, F. (2005), *Le social et le sensible: introduction à une anthropologie modale,* Paris: Téraèdre.
Le Bart, C., with the collaboration of J.-C. Ambroise (2000), *Les fans des Beatles, sociologie d'une passion,* Rennes: Presses Universitaires de Rennes.
Le Breton, D. (2002), *Conduites à risque. Des jeux de mort au jeu de vivre,* Paris: PUF.
Le Douarin, L. (2005), 'L'ordinateur et les relations père–fils', in D. Le Gall, *Genres de vie et intimités. Chroniques d'une autre France,* Paris: L'Harmattan.
Lemarchant, C. (1999), *Belles-filles. Avec les beaux-parents, trouver la bonne distance,* Rennes: Presses Universitaires de Rennes.
Markus, H. (1977), 'Self-schemata and processing information about self', *Journal of Personality and Social Psychology,* vol 35, 2.
Martuccelli, D. (2006), *Forgé par l'épreuve. L'individu dans la France contemporaine,* Paris: Armand Colin.
Maschino, M. (1995), *Mensonges à deux,* Paris: Calmann-Lévy.
Mons, J. (1998), *Séparer ses poubelles: une scène de ménage? Analyse du couple par sa gestion des déchets,* dissertation on family studies, under the supervision of Françoise Bartiaux, Louvain Catholic University.
Perrot, M. (2000), *Présenter son conjoint: l'épreuve du repas de famille,* post-graduate diploma in Sociology, under the supervision of Jean-Hugues Déchaux, Paris IEP.
Picard, D. and Marc, E. (2006), *Petit traité des conflits ordinaires,* Paris: Seuil.
Poitou, J.-P. (1974), *La dissonance cognitive,* Paris: Armand Colin.
Ricœur, P. (1990), *Soi-même comme un autre,* 'Points' collection, Paris: Seuil.
Sauvageot, A. (2003), *L'épreuve des sens. De l'action sociale à la réalité virtuelle,* Paris: PUF.
Schwartz, O. (1990), *Le monde privé des ouvriers. Hommes et femmes du Nord,* Paris: PUF.

Séverac, N. (2005), 'La violence conjugale, une relation qui ne peut se comprendre que de l'intérieur', in D. Le Gall, *Genres de vie et intimités. Chroniques d'une autre France*, Paris: l'Harmattan.

Singly, F. de (1987), *Fortune et infortune de la femme mariée*, Paris: PUF.

— (2000), *Libres ensemble. L'individualisme dans la vie commune*, Paris: Nathan.

— (2005), *L'individualisme est un humanisme*, La Tour d'Aigues: Éditions de l'Aube.

Stevens, H. (1996), *Les couples et la politique. Double je ou double jeu?* Sociology dissertation, under the supervision of A. Quémin, University of Versailles-Saint-Quentin-en-Yvelines.

Thévenot, L. (1994), 'Le régime de familiarité. Des choses en personne', *Genèses*, 17.

— (2006), *L'Action au pluriel. Sociologie des régimes d'engagement*, Paris: La Découverte.

Welzer-Lang, D. (2004), *Les hommes aussi changent*, Paris: Payot.

INDEX

INDEX

mealtimes: beginning and early stages of
conjugal life 14, 17; cause of irritation
24–5, 72–3, 76, 82, 86–7, 122, 145;
comfort zone of conjugal life 24–5; coping
techniques 143–4, 145; disgust 133–5
Melody and HE: causes of irritation 24–5,
81–2; coping techniques 143–4, 145, 154;
disgust 135, 143; gender difference 48;
positive responses 163–4, 165, 166, 167,
169–70, 171–2, 173, 177, 184–5; research
subjects 194, 207–8
men: independence 84; irritation 45–9; macho
attitudes 57–61; mothers 114–21, 196;
perceived to be like children 51, 52–7, 61,
115, 180, 196, 197–8, 203, 210
Mimie and Mickaël: causes of irritation 70,
144; research subjects 208–9
Mireille 209
modernity, and irritation 186–90
money: cause of irritation 79–80, 138; gender
difference 61
Mons, Johanne 79n, 95n, 148n, 213, 214
Monsieur Berg 30, 214
morality 45, 77
mothers-in-law 113–21, 196
moving house 29
Mr Berg, 30, 214
Mrs Blanc 31, 213
Mrs Louis 30, 213
Mrs Tinsart 119–20, 214
Mrs Vannier 30, 214

Nathalie 161, 214
negative feelings 4, 22, 49, 61, 87, 176, 183;
beginning of conjugal life 14–15; see also
anger; anxiety; disgust; dissatisfaction;
frustration; hatred; jealousy; malaise;
resentment
neutrality 173, 175
Nicole: causes of irritation 76, 96; disgust
134; positive responses 169, 177; research
subject 209
Ninette see Pascal and Ninette

objects: cause of irritation 9, 25–33, 65, 66–8,
69, 70–2, 74; crystallization 97–8; everyday
relationship with 10–14; manipulation as
response to irritation 148–50, 170–2, 183
Olivia 136–7, 214
openness, culture of 16
order, desire for 106

Pascal and Ninette 99, 212, 214
Pat see Anaïs and Pat
pathological irritability 4–5, 135–7
Pedro see Fidelia and Pedro
Pénélope 115–16, 214
personal space 82–5, 97, 178, 179
personal time, as means of absorbing
irritation 17–18, 169

Peter see Sarah and Peter
pets, cause of irritation 16, 78
La peur et la porte (Kaufmann) 213
physical intimacy see proximity
physical therapy 169–72, 176, 183
Pierre see Claudie and Pierre
Pittet, Sylviane 191
politics, cause of irritation 28, 81
power: cause of irritation 83; early stages of
conjugal life 19–20; gender difference 53–4,
56–7, 58–61; inattentiveness and 126
Premier Matin (Kaufmann) 82–3, 212, 213, 214
privacy 83, 84; see also personal space
progress 118
proximity: cause of irritation 31, 68–73, 74,
78, 82–5; disgust 133-5; family issues 123;
social circumstances 138
public sphere: conjugal self-mockery 151;
humiliation 129, 130; revenge 160
punctuality, cause of irritation 39, 45, 154–6

Raf and Dolorès 138–9, 214
rationality 9; coping technique 11, 108–9,
110; response to irritation 146–7, 169,
176–8, 183
reality, accentuating positive aspects 183–5
reassurance: in conjugal life 23, 125; family
issues 114, 117
rebellion see revolt
reflex movements 10–11, 12–14, 34, 35–6,
112, 128
reflexivity 171
reform, early stages of conjugal life 17–22
regression in conjugal life 23, 57
regret 98
relaxed approach see cool approach
remorse 101, 160, 175
research 186
research methodology 191–214; chat room
sources 212–13, 214; direct sources
194–212; e-mail technique 191–3; lists of
irritations 89–95; material from previous
research 212–14
resentment 4, 127, 129, 131, 132
responsibility versus relaxation 54–7
retirement 30–1; complementary roles 40; see
also ageing
revenge: complementary roles 39; gender
difference 52; as response to irritation 3,
102, 152, 156–62, 169, 177, 183
revolt 48, 65, 101, 177
Richard see Malvina and Richard
rituals: emotional outburst as 97–9; as
responses 151, 155, 179
rival relationships 118, 131; see also family
Robert see Eliza and Robert; Elsa and Robert
Roberto see Dorothée and Roberto
roles 19–20, 34, 47, 59, 186, 189–90, 205;
reversal of 76; see also complementary
roles; supporting role

223